Banking on Privilege

Banking on Privilege

THE POLITICS
OF SPANISH
FINANCIAL
REFORM

Sofía A. Pérez

Cornell University Press

ITHACA AND LONDON

*HG
186.
S6
P45
1997*

This book is published with the aid of a grant from the Program for Cultural Cooperation between Spain's Ministry of Culture and Education and United States Universities.

First published 1997 by Cornell University Press.

Printed in the United States of America.

Library of Congress Cataloging-in-Publication Data
Pérez, Sofía A. (Sofía Ana), 1963–
    Banking on privilege : the politics of Spanish financial reform /
Sofía A. Pérez.
        p.   cm.
    Includes index.
    ISBN 0-8014-3323-1 (alk. paper)
    1. Finance—Spain.   2. Financial institutions—Spain.
3. Financial institutions—Deregulation—Spain.   I. Title.
HG186.S6P45 1997
332.1'0946—dc21   97-17554

Cloth printing   10 9 8 7 6 5 4 3 2 1

To my grandfather,
  José Pérez Llorca,
    and my grandmother,
      Rotraut Wolfram

Contents

Tables

Preface

The regulation of banking and finance is often perceived as an abstruse if not arcane subject. Because of the technical issues that it involves, financial regulation seems less amenable to the tools of political or sociological analysis than other realms of the political economy, such as labor relations and trade policy, where the lines of conflict appear to be more clearly defined and where the identities of the relevant actors reflect better understood cleavages. When the subject of financial regulation is taken up by political economists, it tends to be addressed almost solely in terms of structural economic forces, such as the inherent power of finance capital or the inexorable force of international financial market integration. The presumption is that the technical nature of financial regulation makes political variables, such as the identities of policymaking elites and their ideological agendas, irrelevant. This is especially the case when it comes to the way political economists think about the phenomenon of financial "liberalization" in a country such as Spain, where market-oriented reform coincided with political democratization, lending support to the idea that it was simply the natural, ahistorical corollary of the interplay of economic and political market forces in a new democracy.

In this book I take issue with many of these common assumptions about the political underpinnings of financial regulation and in particular those of financial liberalization. My analysis grew out of an effort to understand why the liberalization of the domestic financial system instituted in Spain during the late 1970s and early 1980s did not bear the fruits that neoliberal reform is expected to produce: a truly competitive financial system. My effort to understand this outcome led first to the observation of an underlying reality: that the highly oligopolistic private banking sector in Spain was afforded almost as much protection during the reform process as it had enjoyed for nearly a century under a succession of political and regulatory regimes of very different ideological hues. The explanation, I discovered, was not to be found simply in the structural economic "power" that the financial sector held within Spanish capital, as Spanish reformers had tools at their disposal to break that power during the 1980s. It was to be found, rather, in the historical origins of the reform agenda in Spain and in the political dynamic to which this agenda gave rise in the course of the reform process. Financial liberalization in Spain was brought about neither by international market forces nor by democratization, even if these factors played into it in important ways. It represents rather the culmination of a long historical process of competition within the state and of accommodation between succeeding groups of state elites with different political and ideological agendas and the private banking sector, a process that goes back to the early days of Spanish industrialization at the beginning of the twentieth century.

Like all books, this one benefited greatly from the input, critique, and assistance of people to whom I am very grateful. Foremost among them is Harvey B. Feigenbaum, whose keen and unapologetic expositions of the political economy perspective served to focus my mind on the subtleties of economic power and its relation to political processes in contemporary market economies. Thus I became interested in an aspect of Spain's contemporary political economy that has been all but ignored by scholars, though it is critical to an understanding of that country's contemporary economic problems. Throughout the course of my work, Harvey has been a steady source of encouragement, a helpful critic, and a good friend.

Others who have contributed generously with their comments and whose input has helped to shape my ideas are Christopher S. Allen, Tom Cusack, Douglas Forsyth, Jeffry Frieden, John Griffin, Mauro Guillen, John Ikenberry, Richard Locke, Michael Loriaux, Brian

Loynd, Sylvia Maxfield, Cynthia McClintock, Eusebio Mujal-León, Henry R. Nau, Ton Notermans, Juan Carlos Rodríguez, Susan Sell, Stephen S. Smith, David Soskice, Sigurt Vitols, and John Zysman. All offered valuable advice and critique on various versions of the argument that I develop in this book. Special thanks are due to Gabriel Tortella, to Michael Loriaux, and to an anonymous reviewer for Cornell University Press, all of whom offered important suggestions that helped in the final revision of the manuscript. I am also especially grateful to Roger Haydon of Cornell University Press for his early and persistent interest in the project and for his steady hand in guiding to fruition.

The list of persons who assisted in my field research in Madrid includes a large number of government and private bank officials who were intimately involved in the reform process, all of whom were extremely generous with their time and their interest. I am convinced that the strategic choices of this group of reformers were guided by strong personal convictions and intellectual sincerity, and that they can be properly understood only in the light of history.

Members of the academic community in Madrid offered their own insight and helped in a variety of ways. I am particularly grateful to Ramón Tamames for an early interview and for his encouragement; to Víctor Pérez Díaz for his support of the project and for giving me a home base at the Fundación Juan March's Centro de Estudios Avanzados en Ciencias Sociales (CEACS); to Ricardo Cortes and José Pedro Pérez-Llorca for their time and help in facilitating critical interviews; to Professor Enrique Fuentes Quintana for making time for an extensive interview in his extremely busy schedule; to Martha Peach, Jesús Cuéllar, Almudena Knecht, and the rest of the staff at the CEACS library for their assistance; to Paloma Gómez of the Bank of Spain's library for last-minute bibliographical assistance; and to Juan Carlos Rodríguez, who helped me develop the historical analysis through endless conversations.

I am indebted as well to institutions that provided financial and technical support. A fellowship from the Western Europe Program of the Social Science Research Council in New York and another from the Institute of World Politics in Washington, D.C., financed two stays in Madrid for field research. The Fundación Juan March afforded a collegial work environment, along with its extensive computer and library resources. After leaving Madrid, I found another excellent setting for work at the Wissenschaftszentrum-Berlin für Sozialforschung in Berlin. I extend special thanks to David Soskice for inviting me there and for his always brilliant contributions to my thinking, past and present. I also thank my colleagues in the Political Science Department at Boston University for providing a cordial and receptive work environment.

On a more personal note, I thank David Bositis and James Lebovic, who helped me to think clearly about social science; my parents, who always made it clear that not thinking about politics was not an option; and Brian Loynd, for making life fun along the way. The two people to whom I dedicate this book are responsible for pulling two families through the upheavals of the 1930s and 1940s, and hence played no small role in allowing me to complete it.

SOFÍA A. PÉREZ

Boston, Massachusetts

Banking on Privilege

Introduction: Invisible Hand
and Political Legacy

The abandonment of state interventionism and the embrace of market-oriented reform are two of the dominant themes of the late twentieth century. The two concepts are often seen as sides of the same coin and as developments driven principally by the relentless pressure of international market integration. The assumption that it is markets that drive change in domestic regulatory institutions is reflected directly in political scientists' explanations of how the regulatory shift away from interventionism comes about. Market integration, so goes the conventional argument, is compelling liberalization by undermining the capacity of governments to insulate their economies and by increasing pressure from economic actors in favor of institutions that lead to greater allocative efficiency.

This debasement of politics in our understanding of contemporary regulatory trends has a variety of consequences. One is the widespread belief that the same economic pressures that lead governments to abandon interventionism will also lead them to reform domestic market structures, thereby strengthening the capacity for adjustment of national economies. Another is the tendency to assume that the specific characteristics and motivations of state elites, deemed critical to an understanding of interventionism, are far less relevant to our understanding of market-oriented reform. If anything, the historical development of the state may be seen to explain resistance or residual variation in a systemic process of market-driven regulatory convergence. All these conceptions are particularly prevalent in discussions of national financial systems, where market pressures are believed to be imposing a "depoliticization" of financial flows on formerly activist states, because of the exit options that offshore markets and technological innovations offer to investors.

This book challenges the relegation of politics in our understanding of contemporary regulatory trends through a historical analysis of the politics of financial regulation in Spain—a country where the decision to abandon the postwar framework of state-directed credit allocation was taken relatively early and coincided with a transition from an authoritarian regime to a parliamentary democracy. Spain, I argue, offers a telling contrast to France, the country on which the interventionist framework of financial regulation adopted under the Franco regime was modeled and whose experience serves as a point of reference for my analysis. Like post-Franco governments in Spain, the Socialist government in France chose to abandon selective forms of credit regulation in the mid-1980s. Yet this decision was accompanied by a deliberate and aggressive effort to expand the role of the capital market as a source of financing for French firms at the same time that traditional sources of state-directed bank credit to industry were being phased out. This overhaul of the domestic financial market was important to the success of the French government's policy of "competitive disinflation" in the late 1980s and early 1990s. In Spain, by contrast, where the commitment to abandon interventionism was made almost a decade earlier than in France, the reform process was characterized by a protracted failure to accompany credit deregulation with assertive measures to alter the oligopolistic structure of the domestic financial system. As a consequence, financial liberalization exacerbated the burden of adjustment for nonfinancial firms, creating an underlying bias in the economy that ultimately undermined the neoliberally inspired policy strategy of the Socialist government that came to power in 1982.

This contrast in the outcome and consequences of domestic financial liberalization, I suggest, reflects the fact that the abandonment of interventionism in these two European countries was driven in a first order not by changing sectoral pressures or allocative efficiency concerns (although those concerns featured prominently in the arguments of reformers) but by the problematic of macroeconomic, and in particular monetary, control. The common trend away from interventionism in these countries, often adduced as evidence that current regulatory changes are being determined by systemic market pressures, is best understood as a choice by political or elected authorities to extricate the state from the allocation of credit in order to reduce the political costs of macroeconomic adjustment or austerity. Yet because this decision is a negative one, the abandonment of interventionism does not necessarily result in adequate reform of market structures. Indeed, the domestic political dynamic behind the abandonment of interventionism may even militate against such "market" reform. The result of liberalization will in any case depend heavily on the character of the domestic policymaking community and on the way financial reform feeds into the configuration of conflict and identities among state elites. Such an understanding of the trend away from interventionism challenges liberal "convergence" arguments. And it suggests that variation in the outcomes of liberalization may be not just residual but in fact the consequences of the very same political dynamic that fosters the abandonment of interventionism.

To say that the politics of market-oriented reform is tied to the character of the domestic policymaking community and to the configuration of conflict and identities among state elites also is to say that it is historically rooted. The chapters covering the anti-interventionist reform process in this book are therefore preceded by a close look at the origins of the contemporary Spanish financial system and the interventionist regulatory framework instituted under the Franco regime. The politics of both interventionism and liberalization in Spain were conditioned by the way in which the development of the domestic banking sector and its role in Spanish industrialization were linked to the inflationary finances of a waning, and later defeated, colonial state. This linkage among public finance, the banks, and industrialization in Spanish history had two kinds of consequences. First, it turned a private banking cartel into the dominant element of national capital, and at the same time imbued the relationship between these banks and Spanish industry with a very tenuous character. Second, it played a central role in configuring the conflicts and battles within the state elite that would drive both of the major regulatory shifts of this century—toward interventionism in the early 1960s and against it in the 1970s and 1980s. The early relationship between the state and the banks thus gave rise to a latent conflict in the Spanish political economy between the interests of finance and those of producers, and at the same time set in motion a pattern of political accommodation between public officials and the banks that persisted through major regulatory overhauls and through the political transition.

Although this book focuses on the politics of financial interventionism and liberalization and on the way in which the Spanish experience challenges our understanding of these questions, it also offers a specific historical perspective on Spain's present-day economic problems. Political scientists tend to focus on the experience of post-Franco Spain as an instance of success. The literature on political regime transitions regularly highlights the reformist character of the Spanish transition in the 1970s and its successful consolidation during the 1980s. Since the principal aim of this literature is to establish the conditions under which democratic institutions consolidate, it also tends to pair Spain exclusively with other recent democracies. This, however, may not be the best light in which to view other aspects of the recent Spanish experience.

Without contesting the importance of the political transformation that has taken place in Spain since the mid-1970s, this book presents a somewhat less sanguine view of the outcomes of the Spanish transition. It starts with the economic situation in Spain a decade and a half after the end of the Franco regime, revealing a record that includes important economic performance failures: a stagnating rate of technological innovation and productivity growth, "inflation-proneness" in the face of high interest rates, and a dismal record in the creation of employment. Though these economic problems do not negate the successful transformation of Spanish political institutions, they nonetheless raise important questions about just how the legacy of the Franco regime and the character of the regime transition have impinged on the political economy of democratic Spain. My analysis suggests that the Franco regime's legacy was not just one of failed policies or obsolete economic structures. It also involved the emergence of specific cleavages and agendas within the Spanish economic policymaking elite that proved critical in determining the choices of reformers during and after the transition.

The story of Spanish financial reform represents a crucial yet commonly overlooked explanation for Spain's economic problems. It points to the cost of investment finance faced by firms to explain why the costs of adjustment have been so much higher in Spain than elsewhere in the Organization for Economic Cooperation and Development (OECD). It also suggests that analyses that focus exclusively on the creation of participatory institutions exclude an important aspect of the Spanish regime transition. Much of the economic policy course pursued by democratic governments in Spain since 1977, I suggest, has been determined not by participatory institutions but by a contest within the state's policymaking elite that began well before 1977, and by a pattern of accommodations between state elites and the domestic financial sector that has roots even farther back in Spanish history.

The argument advanced in this book develops in the form of a historical analysis. This approach allows us to explore not only the origins of Spain's contemporary problems but also the antecedents and timing of major regulatory decisions, both of which are critical to the questions that I seek to confront. The first chapter lays out the present-day empirical puzzle and places the outcomes of the Spanish reform process in the context of prevalent explanations of financial liberalization.

In chapter 2 I analyze the evolution of Spanish financial regulation before the introduction of an interventionist framework. This chapter explains the basic institutional characteristics of the financial system that emerged in Spain at the beginning of the twentieth century and reveals the origins of the pattern of accommodations between state elites and the domestic banking cartel that persisted through subsequent regulatory overhauls. I place particular emphasis in both cases on the role of inflationary public finance in the early stages of Spanish industrialization. In chapter 3 I turn to the construction of an interventionist framework of selective credit regulation in the early 1960s focusing both on the continuing pattern of accommodation and on the similarities between the Spanish and French postwar experiences. In spite of differences in the existing institutional frameworks, the political goals of ascendant state elites and their economic policy choices in the two countries produced a remarkable degree of regulatory convergence during this period.

I then describe the beginnings of the regulatory turn away from interventionism in Spain, linking it to a subtle shift within the state in favor of central-bank reformers that began in the late 1960s. As in an earlier shift within the Francoist elite, which led to the introduction of French-styled indicative planning and an interventionist regulatory framework, changes in the economic context (both domestic and international) played an important role in abetting the shift at the end of the 1960s. Yet they did so because they impinged upon a particular political configuration within the Spanish policymaking elite. Although the shift away from interventionism in Spain thus can easily be construed to support a market-driven view of liberalization, I seek to demonstrate that such an exercise obscures the domestic political dynamics behind the initiation of reform.

In chapters 5 and 6 I follow the evolution of financial reform through the Spanish regime transition and the Socialist victory of 1982. The transition created a window of opportunity that the reformers were able to use to advance both their agenda for institutional reform and the central bank's position of influence within the state. However, because they saw themselves as advancing a neoliberal agenda that might be jeopardized by the new political process, they also sought to establish a relationship of reciprocal consent with the private banks to strengthen their influence within the transition governments. The outcome was a highly biased course of reform. The Socialist electoral victory of 1982 served to consolidate the shift within the policymaking elite, producing continued accommodation with the banking sector in the process of regulatory reform, and a distinctly nationalist stance toward that sector following Spanish entry into the European Community (EC) in 1986. In chapter 7, I explore the links between financial reform and the macroeconomic policy strategy pursued under the Partido Socialista Obrero Español (PSOE) up until the crisis of the European Exchange Rate Mechanism (ERM) in 1992–93, returning in the Conclusion to the insights that the Spanish experience and its contrast to France hold for our understanding of the domestic politics of financial liberalization.

1

The Spanish Economy
and Financial Reform

When, with the death of Francisco Franco in November 1975, Spain emerged from almost forty years of authoritarian rule, the country faced not only its most important political challenge since the Civil War but, simultaneously, its worst economic crisis in over two decades. The nadir of that crisis still lay ahead, in the second oil shock of 1979. But there already was a widespread awareness among the political elites who undertook the political transformation in 1976 that its success would depend on the country's ability to adjust to new economic realities. The two issues, economic adjustment and political change, thus came to be strongly related in the transition process. Almost from the outset, economic policy was placed in the hands of reformist economists within the public administration and the academic community who sought a sharp break with the interventionist orientation of the Franco regime, and for this purpose, set out to ground the process of political change in a commitment to market-oriented economic reforms. Defying widespread expectations, this commitment not only persisted, but was indeed bolstered with the Socialist victory of 1982.

The steady neoliberal orientation in Spanish economic policy since the transition is often credited with bringing the country firmly into the league of advanced industrialized countries. Many observers have sought lessons in the Spanish case for other countries moving away from authoritarian rule. In the literature on political transitions, Spain often appears as the model of a successful "dual transition," of a country that successfully (or even "miraculously") combined democratization and economic adjustment.[1] However, the tendency to think about the Spanish experience primarily in comparison to that of other recent democracies has led comparativists to neglect important signs of failure in the neoliberal economic adjustment strategy pursued by Spain's post-Franco governments. Indeed, the Spanish experience also holds different lessons about the association between political and economic liberalization.

On certain scores, such as the fight against inflation, the performance of the Spanish economy during the 1980s compared favorably to that of other countries that had undergone recent political democratization, such as Greece and Portugal. The laudatory view of the Spanish experience, however, does not give due importance to the fact that Spain's economic starting point in the early 1970s, with an income per capita that stood at 53 percent of the OECD average, was different from that of these other countries. It also disregards the fact that Spain experienced one of the most severe and prolonged recessions in Europe in the first half of the 1980s. Total employment between 1975 and 1985 fell by 19 percent in Spain, compared to only a marginal decline in the rest of OECD Europe, and the unemployment rate at 22 percent in 1985 was more than twice the EC average. GDP per capita, meanwhile, fell precipitously in comparative terms, to as low as 39 percent of the OECD average in 1985.[2] The recession also lasted longer in Spain than in the rest of the OECD. Employment continued to fall through the first half of 1985 and a turnaround was possible only after Spain signed its treaty of accession to the European Community, which set off a massive foreign-investment-driven boom that lasted almost five years.

---

[1] Adam Przeworski, *Democracy and the Market: Political and Economic Reforms in Eastern Europe and Latin America* (New York: Cambridge University Press, 1991), pp. 8–9; and Nancy Bermeo, "Sacrifice, Sequence, and Strength in Successful Dual Transitions: Lessons from Spain," *Journal of Politics*, August 1994, pp. 601–27. Bermeo emphasizes the extent to which macroeconomic adjustment was postponed in Spain until after the Socialist victory, which she argues was critical to the success of the political transition. Although I do not disagree with her assessment of how policy accommodated political considerations before the Socialist victory, I focus on the agenda of institutional reform of the individuals in charge of economic policy since the first Suárez government in 1976.
[2] OECD, *Economic Surveys: Spain* (Paris, 1986, 1991).

Even as it came out of recession the Spanish economy exhibited signs of important underlying problems. An average annual growth rate of almost 5 percent from 1986 through 1989 allowed per capita income to rise again to 56 percent of the OECD average, earning the Socialist government much praise for the acumen of its neoliberal policy stance from international observers. Yet by 1990, this second Spanish economic miracle had given way to profound pessimism. Reports by various economic agencies noted virtually complete stagnation in the rate of productivity growth, a worrisomely low pace of technological innovation, and an abrupt halt to the process of modernization that Spanish firms had begun in the mid-1970s.[3] These problems were compounded by the persisting failure to achieve certain macroeconomic policy objectives, in particular the top priority of the Socialist government in the late 1980s: the reduction of inflation to the level of core countries in the European Monetary System (EMS). The OECD repeatedly noted the "stickiness" of Spanish inflation rates (at around 6.5 percent between 1989 and 1991), despite high interest rates and a tight monetary policy stance, and the inflation proneness of the Spanish economy. According to one of its estimates, "the rise in unemployment or loss of output necessary to bring inflation down by one percentage point" was "twice as large in Spain as in other EMS countries."[4] Other observers pointed out that the Spanish economy had acquired all of the central features of a "Dutch disease" economy: a combination of poor export performance, rapid growth of the less competitive sectors of the economy, an overvalued currency, high interest rates, and inflation.[5]

The most troublesome aspect of Spanish economic performance since the late 1970s, however, has been unemployment. It rose from 5 percent in 1976 to 22 percent in 1985 and never declined below 16

---

[3] *El País,* November 12, 1990; Juan Antonio Maroto, "La situación empresarial en España (1982–1989)," *Cuadernos de Información Económica* (FIES), nos. 44/45, 1990.
[4] OECD, *Economic Surveys: Spain* (Paris, 1992), pp. 63–65.
[5] Cándido Muñoz Cidad, "Un ajuste febril," *El País,* March 27, 1991. The source of overvaluation in a "Dutch disease" economy is a sector that is experiencing explosive growth, thereby producing large inflows of foreign capital. The overvaluation of the currency and the inflationary effect of capital inflows create a bias against investment in other tradable sectors and is thus associated with deindustrialization. The term has typically been used to describe instances where a natural energy source played this role, such as the discovery of natural gas in the Netherlands or the windfall profits experienced by oil-producing countries following the price shocks induced by the Organization of Petroleum Exporting Countries (OPEC). In the Spanish case, the effect derived from the inflow of short-term capital responding principally to high Spanish interest rates and from the sale of national assets to foreigners.

percent during the years of rapid growth. This outcome is all the more staggering because the rise in unemployment did not, as in many other European countries, reflect a rise in the work force participation rate. Indeed, the participation rate actually decreased from 1976 through 1985, and in the second half of the decade recovered only modestly because a rise in the female participation rate was almost outweighed by the continued decline in the male participation rate. After the EMS crisis in 1992–93, employment shedding led unemployment to rise even further, to almost 25 percent in 1994. In 1996, at the time of the Socialist government's electoral defeat, it remained above 22 percent (still more than twice the average of the European Union [EU]).[6]

The story of Spanish economic performance thus appears largely as one of frustrated expectations. Economic analyses of Spain's economic problems almost invariably emphasize one (or both) of two factors: (1) labor market rigidities, attributed to the paternalistic labor law framework inherited from the Franco era and blamed for excessive labor costs, and (2) the relatively high levels of public deficits that have appeared in the posttransition period.[7] The former is seen as a direct drag on job creation (and more indirectly on investment), and the latter is generally used to explain the persistence of high real interest rates, which discourage Spanish firms from investing in productive capacity and hence also constrain the creation of new jobs. It is this latter phenomenon that concerns us here.

The overall level of Spanish interest rates during the 1980s is summarized in Table 1. The table suggests that real interest rates in Spain, after being low by international standards up to 1982, shot up thereafter, reaching very high levels after 1986 and through the end of the 1980s. Not only were real interest rates exceptionally high when compared to the rest of the OECD, in particular after 1987, but they appeared to respond little to the changing nature of economic activity,

---

[6]   For an extensive review of the empirical evidence on the unemployment phenomenon in Spain, see Olivier Blanchard et al., *Spanish Unemployment: Is There a Solution?* (London: Centre for Economic Policy Research, 1995). This review does not, however, consider the role of the financial market.

[7]   On the role of labor market variables, see in particular L. Angel Rojo, "Desempleo y factores reales," *Papeles de Economía Española*, no. 8, 1981; Juan Dolado and S. Bentolila, "Labour Flexibility and Wages: Lessons from Spain," *Economic Policy* 18 (1994); and Blanchard et al., *Spanish Unemployment*. On the role of the deficit, see, for example, L. Angel Rojo, "El déficit público," *Papeles de Economía Española*, no. 21, 1984, and José María González-Páramo, José María Roldán, and Miguel Sebastián, *Issues of Fiscal Policy in Spain*, Bank of Spain Working Paper no. 9121 (Madrid, 1991).

Table 1. Nominal and real interest rates, Spain and world, 1980–1992

	1980	1981	1982	1983	1984	1985	1986	1987	1988	1989	1990	1991	1992
Spain													
Return on public debt													
Nominal	16.0%	15.8%	16.0%	16.9%	16.5%	13.4%	11.4%	12.8%	11.7%	13.6%	14.6%	12.6%	12.6%
Real	−0.8	1.4	2.0	4.7	7.5	5.3	3.1	8.2	5.9	6.8	7.9	6.7	6.7
Credit rates (1–3 year)													
Nominal	16.8	17.4	17.5	17.8	18.1	16.7	15.4	15.9	15.2	16.4	17.5	16.5	15.9
Real	1.6	3.0	3.5	5.6	9.1	8.6	7.1	11.3	9.4	9.6	10.5	10.6	10.0
Memorandum items													
Consumer Price Index	15.2	14.4	14.0	12.2	9.0	8.1	8.3	4.6	5.8	6.8	6.7	5.9	5.9
General government deficit (as % of GDP)	2.6	3.9	5.6	4.8	5.5	7.0	6.1	3.2	3.2	2.8	3.9	4.9	4.5
Rest of world													
Nominal	10.0	11.9	11.0	9.3	9.6	9.3	7.3	7.5	8.3	8.6	9.2	8.1	6.8
Real	−0.9	2.7	5.1	6.0	5.8	6.0	5.9	4.8	4.8	3.5	4.2	3.3	2.8
Interbank rate differential with rest of EC										4.5	3.9	2.8	4.1

Source: Adapted from Antonio Torrero, "La formación de los tipos de interés y los problemas actuales de la economía española," *Economistas* (Madrid), no. 39, 1989, with data from OECD, *Financial Statistics* and *Economic Surveys: Spain* 1991 and 1994; and Banco de España, *Cuentas financieras de la economía española (1984–1993)*.

inflation, and public deficits during the second half of the 1980s and the early 1990s. Table 1 also shows that, although both real credit rates and the real return on Spanish public debt were high after 1982, Treasury rates experienced greater variation at the end of the decade, yet they had only a limited effect on credit rates, a point that I return to later.

The interest rate data in Table 1 illustrate the high cost of credit and the high return on financial assets in the Spanish economy during the late 1980s and early 1990s. Both of these variables are important determinants of firms' investment behavior. However, a more direct measure of the impact of interest rates on investment and economic activity is the actual cost of financing that firms incur to finance investment in productive capacity. Because of differences in accounting and reporting standards, reliable comparable data of this sort are difficult to come by. One of the few sources is the European Commission's BACH project, which harmonizes data collected by European central banks on the balance sheets of large nonfinancial firms. Table 2 shows the evolution of the ratio of financial costs to external financing in different industrialized countries, as computed from this data set.

The BACH project data indicate that the average cost of investment finance born by Spanish firms (even very large ones) was high in comparison with that of firms in other EC countries from the mid-1980s on. In the absence of perfect international capital mobility, this might be attributed to the greater scarcity of capital in Spain than in the other countries covered by the data. Two observations, however, speak against such a simple explanation. One is that the financial costs of Spanish firms not only were high; they also responded far less than the financial costs of firms in the other countries to major improvements in economic conditions over the course of the decade. Many of the standard economic fundamentals commonly associated with high interest rates—the public deficit, inflation, and excessive indebtedness on the part of firms—improved significantly in Spain over the period. The overall public deficit (including that of both the central and territorial governments and the social security system) was cut from almost 7 percent in 1985 to 3.1 percent in 1987 and remained below 3.5 percent through the end of the 1980s. Inflation was reduced from 8.8 percent in 1985 to 4.8 percent in 1988, rising by 2 percent in 1989, but steadily moderating again thereafter. Over the same period, Spanish firms dramatically increased their self-financing ratio, which had plummeted

Table 2. Financial cost ratios of manufcturing firms in seven countries, 1982–1992

	1981	1982	1983	1984	1985	1986	1987	1988	1989	1990	1991	1992
Spain	—	13.5%	12.9%	13.5%	12.3%	11.2%	11.1%	9.9%	10.2%	10.5%	13.8%	15.1%
Germany	8.0%	7.9	6.0	5.8	5.6	5.2	4.7	4.5	5.1	5.8	—	—
France	16.6	14.1	12.8	10.7	10.8	10.0	9.5	8.8	8.9	9.7	9.3	10.1
Italy	—	14.8	14.6	13.0	12.2	10.2	8.1	8.2	8.5	8.9	9.0	10.7
U.K.	20.2	10.2	8.9	8.3	8.8	5.6	5.1	4.7	6.1	7.1	6.2	5.4
U.S.	—	—	—	—	—	1.4	0.8	0.9	1.6	2.5	3.7	8.6
Japan	10.5	9.6	9.1	8.5	8.2	7.6	6.9	6.4	6.8	7.4	7.7	6.6

Source: BACH project data (EC Commission), in Banco de España, *Central de Balances*, various years.

from 31 percent in the late 1970s to an extremely low negative 12 percent at the beginning of the 1980s, but rose sharply thereafter to an average of 52 percent from 1983 through 1985 and an average of 92 percent for the boom period of 1986 through 1990.[8]

The second critical observation is that the cost of investment finance borne by Spanish firms over the period was high not only in comparison with that of firms in other countries but also in relation to the rate of return on investments. This point is captured by a parameter called the "leverage effect," which measures the difference between the average economic rate of return of firms and the apparent cost of external financing or real interest rate.[9] In a perfect financial market, this differential should be at or near zero. If it is positive, firms can (on average) increase the profitability (or rate of return) of their equity simply by borrowing money. This creates a perverse incentive for firms to borrow beyond the level justified by the profitability of their investments, a point often raised as one of the principal arguments against intervention in financial markets. If the leverage effect is negative, however, firms will on average be decreasing the profitability of their equity by borrowing or taking on other forms of external financing to finance their investments—a possibility that receives less attention in the literature on financial regulation, although it has its own serious implications.

A series of analyses on the same sample of firms represented in the BACH project reveals a negative leverage effect in Spain of very serious proportions, beginning in 1978 and lasting through the early 1990s. The magnitude of the effect declines as the economy turns to boom in the mid-1980s, but the sign of the ratio remains negative throughout the decade. The positive trend, moreover, ends at the very height of the boom in 1988, and there is a sharp increase in the negative magnitude of the effect thereafter.[10] Though these analyses are based on data collected by the Bank of Spain, they received remarkably little attention

---

[8]   OECD, *Economic Surveys: Spain*, 1988, p. 48. The self-financing ratio is the ratio of "retained income gross of depreciation and provisions divided by investment in non-financial assets." The 1986–1990 figure is based on data from OECD, *Financial Statistics: Financial Account of Non-Financial Enterprises* (Paris, 1995), pp. 40–42.

[9]   The leverage effect ratio is this difference weighted by the net debt-to-equity ratio of firms.

[10]   Juan Antonio Maroto Acín, "La financiación empresarial en España y el sistema financiero," *Economía Industrial*, no. 293, 1993; Alvaro Cuervo, "Análisis económico-financiero de la empresa española," *Papeles de Economía Española*, no. 3, 1980.

in the economic literature on Spain. Nor did they feature prominently in Spanish public debate during the 1980s.[11] Yet, the finding of an enduring and significant negative leverage effect is of indisputable significance for understanding the performance of the Spanish economy, as it suggests that, for well over a decade, Spanish firms on average were decreasing the return on their capital when they took on external financing to invest in productive capacity.

The persistence of these conditions over such a long time represents a strong disincentive for investment in productive capacity, technological innovation, and job creation, in particular in sectors that were subject to external competition and could therefore not easily pass on their costs to consumers. Firms that were able to ride out the recession of the early 1980s responded by drastically reducing their recourse to external financing. This is commonly seen as a salutary development, since it brought about a reduction in the financial vulnerability of Spanish enterprises. Yet the incentives entailed in the negative leverage effect apply not only to the decision to take on external financing but also to the way businesses allocate their own retained earnings. The balance sheet data of nonfinancial firms in Spain during the mid- to late 1980s shows that the income firms derived from investing in financial assets grew far more rapidly than the return they made on their own operations (see Table 3). A large share of the profits accrued by Spanish industry during the boom years was therefore "ploughed [either directly or through the financial system] into the creation of speculative service industry ventures—mainly in the property market—rather than into production."[12] The high cost of investment finance, as reflected in the persistence of the negative leverage effect, was thus limiting the share of the financial system's resources that was directed toward productive investments in competitive sectors.

There has been little research into the causes of this problem in Spain. In theory, the leverage effect is as much a function of the factors determining the economic return to investment as of the cost of finance. Among the latter are labor costs, the variable emphasized by the gov-

---

[11] According to officials I interviewed in Madrid during 1991–1992, this may have been the result of the general dearth of firm-level economic research in Spain, an outcome related to the overwhelming concentration of economic expertise in the central bank and the financial sector.

[12] *Financial Times*, March 15, 1991.

Table 3. Balance sheet returns of nonfinancial firms, 1985–1990 (growth over previous years)

Balance sheet items	1985	1986	1987	1988	1989	1990
Gross operating profits	10.9%	12.8%	18.2%	14.3%	5.8%	0.2%
Net operating profits	7.7	13.7	23.3	19.4	3.7	−4.4
Income on financial assets	14.2	24.5	34.7	14.0	26.3	8.0

Source: Banco de España, *Central de Balances,* 1990, p. 20, Table II.A.1.3. Item 2 is equal to item 1 minus provisions.

Table 4. Rate of return on capital of U.S. firms abroad, 1985–1988

	1985	1986	1987	1988	Average
Spain	14.1%	17.3%	39.8%	34.2%	26.3%
World	15.0	15.7	19.3	15.2	16.3
EC	21.6	21.6	25.6	14.7	20.9
Portugal	22.2	32.4	26.9	32.9	28.6
Italy	19.5	39.8	25.8	12.4	24.4
Greece	−8.5	−82.2	30.1	35.0	−6.4

Source: U.S. Department of Commerce, in OECD, *Economic Surveys: Spain,* 1991.

ernment as the key to the competitiveness of the Spanish economy. Several facts, however, suggest that what was exceptional in Spain during the 1980s were the financial costs faced by firms rather than any other factor affecting the return on investment. The profit margins of Spanish manufacturing firms were, at an average of almost 4 percent for the 1980s, considerably higher than those of other EMS countries (which averaged 1.5 percent for the decade). And comparative data on the rate of return on investment by American multinationals (Table 4) show that the return on their Spanish operations rose dramatically over the course of the decade, doubling their world average at its end. External assessments of Spanish labor costs, moreover, tended to highlight the moderating effect of wages on inflation. And although wage growth accelerated after 1989, Spain continued to be identified as a country with very favorable gross wage levels and profit rates by the OECD as late as 1991.[13]

If the exceptional factor behind the strong negative leverage effect in Spain was the cost of investment finance, then the explanation is to be found in the determinants of that cost. In any economy, the cost of finance is determined by a combination of macroeconomic policy deci-

---

[13]   OECD, *Economic Surveys: Spain,* 1992, pp. 59–60, 63–64.

sions, opportunity costs, and structural features of the financial market. In Spain, where the capital market remained extremely narrow through the 1980s (a key structural feature), the cost of finance was mainly defined by the rates charged by banks on credit, which remained by far the principal source of external financing for firms. Credit rates are a function of macroeconomic policy and of those structural aspects of the financial market that determine the degree of market power of borrowers and lenders, as well as those that impinge on the price that the public treasury has to pay on its debt.

Most attempts to explain the high level of credit rates in Spain focus on macroeconomic policy, particularly the level of public spending and public deficits.[14] More specifically, the prevalent view among Spanish officials during the 1980s was that interest rates were high because monetary policy was forced to counteract a lack of fiscal restraint in the government's fight against inflation. The political dimension of the problem would accordingly have to be found in the government's inability to impose a sufficient degree of fiscal restraint. In chapter 7 I argue that the policy strategy pursued by the Socialist (PSOE) government during the 1980s and the unorthodox policy mix that this brought about did indeed play an important role in aggravating the financial costs faced by Spanish firms, although my interpretation of the causes of that mix differ from the ones implied in the economic analyses referred to. For now, however, I will only point out several reasons why the "failure of fiscal restraint" thesis constitutes at best a very incomplete explanation of the level of financial costs in Spain.

First, if the high level of credit rates in Spain was a result of "crowding-out" by the public treasury, then this crowding-out effect itself seems to have carried an important structural component (i.e., one that cannot be attributed to the character of fiscal policy, present or past). Although the level of Spanish budget deficits—at an average of 3.5 percent of GDP for 1987–91—was not low, it was not particularly high by OECD standards. Moreover, the real cost of financing the deficit in Spain (as reflected in the differential between real Spanish Treasury

---

[14] See, for example, José Luis Raymond Bara and José Palet, "Factores determinantes de los tipos reales de interés en España," *Papeles de Economía Española*, no. 43, 1990; González-Páramo et al., *Issues of Fiscal Policy in Spain;* and the OECD surveys of Spain for 1988–90. The explanatory role of fiscal policy is questioned in Fernando Ballábriga and Miguel Sebastián, "Déficit público y tipos de interés en la economía española: ¿Existe evidencia de causalidad?" *Revista de Economía Española* 10, no. 2 (1993).

rates and international rates in the late 1980s and early 1990s was disproportionate with the modest level of the Spanish public debt, which at 47 percent of GDP in 1991 remained well below the EC average (and Maastricht convergence criterion) of 60 percent.

Second, the overriding importance attributed to fiscal variables also is challenged by the limited degree of variation in credit rates. Although the level of public deficits rose significantly during the regime, transition, it also varied considerably over the 1980s, whereas the level of credit rates charged by banks hardly budged. As table 1 shows, real credit rates increased and remained very high in the second half of the 1980s, when the general government deficit (which includes the territorial government deficit and social security system) was being drastically cut, from almost 7 percent in 1985 to 3.2 percent in 1987. Credit rates also varied little in relation to reference rates such as the rediscount and Treasury rates. The "feed-through of cuts in money and security market rates to credit institutions' rates vis-à-vis customers," one Bank of Spain analysis noted, was very weak.[15] All of this suggests that something other than the macroeconomic magnitudes so persistently emphasized by Spanish officials accounted for the high cost of investment credit. This something else is to be found in the character of the Spanish financial market.

In one of the few analyses that depart from the standard emphasis on macroeconomic variables, economist Antonio Torrero offers a closer look at how commercial banks in the 1980s were able to maintain high credit rates in the face of sharply changing economic conditions.[16] He suggests that the principal cause of high rates in Spain in fact changed repeatedly. In a first phase, lasting from 1977 to 1982, the main factor allowing banks to charge high credit rates in the throes of a deep industrial recession was to be found in the desperate situation faced by Spanish businesses and in their high level of indebtedness. "This dependence on external financing, the economic crisis, and high interest rates themselves, left Spanish firms struggling to survive with no option to negotiate costs," lowering their self-financing ratio to the extremely low − 12 percent referred to earlier.

In a second phase, from 1983 through 1985, firms managed to re-

---

15 "Quarterly Report on the Spanish Economy," *Economic Bulletin*, Bank of Spain, April 1992, p. 27.
16 Antonio Torrero, "La formación de los tipos de interés y los problemas actuales de la economía española," *Economistas* (Madrid), no. 39, 1989.

Table 5. Banks' credit portfolios, 1985–1989 (billions of pesetas)

	1/1/85	3/31/89	Percent variation
Credit to businesses			
Total	10,208.8	13,982.3	37.0
Agricultural activities	422.1	699.0	65.3
Energy (nonutilities)	341.5	185.1	− 46.8
Utilities (electricity, gas, water)	688.1	1,429.9	107.8
Mineral extraction/transformation	620.3	469.4	− 24.3
Chemical industries	475.2	432.2	− 9.1
Metal	985.3	1054.0	7.0
Construction materials	960.0	452.3	− 52.9
Food and tobacco	551.6	700.8	27.1
Other manufacturing	1,119.9	1,477.3	31.9
Construction	1,119.7	1,738.4	55.3
Commerce	1,267.7	2,255.6	77.9
Transport and communication	415.6	694.9	67.2
Real estate ventures	387.0	650.8	68.2
Other activities (except financing to other financial institutions)	853.8	1,772.5	107.6
Credit to individuals	2,182.7	5,552.2	154.4
For housing	1,273.1	2,690.2	111.3
For consumer goods and services	437.1	1,571.8	256.0
Other (including purchase of assets)	475.5	1289.8	171.3

Source: Adapted from Antonio Torrero, "La formación de los tipos de interés y los problemas actuales de la economía española," *Economistas* (Madrid), no. 39, 1989, Table 3, p. 40.

duce their borrowing requirements drastically, increasing their self-financing level to as much as 52 percent by 1985. During this phase, however, the banks were able to prevent a significant fall in their interest margins despite the collapse of credit demand from firms by shifting their resources into public debt. In a third phase, starting with the demand boom in 1986, the economy recouped and the return on public debt became less attractive. Nonfinancial firms, scathed by the traumatic experience of the early 1990s, continued to rely heavily on self-financing. However, the banks were able to raise both their interest and earning margins without cutting their operating costs by shifting a substantial amount of their resources to those credit users that were least sensitive to high interest rates: utilities and service ventures that were not exposed to foreign competition and hence could pass on high financial costs to consumers (see the breakdown of credit recipients in Table 5) and households. Indeed, one of the most dramatic developments associated with this redeployment of bank credit was a boom in new consumer credit to individuals, which at 2.8 percent of GDP in

1988 was triple the rate of 0.9 percent found in the United States.[17] Meanwhile, the net lending capacity (or savings) of households declined from 5.2 percent in 1985 to 1.4 percent in 1988.[18]

Torrero's analysis identifies the changing sources of credit demand that allowed Spanish banks to maintain their credit rates through the 1980s despite the altered behavior of nonfinancial firms. However, such demand factors resulted in extraordinary credit rate levels only because of the existence of an oligopolistic financial market structure. This structure is reflected in cross-national data on commercial bank cost and profit margins in Table 6, which shows that Spanish banks had far higher cost, interest, and earning margins than other West European countries. The evolution of those margins for Spanish banks since the mid-1970s (see Table 7) indicates that the banks were able to increase significantly both their interest and earning margins without decreasing their costs during the onset of the recession in the 1970s and that they did not have to adjust these ratios in any significant way during the 1980s. As one OECD report noted, "relatively high unit costs [had] not prevented banks from enjoying sizeable intermediation margins," and "high profits in a context of relatively high costs are a symptom of monopolistic behavior within the banking sector and of a monopolistic position of banks within the wider financial system."[19]

Whatever the effect of macroeconomic policy, any explanation of the high financial costs born by Spanish firms in the 1980s must include the impact of the financial market structure. The puzzle arises from the fact that the most perverse effects of that structure—the rise in the banks' cost and earnings margins in the midst of a deep recession—occurred in the context of a financial liberalization process and persisted more than a decade after the initiation of that process. Indeed, the persistence of oligopolistic conditions in the market for corporate finance might surprise anyone who followed journalistic accounts of developments in Spain during the 1980s, which invariably emphasized the changes that

---

[17] Ibid., p. 43.

[18] OECD, *Economic Surveys: Spain*, 1991, p. 67. The decline in household savings also was clearly affected by other variables, such as changes in taxation, but the role of the banks in promoting such credit is an important factor in this change in the saving propensity of households.

[19] OECD, *Economic Surveys: Spain*, 1988, p. 58. See also *Economic Surveys: Spain*, 1986, pp. 44–48; *Economic Surveys: Spain*, 1992, p. 33; and Ramón Caminal, Jordi Gual, and Xavier Vives, "Competition in Spanish Banking," in Jean Dermine, ed., *European Banking in the 1990s* (Oxford: Basil Blackwell, 1990), p. 292.

Table 6. Cost and earnings margins of large commercial banks in seven countries, 1990 (percent of average balance sheet total)

	Spain	France	Germany	Belgium	Italy	Netherlands	U.K.
Gross earnings margin	5.62%	2.39%	3.56%	1.75%	4.16%	2.69%	5.03%
Interest margin	4.36	1.79	2.31	1.35	2.91	1.92	3.01
Other income	1.26	0.60	1.24	0.40	1.25	0.77	2.02
Operating costs	3.29	1.56	2.25	1.21	2.72	1.86	3.37
Net earnings	2.33	0.83	1.31	0.54	1.44	0.83	1.66
Profit pretax	1.72	0.31	0.83	0.33	0.90	0.51	0.65
Profit after tax	1.22	0.36	0.49	0.27	0.70	0.38	0.34

Source: OECD, *Bank Profitability, 1981–1990* (Paris, 1992).

Table 7. Income statements of large Spanish commercial banks, 1974–1990 (percent)

Year	Interest margin	Gross earnings margin[a]	Operating costs[a]	Net earnings[b]
1974	3.96%	3.97%	2.43%	1.54%
—	—	—	—	—
—	—	—	—	—
1978	4.66	5.43	3.53	1.90
1979	4.33	5.53	3.49	2.04
1980	5.14	6.15	3.97	2.17
1981	5.15	6.10	4.02	2.08
1982	4.82	5.82	3.80	2.03
1983	4.48	5.47	3.40	2.08
1984	4.34	5.25	3.27	1.98
1985	4.18	5.22	3.28	1.94
1986	4.50	5.44	3.71	1.72
1987	4.72	6.02	3.74	2.28
1988	4.73	6.07	3.46	2.61
1989	4.61	5.70	3.29	2.41
1990	4.61	5.62	3.29	2.33

[a]Percent of average assets.
[b]Before provisions and tax.
Sources: 1974–79: Antonio Torrero, *Tendencias del sistema financiero español* (Madrid: H. Blume, 1982), p. 19; 1980: OECD, *Bank Profitability, 1980–1984* (Paris, 1987); 1981–90: OECD, *Bank Profitability, 1981–1990* (Paris, 1992).

liberalization entailed and the way in which it challenged the status quo in the banking sector. A closer examination of developments in the Spanish financial sector, however, shows how regulatory change was calibrated to sustain the banks' position within the system through the end of the decade.

The perverse repercussions of financial liberalization in Spain derived from a reform process characterized by a fundamental set of biases. Credit deregulation, which was forcefully initiated in the late 1970s, failed to be accompanied for more than a decade by measures that would have breathed any real competition into the domestic corporate finance market. Although other financial intermediaries, most notably foreign banks and domestic savings institutions, were allowed to expand their activities, they remained hampered by operational restrictions that discouraged them from exerting downward pressure on credit rates during the 1980s. Foreign banks were made to depend for resources on a domestic interbank money market that was tightly controlled by the Big Seven commercial banks. Although they played a leading role in organizing syndicated loans and in other financial innovations, foreign banks were therefore not able, despite several attempts, to exert downward pressure on credit rates in the market at large. Savings banks expanded their deposit base significantly at the expense of the domestic commercial banks, thanks to changes in their regulatory treatment. Yet they were prevented from expanding beyond their regional base until 1989. Moreover, because they had even higher operating costs than the commercial banks, they were inclined to allocate their resources in the same manner as the latter (toward public debt and consumer credit) rather than to compete aggressively in the market for corporate finance by cutting credit rates. The narrow and archaic Spanish stock market, meanwhile, was left virtually intact for more than a decade after the initiation of credit deregulation.

The reform effort thus did little to create alternative sources of finance for the great majority of Spanish firms that were not large enough to access the Euromarkets, and it even skewed the financial cost structure of the large firms represented in the BACH project data.[20] The effects of this first bias were exacerbated by a second aspect of the reform process pertaining to the public debt market. As noted, the shift into public debt served as a compensatory mechanism for the banks during the 1980s. It allowed them to prepare the shift into consumer

---

[20] There was a substantial rise in the financing raised by Spanish firms on the Euromarkets after 1979, but it was limited to a very small number of firms. Twenty-five firms (predominantly electric utilities and highway construction companies) accounted for over 80 percent of Eurocredits raised between 1974 and 1986. See Angel Berges and Emilio Ontiveros, "El coste del endeudamiento exterior," *Papeles de Economía Española, Suplementos sobre el Sistema Financiero*, no. 22, 1988.

lending in the face of drastically changed borrowing behavior by Spanish firms, without undergoing any significant change in their margins. This strategy by the banks was facilitated by the government's resort to "negotiated" solutions to its deficit financing problem in the mid-1980s (see chapter 6) and its decision not to promote an independent public debt market more aggressively. The high return that the banks received on their public debt holdings as a result supported their earnings at a point in the economic cycle when the collapse of credit demand would otherwise have forced them to cut credit rates and reduce costs. It thus provided a pause in the reform process that had lasting consequences for the banks' behavior as lenders.

The process of domestic financial liberalization carried out over the late 1970s and 1980s in Spain thus placed deregulation ahead of market reform, exacerbating the burden of adjustment for Spanish firms and creating an underlying bias in the economy against investment in productive capacity (at least in those sectors most exposed to foreign competition and thus less able to pass on their costs). This outcome contrasts significantly with that of market-oriented financial reform in another formerly interventionist European state, France.[21] The framework of state-directed credit allocation instituted in Spain in the early 1960s was directly modeled on that constructed in France during the early post–World War II period. As in Spain, the regulatory framework in France underwent a radical overhaul during the 1980s, in which the principle of state-directed credit allocation was abandoned in favor of market-based allocation. Because France was so widely touted as the archetypical *dirigiste* state in Europe, the move away from interventionism in that country often is cited as evidence that financial liberalization is determined by systemic market forces that compel governments to adopt efficiency-maximizing institutions which result in better eco-

---

[21] French financial reform has received significant attention from political scientists. Throughout this book, I rely on this secondary literature. An overview of the politics of reform in France is offered in Stephen S. Cohen, James Galbraith, and John Zysman, "Rehabbing the Labyrinth: The Financial System and Industrial Policy in France," in Stephen S. Cohen and Peter A. Gourevitch, eds., *France in the Troubled World Economy* (London: Butterworth, 1982); Philip G. Cerny, "The 'Little Big Bang' in Paris: Financial Market Deregulation in a Dirigiste System," *European Journal of Political Research*, no. 17, 1989; Jacques Melitz, "Financial Deregulation in France," *European Economic Review* 34 (1990); Michael Loriaux, *France after Hegemony: International Change and Financial Reform* (Ithaca: Cornell University Press, 1991); and William Coleman, "Reforming Corporatism: The French Banking Policy Community, 1941–1990," *West European Politics*, April 1993.

nomic performance. This conclusion is boosted by the fact that the abandonment of state-directed credit allocation in France was closely tied (both in theory and in time) to the expansion of alternative forms of financing for nonfinancial firms. Indeed, efforts to promote the capital markets as a source of financing for firms preceded the abandonment of selective credit regulation in France. One of the first reform measures, the Loi Monory of 1978, thus expanded the stock market's potential as a source of financing for firms by offering French citizens a substantial tax deduction for share purchases, giving rise to a dynamic market in mutual funds. And when French policymakers decided to abandon *dirigiste* credit regulation in the mid-1980s, they simultaneously undertook a comprehensive overhaul of the domestic capital market.[22]

The abandonment of interventionism in France was thus accompanied by what appears as a clear thrust toward an alternative model of corporate finance that could support the adjustment efforts of nonfinancial firms, whether this be the "German model" of bank-organized industrial finance or the "Anglo-Saxon" model of aggressive capital markets. The reality of the French reform may have confounded these two alternatives and fallen a good distance from either lofty ideal. Yet, the contrast between the French and Spanish cases is nonetheless stark. As Table 8 demonstrates, French efforts to expand the availability of non-credit-based forms of corporate finance resulted in a very significant increase in the proportion of funds that nonfinancial enterprises were able to raise in the form of securities, bonds, and shares by the end of the 1980s. The Spanish reform effort, by contrast, had resulted in only a marginal increase in non-credit-based financing, even though the deregulation of credit had begun much earlier than in France. Equally significant is the contrast in the cost of investment finance in the two countries. Both France and Spain started the decade with higher costs then other OECD countries, but the financial costs of French firms substantially declined, whereas those of Spanish firms decreased significantly only at the very height of the economic boom in 1988–1990 and rose again dramatically thereafter.

The contrast between the Spanish and French experiences with domestic financial liberalization is all the more interesting because it is found in what otherwise constitutes a most-similar-case comparison.

---

[22]   Cerny, "'Little Big Bang' in Paris," p. 177.

Table 8. Net funds raised by nonfinancial enterprises, France and Spain, 1977–1989 (percent of total)

France	1977	1982	1989
Loans	79%	72%	47%
Securities, bonds, and shares	21	28	53
Spain			
Loans	82	82	77[a]
Securities, bonds, and shares	18	18	23[a]

[a]1989–90 average.
Source: OECD, *Financial Accounts* (France 1990, Spain 1992).

As I argue in chapter 3, the edifice of financial interventionism erected in Spain in the early 1960s not only mimicked the institutional structure of the French framework, but also served very similar political purposes. The adoption of interventionist credit regulation in the two countries followed a similar decision to place political stability ahead of economic stabilization, at a time when the two countries were governed by very different political regimes. The liberalization efforts, however, seem to reflect differing priorities, a divergence that occurred paradoxically at a time when Spain was undergoing its transition to democracy.

These contrasts raise important questions about the theoretical arguments offered by political economists to explain the cross-national trend toward financial deregulation, in particular the decision by governments to abandon financial interventionism. Indeed, they offer a unique opportunity to test our theoretical understanding of the politics of interventionism and of liberalization in formerly interventionist states. Such an understanding also is required if we are to draw any useful lessons from the biased course of reform in Spain. The next section therefore considers the outcomes I have discussed in the light of prevalent arguments about the politics of liberalization.

Explaining Financial Liberalization

The outcome of the Spanish financial reform process—and its contrast with the "most similar" French case—presents not just a problem for the Spanish economy but also a theoretical puzzle about why and how formerly activist states abandon state-directed credit regulation. This section therefore turns to a discussion of the theoretical literature that addresses such a regulatory shift. The discussion departs from the assumption that any regulatory change as significant as the wholesale abandonment of state-directed credit allocation cannot be explained simply as a public policy decision. It necessarily carries an important political component. As Frances Rosenbluth writes, "undiscriminating and relentless as market forces may be, they generate policy changes only to the extent that they incite important players in the domestic polity to alter the regulatory framework."[23] Or as Louis Pauly puts it, economic analysis may "demonstrate why policies should change, but only detailed examination of domestic policy making can explain how and why changes actually do occur."[24] It may be up to the economist to explain the consequences of various modes of financial regulation, but the challenge of explaining why such varying modes of reform are undertaken in different countries and at different times falls to the political economists.

One of the writers who has drawn political scientists' attention to these questions is John Zysman, who has argued that differences in the way advanced industrialized countries adjusted to the external shocks of the 1970s were linked to differences in national financial systems.[25] Building on the work of the economist Andrew Shonfield, Zysman offered a typology that revolved around the contrast between two types of financial systems: (1) the capital market-based financial system found in the Anglo-Saxon countries, in which the price and availability of corporate finance were left to the markets and; (2) a system of state-directed credit allocation, as found in France and Japan, in which state authorities administered prices in such a way as to direct financial resources to specific users. Alongside these two diametrically opposed systems, Zysman's typology also included a third type: a credit-based system in which financial flows were organized not by the state but by a few large private banks, as found in Germany.

The distinctions in national financial systems drawn by Zysman came to play a very important role in the "institutionalist" and "na-

---

[23] Frances McCall Rosenbluth, *Financial Politics in Contemporary Japan* (Ithaca: Cornell University Press, 1989), p. 1.
[24] Louis Pauly, *Opening Financial Markets: Banking Politics on the Pacific Rim* (Ithaca: Cornell University Press, 1988), p. 6.
[25] John Zysman, *Governments, Markets, and Growth: Financial Systems and the Politics of Industrial Change* (Ithaca: Cornell University Press, 1983).

tional models" approaches that became popular during the 1980s.[26] At the very same time, however, domestic financial regulation in many parts of the world was becoming the subject of reform efforts that were promoted with a remarkable degree of doctrinal and idiomatic consistency across countries. In almost all cases, such reform was cast under the labels of "liberalization" and "deregulation," two terms that appeared to militate against the continued relevance of historical differences in national regulatory institutions. Political scientists who focused specifically on the subject of financial regulation therefore soon centered their attention on the apparent unraveling of the postwar pattern of divergence in regulatory institutions that had been captured in Zysman's typology.

The actual measures to which the labels of domestic financial "liberalization" and "deregulation" have been attached have differed greatly from country to country. They include everything from the simple deregulation of credit rates or lifting of credit ceilings to changes in the kinds of financial transactions that different economic agents (commercial, investment, and savings banks, insurance companies, and brokerage firms) are allowed to engage in, to the creation of new instruments and markets for both corporate and public finance. Given this complexity, it is not surprising that most of the original work by political scientists on this subject has focused on the experiences of single countries or regions.[27]

---

[26] See, for example, Jeffrey A. Hart, *Rival Capitalists: International Competitiveness in the United States, Japan, and Western Europe* (Ithaca: Cornell University Press, 1992), pp. 4–5. Peter A. Hall's concept of the "organization of capital" in various European countries and Michel Albert's discussion of different modes of capitalism, while centering more on the nature of corporate governance than on the state/market divide, parallel Zysman's typology to a significant extent. See Hall, *Governing the Economy* (New York: Oxford University Press, 1986), pp. 38–39, 231–58; and Albert, *Capitalisme contre capitalisme* (Paris: Seuil, 1991).

[27] Some examples of this literature are Pauly, *Opening Financial Markets;* Rosenbluth, *Financial Politics;* Benjamin J. Cohen, "European Financial Integration and National Banking Interests," in Paolo Guerrieri and Pier Carlo Padoan, eds., *The Political Economy of European Integration: States, Markets, and Institutions* (Savage, Md.: Barnes & Noble, 1989); Sylvia Maxfield, *Governing Capital: International Finance and Mexican Politics* (Ithaca: Cornell University Press, 1990); Loriaux, *France after Hegemony;* Jungen Woo, *Race to the Swift: State and Finance in Korean Industrialization* (New York: Columbia University Press, 1991); and Kent E. Calder, *Strategic Capitalism: Private Business and Public Purpose in Japanese Industrial Finance* (Princeton: Princeton University Press, 1993).

More often than not, this literature suggests, the reduction in regulation implied by the neoliberal labels under which reform has been promoted masks actual "re-regulation" or even an intensification of the regulation of financial market transactions.[28] One feature that can nonetheless be clearly distinguished in the reform wave of the 1980s is the trend away from the state-led/price-administered model of financial regulation that was so central to Zysman's classification. This trend away from selective credit regulation represents an important change in the domestic political economy of previously interventionist states because it redefines the domain of political authority in the domestic economy. It is therefore an important development for political scientists to understand.

Attempts to explain the trend away from financial interventionism as a cross-national phenomenon place overriding importance on the role of international market developments in bringing about this type of regulatory change.[29] Indeed, the causal link between the growth of international capital markets and regulatory reform in formerly interventionist states is treated almost as conventional wisdom in much of the contemporary political economy literature. This stance, however, also leads to the sometimes unquestioned acceptance of a particular political model of how and why the abandonment of interventionism comes about, a model that has important implications for our expectations about such reform and that I refer to as the "market-driven" model of liberalization.

The market-driven model is one in which change in domestic regulation is determined by a relentless process of market integration (one that takes shape by way of new regulation-evading financial technologies), while the persistence of national differences is treated as residual variation that can be ascribed to institutional resistance or mediation of market forces. Two kinds of arguments are commonly

---

[28] See, for example, Michael Moran, *The Politics of the Financial Services Revolution: The USA, UK, and Japan* (New York: St. Martin's Press, 1991); and Steven K. Vogel's discussion of financial reform in various OECD countries in *Freer Markets, More Rules: Regulatory Reform in Advanced Industrial Countries* (Ithaca: Cornell University Press, 1996).

[29] See in particular John B. Goodman and Louis W. Pauly, "The Obsolescence of Capital Controls? Economic Management in an Age of Global Markets," *World Politics* 46 (October 1993); Jeffry A. Frieden, "Invested Interests: The Politics of National Economic Policies in a World of Global Finance," *International Organization* 45, no. 4 (1991): 439.

offered to make the causal connection between international market forces and domestic regulatory reform.

The first involves the emergence of politically mobilized (or at least tappable) sectoral interests that favor liberalization. These interests may or may not be narrow (i.e., limited to the financial sector itself). In the narrow version of this argument, it is national financial institutions that seek a breakdown of national barriers to capital mobility and deregulation of domestic financial flows to enhance their ability to compete internationally.[30] In the broader version, such reform is sought by holders of liquid assets (which include not only domestic financial institutions, but also multinational corporations) as opposed to holders of fixed assets (national industry and labor).[31] Foremost among the changes sought by the sectoral actors is the abandonment of international capital controls. Yet, as Jeffry Frieden and Ronald Rogowski have argued, the argument extends to any institutional arrangement that impedes the ability of those favored by liberalization to reap the full benefits of market integration.[32] Institutions that give governments control over domestic capital flows clearly represent such a barrier. Because barriers to capital mobility are assumed to entail market efficiency costs, political entrepreneurs are predicted to seek to exploit the potential aggregate welfare gains of liberalization as a way to garner political support.

The second kind of argument that is commonly offered to draw the connection between international market forces and domestic reform involves negative constraints on governments that result from uncoordinated action by economic agents, rather than positive political action or pressure. Financial integration, not only alters the interests of sectoral actors but also increases their exit options. Stephan Haggard and Sylvia Maxfield, for example, write that "changes in the opportunities

---

[30]   Such an argument is made by, for example, David Dollar and Jeffry Frieden in "The Political Economy of Financial Deregulation in the United States and Japan," in Giacomo Luciani, ed., *Structural Change in the American Financial System* (Rome: Fondazione Olivetti, 1990), and by Benjamin J. Cohen in "European Financial Integration and National Banking Interests," in Guerrieri and Padoan, *Political Economy of European Integration.*

[31]   Frieden, "Invested Interests."

[32]   Jeffry Frieden and Ronald Rogowski, "The Impact of the International Economy on National Policies: An Analytic Overview," in Robert O. Keohane and Helen V. Milner, eds., *Internationalization and Domestic Politics* (New York: Cambridge University Press, 1996).

for savers—whether through the growth of parallel markets, access to international markets, or partial financial market reform—decrease the viability of state controls."[33] And John Goodman and Louis Pauly write that the liberalization of capital "has been driven by fundamental changes in the structures of international production and financial intermediation, which made it easier and more urgent for private firms—specifically corporations and financial institutions whose aspirations had become increasingly global—effectively to pursue strategies of evasion and exit."[34] Whether or not they are receptive to sectoral pressures in favor of liberalization, governments are thus forced to adapt their policies to take into account the interests of liquid asset holders.

These two arguments emphasize causal paths that have fairly different implications. Yet they coincide in ways that often lead them to be conflated. Regulatory reform, in both pictures, is forced on reluctant governments by economic actors who are seeking to exploit new market opportunities. It also is expected to conform in broad strokes to the logic of a wider, more competitive marketplace. This collective acceptance of the premise that it is markets that determine the nature of regulatory change also has other implications for the way political scientists think about the politics of liberalization in formerly interventionist states. To the extent that liberalization is promoted by reformers within the state, the motivations of these reformers are assumed to correspond with the logic of competitive market forces—either because they respond directly to sectoral pressure or because they act as political entrepreneurs seeking to internalize the aggregate social welfare gain that liberalization is assumed to entail. The same dynamic that leads them to seek the abandonment of interventionism hence is also assumed to lead to the kinds of market reforms that make these aggregate economic benefits possible. Liberalization is therefore expected to support an economy's performance, because whatever its distributional consequences, it is expected to render aggregate efficiency gains even if it causes dislocation along the way. Finally, there is the all-pervasive tendency to assume that liberalization (or for that matter change) is

---

[33]   Stephan Haggard and Sylvia Maxfield, "Political Explanations of Financial Policy in Developing Countries," in Stephan Haggard, Chung H. Lee, and Sylvia Maxfield, eds., *The Politics of Finance in Developing Countries* (Ithaca: Cornell University Press, 1994), p. 316.
[34]   Goodman and Pauly, "Obsolescence of Capital Controls?" p. 51.

driven by economic forces, whereas only resistance to liberalization has its roots in politics.

The market-driven model of liberalization links up with a rent-seeking view of interventionism and fits well with the view of politics in much of the economic literature. Financial liberalization as an outcome is believed to reflect the intrinsic incentives of market forces. If it does not occur, its absence is attributed to resistance by rent-seeking agents who benefit from interventionist institutions. In this manner, political scientists construct an explanation of political decisions (actual liberalization measures or the lack thereof) that is derived from the normative implications of economic models. Yet however compelling such cross-disciplinary congruence may be for those seeking a systemic explanation of contemporary regulatory trends, the market-driven model of domestic financial liberalization entails some serious problems as a political model of domestic regulatory reform.

We can best understand these problems by looking at the various proposed causal links individually. First, the narrow version of the sectoral pressure model offers a fairly convincing explanation for the kind of regulatory reforms that have been implemented in countries whose domestic financial institutions are, to begin with, major players in international financial markets (the United States, the United Kingdom, and Japan).[35] In the case of most other countries, however, the competitive pressure exerted by large financial institutions through the Euromarkets should be more likely to lead domestic financial institutions to want to preserve regulatory institutions that reserved the domestic financial market to them, rather than to want to dismantle them. The narrow version of the sectoral pressure argument thus seems to apply to a relatively limited range of cases in explaining market-oriented regulatory reforms.

The broader formulation offered by Frieden and Rogowski seeks to overcome this limitation by expanding on the range of potential economic actors that may stand to benefit from liberalization. Yet, this

---

[35] As several authors have argued, however, the growth of these markets was itself the result of regulatory decisions taken in the United States, the United Kingdom, and Japan. See Geoffrey R. D. Underhill, "Markets beyond Politics? The State and the Internationalization of Financial Markets," *European Journal of Political Research*, March/April 1991; and Eric Helleiner, *States and the Reemergence of Global Finance: From Bretton Woods to the 1990s* (Ithaca: Cornell University Press, 1994).

more deductive model has its own problems as an explanation of actual regulatory reform. It translates putative costs and benefits postulated in economic models under very strict assumptions into a model of political action that begins with sectoral actors (whose preferences are defined in terms of alternative ideal worlds that correspond to the assumptions of neoliberal economic models) and ends with a conceptual figure (that of the political entrepreneur) that serves as the analytic mechanism whereby latent interests are hypothesized to translate into political action. This analytic leap has the advantage of rendering the sectoral interest–based explanation universally applicable. But it runs against the grain of much of what political scientists believe to be true about the formation of political coalitions and the dynamics of preference formation. The stipulation that potential social welfare gains will tend to bring about political action in favor of liberalization is challenged by the fact that the potential gains from liberalization are likely to be diffuse and relatively remote, whereas the costs are likely to be heavily concentrated and immediate. It also seems to hinge on the assumption that "numbers matter," and hence is meant to apply in particular to polities in which political power is based on electoral results. Yet, the technical nature of financial regulation and the diffuse nature of the benefits of liberalization make this an unlikely rallying point for the formation of electoral coalitions.

If international markets are driving regulatory reform and the abandonment of interventionism, it is thus much more likely to be by way of uncoordinated economic action (i.e., the exercise of exit options by economic agents) than by way of positive political pressure from mobilized sectoral coalitions. This second argument, which I term the "capital mobility–induced constraint" argument, offers an explanation for liberalization where domestic financial institutions have more to gain from resisting liberalization than from promoting it, and where the initiative for such reform comes from within the policymaking bureaucracy. Contrary to the first argument, it implies a state-centric, or technocratic, model of regulatory reform, in which public officials rather than economic groups are the principal agents behind market-oriented reforms. Many accounts of contemporary financial reform in France, Japan, and the Scandinavian countries support this view, as does the account of liberalization in Spain given in later chapters of this book. Nonetheless, the capital mobility–induced constraint argument is not entirely convincing as an explanation of actual financial liberalization efforts.

Because the growth of international financial markets is bound to affect the way in which governments are able to regulate domestic financial flows, it is appealing to conclude that, if there is a trend toward the abandonment of interventionism, it must be determined in some systematic manner by the secular rise in cross-national financial flows over the last few decades. However, only if regulation-evading technologies had raised capital mobility to an order that rendered external controls effectively obsolete, or so ineffective that their costs outweighed any potential benefits, would this itself explain liberalization. Despite the widespread tendency to accept this assumption, there is significant evidence to the contrary. A number of empirical studies on the question suggest that controls were quite effective in allowing governments to maintain interest rate differentials between domestic and international financial markets through the 1980s and that they were hardly as effectively evaded as is commonly assumed.[36] This fact also was dramatically illustrated by the experience of the European Monetary System after several countries in the Exchange Rate Mechanism (ERM) lifted capital controls in compliance with the Single European Act at the end of the 1980s. Had capital controls been effectively obsolete, their lifting should have had at most a limited impact on the volume of flows and the stability of ERM currencies. In fact, however, it brought about a massive rise in speculative capital flows, setting the stage for the system's crash in 1993.[37] Moreover, because the causal path of the capital mobility–induced constraint argument moves from the growth of international capital markets to the unsustainability of external capital controls to the undermining of domestic credit regulation, we would expect that the lifting of external controls would be

[36] Gerald A. Epstein and Juliet B. Schor, "Structural Determinants and Economic Effects of Capital Controls in OECD Countries," in Tariq Banuri and Juliet B. Schor, eds. *Financial Openness and National Autonomy: Opportunities and Constraints* (Oxford: Clarendon, 1992); Paul de Grauwe, "The Liberalization of Capital Movements and the EMS," in Piero Ferri, ed., *Prospects for the European Monetary System* (New York: St. Martin's Press, 1990), p. 171.

[37] On this point see Francesco Giavazzi and Luigi Spaventa, "The 'New' EMS," in Paul De Grauwe and Lucas Papadeos, eds., *The European Monetary System in the 1990s* (New York: Longman, 1990); and Barry Eichengreen and Charles Wyplosz, "The Unstable EMS," *Brookings Papers on Economic Activity* no. 1 (1993).

closely connected in time to domestic credit deregulation. Yet among interventionist states, external capital controls have often been lifted quite a long time after the initiation of domestic liberalization. This observation suggests that if the lifting of capital controls correlates roughly with an increase in international financial flows, the former may be giving rise to the latter, and not the opposite.

The most important thing to note about the capital mobility–induced constraint argument, however, is that it offers little reason to expect that the abandonment of interventionism will produce the aggregate efficiency or competitiveness gains that are commonly assumed. The threat of capital hemorrhage is likely to induce governments to tighten macroeconomic (and in particular monetary) policy, which in turn creates incentives for elected authorities to abandon selective credit regulation. But it does not create any similarly automatic or powerful incentives for "market" reform; that is, reforms that create markets where they do not exist—such as venture capital for new firms or patient capital for the restructuring of firms—or that counter oligopolistic conditions in existing markets so as to approximate the assumptions on competition and external effects of neoclassical economic models. In the area of financial regulation, this problem is moreover complicated by the asymmetric relationship between nonfinancial firms and financial investors. As Fritz Scharpf writes, "the market clearing price for capital is not exclusively defined by the relationship of relative scarcity between the supply of capital and the supply of profitable opportunities for productive investment." The supply side of the capital market has a choice between productive and nonproductive monetary investments, and "if interest rates climb while business profits are unchanged, savers will redirect their assets to unproductive monetary investment, thereby constraining the economy's capacity to produce," and leading to involuntary unemployment.[38]

Under the kind of selective credit regulation instituted in countries such as France and Spain after World War II, the potential pitfalls of this asymmetry were addressed through credit and capital controls that created specific incentives and obligations for financial institutions to channel savings toward productive investments. This solution, however, required the state to underwrite the risk to the financial sector of

[38] Fritz Scharpf, *Crisis and Choice in European Social Democracy* (Ithaca: Cornell University Press, 1991), p. 19.

transforming short-term savings into long-term lending.[39] Selective credit regulation was thus generally linked to generous rediscounting of credits by the central bank. Where such policies did not result in growing financial self-sufficiency among nonfinancial firms (as they did do in Japan), one of the side effects was the erosion of domestic capital markets. The effort to avoid the Keynesian liquidity trap and to promote productive investments under such regimes therefore often produced a concentration of power in the banking sector and the creation of an oligopolostic financial market structure that intensified the latent asymmetry in the relationship between financial institutions and nonfinancial firms.

For financial reform in formerly interventionist states to result in an efficient and optimal use of savings thus requires an independent and proactive political will to reform the structure of the domestic financial market in a manner that addresses the financial needs of nonfinancial firms. However, there is nothing inherent in the kinds of pressures exerted by international financial markets on governments that necessarily induces such reform. The specific motivations and objectives of reformers within the policymaking bureaucracy and their relationship to other members of the domestic political economy therefore are likely to be as important (or more) to the outcome of market-oriented reform as they were to the construction and uses of financial interventionism. This means that the balanced character of liberalization in France may represent the exception rather than the rule, and that it is likely to have depended, in any case, on factors other than market forces. It is also a critical point in understanding the different pattern and repercussions of liberalization in Spain.

Financial Reform and the Motivations of State Elites

In the political economy literature, state elites are commonly conceptualized in one of two ways. One view (that promoted by public choice theorists) casts public officials as either politicians or bureaucrats who have vested interests in maintaining state controls over the economy to satisfy economic and political rents. The other view is that offered

[39] For discussion, see Loriaux, *France after Hegemony*, pp. 112–13; and Jean Pierre Patat and Michel Lutfalla, *A Monetary History of France in the Twentieth Century* (New York: St. Martin's Press, 1990), pp. 122–25.

by scholars who conceptualize the state as an autonomous actor in the domestic political economy; one whose objectives are defined by its place at the intersection of the domestic and international systems and may therefore respond to aggregate rather than particularistic objectives.

The first perspective does not offer much insight into efforts by state elites to dismantle interventionist practices. Authors who take the latter view have argued that such reform efforts may be seen as action taken by state authorities to promote economic adjustment.[40] Because the potential economic benefits of abandoning interventionism depend on the presence of adequate market conditions, this perspective would lead us to expect that state elites who promote the abandonment of interventionism would be equally committed to market reform. The inadequacies of the financial reform effort in Spain might consequently be interpreted as reflecting a lack of state autonomy and/or insurmountable institutional resistance to state action. Such a conclusion, however, misses an important insight offered by the Spanish experience: the way in which the motivations of different, and contending, state elites may interact to bring about the abandonment of interventionism. Financial reform in Spain failed to support economic adjustment in the 1980s not because the Spanish state was intrinsically weak or inescapably captured by the private banking sector but because the reform process was driven by reformers within the state bureaucracy who had an agenda that led them to seek a working alliance with the domestic financial sector.

State-centered analyses often assume that, other things being equal, the motivations of public officials in charge of the reform effort will correspond to the aggregate objective of promoting national economic competitiveness. Such an objective is certain to feature in public justifications of any reform effort. Yet, given that international market pressures are not sufficient to compel any particular pattern of reform away

---

[40] Up until the 1980s, state-centered analyses tended to interpret interventionist forms of regulation principally as a source of state capacity and strength. More recent state-centered analyses, however, argue that interventionism can also limit the ability of state authorities to "impose the market," and this can serve as the motivation for public officials to favor market-oriented reform. See, for example, G. John Ikenberry, *Reasons of State: Oil Politics and the Capacity of American Government* (Ithaca: Cornell University Press, 1991); and Loriaux, *France after Hegemony*. Peter Katzenstein's argument about the "strength of the weak" in *Small States in World Markets: Industrial Policy in Europe* (Ithaca: Cornell University Press, 1985) follows an analogous logic.

from interventionism, aggregate objectives are likely to compete in practice with other objectives. There are reasons to expect, moreover, that the motivations of state elites may deviate systematically from those of a unitary state actor. To get at this point, however, we must first distinguish among different kinds of state elites who are likely to be involved in the reform process.

Regulatory reform in formerly interventionist states involves at least three different kinds of state elites: (1) reformers within the state bureaucracy or broader policymaking community who act as advocates of market-oriented reform; (2) other state elites, including technocratic planners and industrial policy authorities who held a privileged position in policymaking under the regime of selective credit regulation; and (3) political or elected authorities. The decision to abandon financial interventionism entails changes in the intrastate balance of influence between the first two sets (reformers and planners). It also involves an interplay of objectives and decisions on the part of the second two sets (reformers and political or elected authorities). The objectives of these latter two groups are likely to differ from each other and may also depart systematically from the aggregate welfare objectives set out in economic models.

The economic literature on financial regulation emphasizes issues of allocative efficiency and of the total level of savings that is achieved in an economy, but actual financial reform in formerly interventionist states has typically centered on a different, more immediate kind of problem: facilitating monetary control. This issue lay at the heart of both the French and Spanish reform efforts. One of the features of selective credit regulation in these countries (and others) was that it subsumed monetary policy instruments (such as interest rates and central bank rediscounting), placing these under the direction of political authorities and indirectly at the disposal of planning or industrial policy authorities. This merging of monetary and industrial policy instruments was meant to allow governments to reconcile otherwise incompatible policy objectives (such as boosting investment in key sectors while slowing down credit growth). By implication, however, it also subordinated the policymaking role of central bank officials to that of planners or industrial policy authorities. It is therefore not surprising that much of the intellectual groundwork and promotion of market-oriented reform in formerly interventionist states has been done by the research departments of central banks. The common theme in the arguments presented by central bankers against interventionism is that it constituted an obstacle to the pursuit of effective monetary control. The reasons put forth by central bankers as to why this is so are mostly of a technical nature. The most common argument is that monetary aggregates can be properly gauged and controlled only in the context of a fully developed money market, in which the central bank can add and detract liquidity in a routine fashion. Administrative credit ceilings, as were typically used to control liquidity under a system of selective credit regulation, are considered inadequate tools for effective monetary control, because they do not allow adjustments in response to very short term liquidity changes. Because the practice of state-determined credit prices often had the effect of atrophying the market for monetary assets (money market), it hence interfered with effective monetary policy. The single most important objective of the financial reform efforts in countries such as France and Spain accordingly has been the creation of a dynamic money market in which central bank officials exert control over liquidity in an unincumbered fashion.

Despite the widespread acceptance of these technical arguments, it is questionable that they offer a compelling explanation of the transcendental decision on the part of political or elected authorities to abdicate their discretion over credit flows. The superiority of orthodox central bank instruments over other forms of credit controls was hardly established in the mid-1970s, when reform was initiated in Spain. The French government in the late 1970s and early 1980s came just as close, when not closer, to meeting its monetary targets through selective credit ceilings as did the German Bundesbank.[41] And monetary aggregate targeting was being undermined at the time by unpredictable changes in money demand and by financial innovation even in those countries where central banks operated in well-developed money markets (the United Kingdom and the United States).[42] Last, it is unclear why such technical considerations would carry so much more sway in Spain than in France in the 1970s as to explain the difference in the timing of reform in the two countries.

A different argument as to why interventionism hindered monetary control is the one offered by Michael Loriaux in his study of French

[41] OECD, *Economic Surveys: France,* 1983, p. 40; and *Economic Surveys: Germany,* 1984, p. 30.
[42] David Cobham, "Monetary Targeting," in *The New Palgrave Dictionary of Money and Finance* (London: Macmillan, 1992).

financial reform and centering on the "overdraft economy." Rooted in the work of the economist John Hicks and expanded upon by French central bank economists, the concept of the "overdraft economy" is defined by contrast to that of an asset-based economy. Whereas an asset-based economy is characterized by a well-developed financial market in which "firms and banks, when faced by liquidity shortfalls, sell securities previously purchased and held in reserve in order to confront monetary emergencies," an overdraft economy is characterized by the absence of demand for "precautionary assets" on the part of economic agents because of a presumption that credit from institutional lenders is assured. In the French case, Loriaux argues, this "presumption of assured borrowing power" was caused by the state's role in directly regulating the allocation of credit, which created a form of insurance for economic agents, and an overreliance on institutional credit. As a consequence, both firms and banks became both less sensitive to gradual changes in interest rates and more vulnerable to assertive monetary policy measures. Hence, Loriaux argues, government officials in France chose to abandon selective credit regulation to bolster their ability to impose austerity.[43]

The problems of the "overdraft economy" offer a more compelling argument as to why governments would want to dismantle an interventionist regulatory framework. They also suggest, however, that the underlying reasons for abandoning interventionism were political, not technical. The overdraft economy was not a necessary consequence of financial interventionism in a technical sense. Other countries, notably Japan, engaged in similar regulatory practices during the postwar period without experiencing the atrophy of domestic capital markets that occurred in France and Spain. It was rather the consequence of the way in which selective credit regulation was used to defuse social conflict through the extension of cheap credit to firms in the two European countries (see chapter 3). Once there was less room for an expansionary credit stance (because of both international and domestic developments), the regulatory framework created during the postwar boom years had the effect of politicizing the task of macroeconomic adjustment by requiring state officials to make the hard distributive choices that monetary rigor implied. Monetary rigor is politically easier for elected authorities when credit growth is controlled by the central bank

---

[43]   Loriaux, *France after Hegemony,* p. 56.

through routine operations in a money market, because the allocation of hardship is left to the presumed neutrality of the market. If interventionism hindered monetary policy, it thus did so not as much for technical reasons as by raising the political costs of monetary rigor for political authorities.

If the principal motivation for political authorities in abandoning interventionism is to depoliticize macroeconomic adjustment, then the nature of their choice is essentially negative: it ends when governmental authority has been extricated from the task of allocating credit. Other factors are therefore likely to determine what corollary measures are instituted to accompany credit deregulation. Foremost among those other factors are the goals and motivations of anti-interventionist reformers within the policymaking elite. Given the ideological dichotomy between *dirigisme* and monetarism, the specific problems that credit regulation poses for monetary policy, and the subordination of central bank authority to that of other state officials under selective credit regulation, opposition to interventionism is likely to be institutionally anchored in the central bank. Yet, there are reasons to expect that central bankers, like elected authorities, may have motives for advancing market-oriented reform that depart from the purely economic ones emphasized in the policy literature.

Most of the literature by political scientists on the role of central bankers espouses what Nathaniel Beck has called the "public interest theory of monetary policy,"[44] which assumes that central bankers are essentially apolitical actors who, when freed from the electoral process, will pursue aggregate welfare objectives (such as fighting inflationary expectations) in a manner that elected authorities are unable to do. It is the very acceptance of this premise that makes it politically expedient for governments to abdicate control over credit flows and monetary policy to central bankers. Yet central bankers in interventionist financial systems may be guided by at least two kinds of motives in seeking and designing the dismantlement of selective credit regulation. To the extent that they themselves believe in the public interest theory of monetary policy (i.e., in the inability of elected officials to commit to adequate monetary rigor, and, on a more technical plane, in the necessity of a well-developed money market), they will have a strictly ideological motive

[44]   Nathaniel Beck, "Politics and Monetary Policy," in Thomas D. Willett, ed., *Political Business Cycles: The Political Economy of Money, Inflation, and Unemployment* (Durham: Duke University Press, 1988), p. 368.

for seeking the dismantlement of interventionism. However, reforms that create the money market infrastructure that allows central bankers to control liquidity also imply the dismantling of a regulatory structure that gave other state elites a dominant voice in economic policymaking. Such a change may be consistent with the ideological convictions that central bankers espouse. Yet, it also involves a reduction in the influence over economic policy of planning bureaucracies, public enterprises, and other industrial policy elites in favor of the central bank. To the extent that central bankers believe that achieving their ideological objectives depends on such a shift, they therefore also will have strategic and political motives to seek liberalization, and they may be inclined to subordinate market reform to those objectives. A financial reform process dominated by central bankers may therefore fail to support an economy's ultimate capacity for adjustment.

More specifically, if the central bank comes to be targeted by reformers who see themselves as a contending policy network, and if it is able to control the reform process, one of the factors driving the course of liberalization may be simply the objective of curbing the influence of other state actors over economic policy. Another may be the reformers' need to gain the support of powerful social actors in their quest to bolster the authority of the central bank. Because the "natural constituency" of any central bank is the domestic financial sector, a financial reform process dominated by central bankers is likely to become the subject of a search for "reciprocal consent" between central and private bankers,[45] a possibility made all the more likely by the fact that the tighter monetary stance that reform is intended to facilitate places direct pressure on the profitability of banks. Cheap central bank redis-counting in the postwar period allowed banks to lend to industrial

---

[45] The concept of reciprocal consent is developed by Richard Samuels in *The Business of the Japanese State: Energy Markets in Comparative and Historical Perspective* (Ithaca: Cornell University Press, 1987), pp. 8–14. The relationship between central bankers and the financial community, their "natural constituency," is discussed as one of the most important sources of political influence of any central bank in John T. Woolley, "Central Banks and Inflation," in Leon N. Lindberg and Charles S. Maier, eds., *The Politics of Inflation and Economic Stagnation: Theoretical Approaches and International Case Studies* (Washington, D.C.: Brookings Institution, 1985), p. 338. Delivering the cooperation of the big banks was one of the ways in which central bank reformers sought to boost their influence in the course of the Spanish regime transition (see chapter 5). To do so, however, they had to preempt attempts by Adolfo Suárez and other politicians in the transition government to use the financial support of foreign banks as a lever against the private banks' oligopolistic hold over the domestic credit market.

firms at low interest rates, while making considerable profits for themselves, thus suppressing the latent conflict between restricting competition in the financial sector and providing adequately priced financing to industry. To maintain the profitability of the banking sector while moving away from the cheap credit policies under which financial interventionism was instituted, banks either have to become more cost-efficient or be allowed to continue exploiting oligopolistic market conditions, so that they can pass on the higher cost of financing from the central bank to their customers.

A financial reform process aimed at increasing the central bank's influence over economic policy and limiting that of other state actors is thus likely to entail considerable pressure for continued protection rather than aggressive market reform. To some extent this pressure reflects the dual institutional imperative of any central bank: to ensure both monetary rigor and the stability of the financial sector. Because of the tension between these objectives, reforms meant to facilitate monetary rigor will inspire central bankers to mitigate the competitive impact of liberalization on financial institutions. However, the search for a relationship of reciprocal consent between central bankers who seek to increase their influence and an oligopolistic banking sector also is likely to entail a political premium, so that protection is taken further than considerations of financial solvency alone might account for. A reform process dominated by reformers with an agenda to increase the policy influence of the central bank will therefore tend to protect the banking sector at the expense of nonfinancial firms.

The politics behind the abandonment of financial interventionism may thus not be conducive to aggressive market reform. The motivations that lead elected authorities to abandon financial interventionism are not sufficient to bring about such reform, and those that lead central bankers to promote the abandonment of interventionism may militate against adequate market reform. If this is the case, then the likelihood that financial liberalization in formerly interventionist states will enhance a country's capacity for adjustment may be far more limited than is commonly assumed. The inadequacy of market-oriented reform may grow out of the very political dynamic that promotes the abandonment of interventionism.

Stated differently, my stylized account of the likely political dynamic behind liberalization in interventionist states suggests that the success of reform depends heavily on the presence of other intervening factors that can counteract and redirect the tendencies we have considered. Foremost among those factors, I propose, are (1) the way identities, networks, and conflict among state elites are configured over time; (2) the extent to which economic change interacts with domestic political conditions to alter the influence of different groups of policymakers; and (3) the nature of the relationship between the financial sector and nonfinancial firms. The first and second of these factors affect the likelihood that financial reform will become the vehicle of a political drive by activist central bankers to increase their influence within the state and the extent to which central bankers are able to dominate the reform process. The third affects the extent to which the search for reciprocal consent between reformers and the domestic financial sector is likely to come at the expense of nonfinancial firms. It involves the relationship between banks and their industrial clients and the extent to which the former pursue business strategies that are tied to the success of the latter.

All of these factors are historical outcomes, and they may be largely independent of the economic forces that feed into them at any given point. Recognizing this allows for much greater variation in the effect of liberalization than do models that seek to explain the actions of governments and reformers in terms of objective international economic constraints and opportunities. In the Spanish case, the political model that best captures the deregulation process is one in which changing economic and social conditions at the end of the 1960s tipped the balance in favor of a small network of reformers that was beginning to form around the central bank's research department. These reformers viewed themselves as standing in opposition to a particular historic tendency in Spanish economic development in which monetary rigor and market discipline were subordinated to the principles of state discretion and private privilege in the economy. Their main agenda was to reverse the hold of a developmentalist-minded planning bureaucracy over Spanish economic policy by placing the central bank in control of the financial system. The political regime transition propelled these central bank reformers into positions of leadership. Nevertheless, to ensure the centerpieces of their agenda of institutional reform, they actively pursued an accommodation with an initially resistant domestic banking sector.

It is this interplay between the political objectives of contending state elites and the politics of accommodation with the domestic banking sector that explains the character of Spanish financial reform. This story of shifts among the policymaking elite, enhanced (but not determined) by changing economic conditions and premised on accommodations with the banking sector also applies to the creation of an interventionist regulatory framework in the early 1960s. In both instances, political struggles within the state served as the impetus for regulatory change, changing economic conditions as a facilitating factor, and accommodation with the banking sector as a constant. In both cases, the central issue at the heart of domestic political struggles also centered on monetary policy, more specifically, on its political uses. The course of financial regulation in Spain over the present century thus reflects a remarkable degree of continuity across both political regimes and regulatory frameworks.

In the following chapters I seek to illustrate this "continuity within change." In doing so, I hope to show how the politics of Spanish financial liberalization grew out of the politics of interventionism itself. To a much more significant extent than prevalent explanations of liberalization allow for, regulatory changes in Spain have been domestically rooted. Domestic political battles within the state elite not only impinged on changes in Spanish financial regulation, but also drove those changes. Changing economic and social constraints, on the other hand, played mainly a facilitating role. The overall choice in favor of market oriented reform may seem to corroborate the market driven view of liberalization, but I contend that such a conclusion obfuscates the political dynamic at the heart of the process.

The elements of continuity that have persisted in Spain even in the course of seemingly dramatic regulatory overhauls compel an historical analysis. As I seek to illustrate in chapters 2 and 3, the political contest among Spanish state elites that motivated credit deregulation in the 1970s and 1980s was configured a long time ago. This also is true of the regulatory overhaul that led to the establishment of an interventionist framework in the early 1960s, and of the constant that has characterized all forms of financial regulation in Spain during this century: accommodation between state elites and the private banking sector.

2

The Inflationary Origins of
the Spanish Financial System

In 1874, the restoration of the Bourbon monarchy under a parliamentary constitution brought an end to the half-century of political upheaval that had followed Napoleonic occupation in Spain, auguring a relative stability that would last for almost five decades. That same year, the first government of the new political regime known as the *restauración* passed a banking law that granted the monopoly of currency issue to the Bank of Spain, one of fifteen private banks of issue that had come into existence during the nineteenth century.[1] This move set the institutional cornerstone for the creation of a monetary economy and a modern banking system in Spain. Yet, it also embodied the new regime's solution to the problem that had underpinned the long-running conflict between liberal and absolutist forces: how to address the chronic economic indigence of a waning colonial state.

---

[1] The Banco de España came into existence in 1856 when it replaced the former Banco de San Fernando, which had replaced the failed Banco de San Carlos in 1829. It had long had a privileged relationship with the Spanish Treasury, acting as its main creditor. The 1874 law gave the remaining fourteen banks of issue the option of merging with the Bank of Spain (an option taken by all but four) or of limiting their business to other banking activities (the option taken by the banks of Bilbao, Santander, Barcelona, and Tarragona). See Rafael Anes Alvarez, "El Banco de España (1874–1914): Un banco nacional," and Pedro Tedde de Lorca, "La banca privada española en la Restauración," both in Banco de España, *La Banca Española en la Restauración,* vol. 1 (Madrid, 1974).

The political regime of the *restauración* rested on an accommodation between the agrarian and financial interests of the Spanish aristocracy and those of the emerging Catalan, Basque, and Madrilian bourgeoisies. The two premises of this accommodation were protectionism for both agriculture and industry and the forestallment of the radical tax reform that would have been needed to give the state a modern fiscal base.[2] The monopoly of issue was therefore granted to the Bank of Spain as compensation for its agreement to finance the Treasury's chronic deficits, just as foreign creditors had received privileged licenses for ventures in mining, banking, and the construction of railways as payoffs for the crown's debts during the earlier part of the century. The new central bank's criterion for issuing currency was hence that of "answering to all of the credit demands of the State, and to those of solvent private actors within the limits allowed by metallic reserves."[3] Those limits were ampler than those of most of Spain's European trading partners, which in the late nineteenth century adopted the Gold Standard. The governments of the *restauración* stuck to the bimetallic standard that had been adopted in 1868 and that in 1883 became a de facto silver standard after the Bank of Spain revoked the convertibility to gold of peseta bills. The steady decline of the price of silver at the end of the century, moreover, resulted in a growing discrepancy between the value of metallic reserves and that of the currency in circulation, so that the monetary standard in practice was of a fiduciary nature.[4] In this way, "inflation became the expedient that Spanish governments would use to reduce the cost of their debt."[5]

If the Spanish state's indigence served as the basis for the creation of a modern banking system, it would also strongly condition the character of that system. The political solution entailed in the Bank of Spain's

---

[2]   Carlos Moya, *El poder económico en España* (Madrid: Tucar, 1975), pp. 55–91. On the historical evolution of the Spanish tax system, see Josep Fontana, *La historia de la hacienda en la historia de España, 1700–1931* (Madrid: Instituto de Estudios Fiscales, 1980); Enrique Fuentes Quintana, "Los principios del reparto de la carga tributaria en España," *Revista de Derecho Financiero y de Hacienda*, no. 41, 1961, and "Política fiscal y reforma tributaria," in Manuel Fraga, Juan Velarde, and Salustiano del Campo Urbano, eds., *La España de los años 70* (Madrid: Moneda y Crédito, 1974), vol. 3, no. 2.

[3]   Gonzalo Pérez de Armiñán, "La autoridad financiera y la regulación monetaria, crediticia y de cambios," *Revista de Economía Política*, no. 65, 1973, p. 101.

[4]   Ibid., pp. 95–98; Gabriel Tortella, *Desarollo de la España contemporánea* (Madrid: Alianza, 1995), pp. 138–39, 144–45, 177.

[5]   Franciso Comín, "Perfil histórico de la deuda pública española," *Papeles de Economía Española*, no. 33, 1987, p. 96.

new status implied an inflationary model of public finance, and the banking sector that emerged in the context of the new law would be strongly engaged in the provision of public finance. Its activities were therefore inevitably tied to the inflationary process. Until World War I, the sector was overwhelmingly dominated by the Bank of Spain itself, whose assets at the turn of the century outnumber those of other private banks by 3 to 1, and whose activities centered overwhelmingly on channeling resources into public rather than industrial finance.[6] This involvement of the banking sector in the finances of a waning and penurious colonial state is commonly identified as one of the principal causes of the arrested pace of industrialization during the last quarter of the nineteenth century and hence of what some economic historians regard as a critical loss of timing in Spanish economic development.[7]

The first important change in this scenario came during the first two decades of the twentieth century, which, as Table 9 shows, saw the rapid growth of a number of new private commercial banks. By 1929 the Bank of Spain's overriding importance in the financial system had been outweighed by other private banks, reversing the situation that had existed up to 1913. The two most important factors in the growth of these new financial institutions were the repatriation of capital from Cuba after the final colonial defeat of 1898, and Spanish neutrality in World War I. The latter increased the demand for Spanish exports while forcing substantial import substitution, producing an economic boom in Spain that led commercial banks to become actively involved in promoting industrial firms.

[6] See Pablo Martín Aceña, "Development and Modernization of the Financial System, 1844–1935," in Nicolás Sánchez-Albornoz, ed., *The Economic Modernization of Spain, 1830–1930* (New York: New York University Press, 1987); Gabriel Tortella, "Spain, 1829–1874," in Rondo Cameron, ed., *Banking and Economic Development: Some lessons of History* (New York: Oxford University Press, 1972).

[7] See, for example, Rosa Vacarro, "Industrialization in Spain and Italy (1860–1914)," *Journal of European Economic History* 9, no. 3 (Winter 1980); and on the second point Francisco Comín, *Hacienda y economía en la España contemporánea (1800–1936)* (Madrid: Instituto de Estudios Fiscales, 1988), pp. 527–41, 574. Other arguments about the role of the banking sector in Spanish industrialization are discussed in Tortella, "Spain, 1829–1874," and in Tedde de Lorca, "Banca privada." For more general discussions of the failure of industrialization in Spain during the second half of the century, see Jordi Nadal Oller, "The Failure of the Industrial Revolution in Spain, 1830–1913," in C. M. Cipolla, ed., *The Fontana Economic History of Europe*, vol. 4, pt. 2 (London: Collins, 1973); and Gabriel Tortella, "Los Orígenes de la industrialización española, 1950–1931," in *Banco de Bilbao: 125 años de historia (1857–1982)* (Madrid: Banco de Bilbao, 1985).

Table 9. Total assets of Spanish financial institutions, 1854–1935 (millions of pesetas)

	1854	1873	1880	1900	1913	1929	1935
Bank of Spain	128	234	1,067	2,706	2,846	6,304	7,005
Private banks	48	337	431	984	848	11,702	13,296
Savings banks and credit companies		17	59	131	349	1,998	2,886
Public credit institutions		19	59	63	236	2,075	2,720
Total	176	607	1,616	3,984	4,279	2,207	25,907

Source: Pablo Martín Aceña, "Development and Modernization of the Financial System, 1844–1935," in Nicolás Sánchez-Albornoz, ed., *The Economic Modernization of Spain, 1830–1930*, trans. Karen Powers and Manuel Sañudo (New York: New York University Press, 1987), by permission of Banco de España.

As before, however, the activities of the Spanish banking sector continued to be determined by its relationship to public finance. Starting in 1917, the direct monetization of the public debt by the Bank of Spain was replaced by a less conspicuous mechanism known as *pignoración automática,* whereby the private banks could automatically obtain credit from the Bank of Spain for up to 90 percent of the public debt that they subscribed. This change—which meant that the public debt was now effectively monetized through the new commercial banks— gave rise to a "mixed banking" system in Spain once the World War I bonanza had ended. "Thanks to [the *pignoración*]," writes one economic historian, "the Spanish financial institutions, which without the support of the Bank of Spain's printing press would have had to tighten their business to the more modest dimensions of their capital, were able to find unlimited credit margins to promote all types of firms."[8] By the early 1920s, the sector was thus characterized by the "predominance of a small number of large banks practicing "mixed" activities, in the manner of the German "universal" banks: commercial banks that also undertook extensive company promotion and held a sizable proportion of private securities in their portfolio."[9]

The *pignoración* mechanism turned inflationary public finance into a motor of industrialization. As Gabriel Tortella and Jordi Palafox note, it allowed the banks to "increase their ratio of productive to liquid assets . . . at a negligible additional risk" and cost.[10] This encouraged them to invest in industry and promote industrial activities. Yet, be-

[8]   Luis Olariaga, quoted in Juan Velarde, *Sobre la decadencia económica de España* (Madrid: Tecnos, 1969), p. 621.
[9]   Gabriel Tortella and Jordi Palafox, "Banking and Industry in Spain, 1918–1936," *Journal of European Economic History,* 1984 (special issue), p. 88.
[10]   Ibid. See also Velarde, *Decadencia económica de España,* pp. 621–23.

cause industrial promotion was underwritten by inflationary public finance, it also stained the relationship between Spanish banks and the industrial sector with an "original sin": that of rendering industrial investment a source of extraordinary profits for the banks, not requiring them to develop the kind of internal capacity and culture necessary for the development of competitive, long-term industrial investment strategies. The banks' direct investment was heavily concentrated in those sectors that were either natural oligopolies (energy) or that benefited from heavy tariff protection. And, aside from their direct holdings, they financed industrial ventures predominantly through the rollover of short-term debt. There was thus never the "patient capital" link between universal banking and export promotion that has received so much attention in the German case.[11]

If inflationary public finance shaped the relationship between Spanish banks and industry, it also shaped developments in the banking sector itself. The sector's assets experienced rapid growth during the interwar period, and this growth was accompanied by heavy concentration into a small number of banks. "By 1923 the 'big six,' numerically just 6.6% of the bank population, had over 40% of the combined paid-in capital and over 50% of the deposits," thanks to their widespread branch networks.[12] This concentration was accompanied by the creation of extensive networks of interlocking directorships with public utilities and large industrial firms around each of the big banks, so that by 1921 they collectively had directors on the boards of 274 companies, whose combined capital amounted to 49 percent of the paid-in capital of all Spanish corporations.[13] The process also had a geographic dimension. "Madrid and Bilbao housed the headquarters of the 'big six.' Barcelona, once the leading financial center, was a more and more distant third . . . [as] became dramatically evident when the venerable Banco de Barcelona had to close in 1920 and declare bankruptcy soon thereafter."[14]

The "mixed" and increasingly oligopolistic character of the sector

[11] Andrew J. Spindler, *The Politics of International Credit: Private Finance and Foreign Policy in Germany and Japan* (Washington, D.C.: Brookings Institution, 1984); Michael Kreile, "West Germany: The Dynamics of Expansion," in Peter J. Katzenstein, ed., *Between Power and Plenty: Foreign Economic Policies of Advanced Industrial States* (Madison: University of Wisconsin Press, 1978).

[12] Tortella and Palafox, "Banking and Industry," p. 83. The Big Six banks were Hispano Americano, Bilbao, Urquijo, Central, Vizcaya, and Banesto.

[13] Ibid., p. 87.

[14] Ibid., p. 83.

Table 10. Industrial portfolios of private banks, 1922–1934 (millions of constant 1913 pesetas)

Year	All banks (1)	Seven largest banks (2)	Percent of total (2/1)
1922	344.8	185.0	53.7%
1923	392.3	223.7	57.0
—	—	—	—
—	—	—	—
—	—	—	—
1930	824.1	512.4	62.2
1932	801.1	508.8	63.5
1933	849.0	539.0	63.5
1934	867.6	558.4	64.4

Source: Adapted from Gabriel Tortella and Jordi Palafox, "Banking and Industry in Spain, 1918–1936," *Journal of European Economic History* 13 (Fall 1984) (special issue), p. 88.

intensified during the Great Depression, when the large banks took advantage of the depressed stock market to increase their portfolios while the smaller banks did the opposite. From 1922 to 1934 the proportion of industrial assets held by the seven largest banks rose further, from 53.7 percent to 64.4 percent of the total industrial portfolios of the more than ninety registered banks in Spain (Table 10). The importance of industrial assets in the large banks' balance sheets also rose sharply in relation to their ordinary banking activities (compare columns 10 and 11 in Table 11). Table 12 shows the connections between the Big Six and leading Spanish industrial and public utility companies in 1930, illustrating the tendency of the banks to link up with big and heavy industry. Thus, as the economist Juan Velarde writes, "the inflation produced by the budget imbalance of the State [was] diverted [through the *pignoración*] in the benefit of the Great Spanish Banking group, who capitalized the income that was expropriated through this inflation in the form of various [industrial holdings]."[15]

[15] Velarde, *Decadencia económica de España,* p. 623. The Spanish banks maintained strong profits while expanding their industrial holdings during the Great Depression (see Table 11), thanks to the relatively weak impact of the international downturn on the still relatively backward and insulated Spanish economy. Unlike much of the rest of Europe, Spain thus did not experience a generalized banking crisis in the 1920s or 1930s. This put the large banks in a position to take advantage of the investment opportunities afforded by the public works campaign and increased tariff protection instituted by the Primo de Rivera dictatorship (1921–29). See Tortella and Palafox, "Banking and Industry"; and "La banca privada y el proceso de desarollo en España," *Situación* (Banco de Bilbao), no. 3, 1982.

Table 11. Big Six banks: Balance sheet items (millions of 1913 pesetas) and profit rate, 1923–1934

Year	Paid-in capital (1)	Reserves (2)	Total capital (3)	Current accounts (4)	Savings deposits (5)	Total deposits (6)	Discounted bills (7)	Public bonds (8)	Industrial securities (9)	Portfolio (10) (7 + 8 + 9)	Loans (11)	Securities under custody (12)	Profit rate[a] (13)
1923	193.7	81.3	275.0	884.5	180.3	1064.9	368.0	276.5	182.7	827.2	405.1	4,337.5	18.97%
1929	224.4	131.4	355.7	1,501.2	599.9	2,100.5	660.4	713.0	440.7	1,814.1	666.8	6,076.9	18.92
1930	236.8	152.1	389.0	1,547.4	633.3	2,180.8	661.7	811.5	482.7	1,955.9	679.9	6,437.7	18.57
1932	246.0	132.9	378.9	1,360.4	641.8	2,002.3	564.5	863.7	479.6	1,907.8	505.7	6,435.4	13.16
1933	257.5	146.3	403.7	1,493.9	740.3	2,334.2	579.6	939.5	502.5	2,021.6	590.6	6,735.9	12.65
1934	250.9	147.0	397.9	1,359.5	1,047.7	2,407.2	595.0	1,102.9	530.7	2,228.6	587.5	7,100.4	13.08

aRatio of profits to paid-in capital.
Source: Adapted from Gabriel Tortella and Jordi Palafox, "Banking and Industry in Spain, 1918–1936," *Journal of European Economic History* 13 (Fall 1984) (special issue), pp. 93, 107.

Table 12. Interlocking directorates of Big Six banks and heavy industry, 1930

Banco Hispano Americano
Railways
Ferrocarriles Santander Mediterráneo (1; IV)
Electricity
Hidroeléctrica Española (1; III)
Mining
Minero Metalúrgica Los Guindos (1; II)

Banco Urquijo
Railways
Caminos de Hierro del Norte (3; I)
Ferrocarriles de Madrid a Zaragoza y Alicante (1; II)
Ferrocarriles del Oeste de España (1; III)
Iron and steel
Altos Homos de Vizcaya (3; I)
Duro Felguera (4; II)
Industrial Asturiana Santa Bárbara (1; IV)
Basconia, S.A. (1; IV)
Electricity
Hispano Americana de Electricidad (4; I)
Mining
Cia. Española de Petróleos (1; I)

Banco de Vizcaya
Railways
Caminos de Hierro del Norte (2; I)
Ferrocarriles de Madrid a Zaragoza y Alicante (1; II)
Ferrocarriles del Oeste de España (1; III)
Cia. Metropolitano Alfonso XIII (3; V)
Iron and Steel
Altos Homos de Vizcaya (2; I)
Electricity
Hispano Americana de Electricidad (2; I)
Hidroeléctrica Española (6; III)
Cia. Sevillana de Electricidad (2; IV)
Hidroeléctrica Ibérica (7; VI)
Mining
Minero Metalúrgica Los Guindos (1; II)
Cia. Española de Minas del Rif (1; V)

Banco de Bilbao
Railways
Caminos de Hierro del Norte de España (6; I)
Ferrocarriles de Madrid a Zaragoza y a Alicante (1; II)
Ferrocarriles del Oeste de España (3; III)
Iron and steel
Altos Hornos de Vizcaya (3; I)
Cia. Siderúrgica del Mediterráneo (4; III)
Basconia, S.A. (1; IV)
Mining
Cia. Minera de Sierra Menera (3; IV)
Cia. Española de Minas del Rif (1; V)

Banco Central
Railways
Ferrocarriles de Madrid a Zaragoza y Alicante (2; II)
Ferrocarriles Andaluces (2; VI)
Iron and steel
Fábrica de Mieres (1; V)
Electricity
Hispano Americana de Electricidad (1: I)
Hidroeléctrica Española (1; III)
Mining
Cia. Española de Petróleos (3; I)

Banco Español de Crédito (Banesto)
Railways
Caminos de Hierro del Norte (1; I)
Ferrocarriles de Madrid a Zaragoza y Alicante (1; II)
Ferrocarriles Andaluces (1; IV)
Electricity
Hidroeléctrica Española (1; III)
Hidroeléctrica Ibérica (7; VI)
Mining
Cia. Española de Minas del Rif (1; V)

Note: An arabic number indicates number of shared directors (board members); a roman numeral indicates the firm's rank within its sector according to paid-in capital.
Source: Gabriel Tortella and Jordi Palafox, "Banking and Industry in Spain, 1918–1936," *Journal of European Economic History* 13 (Fall 1984) (special issue), pp. 85–87.

The same mechanism that turned inflationary public finance into a motor of industrialization in Spain thus concentrated economic power in the banking sector. Such newfound economic clout was reinforced through strong personal connections between the new financial capital and the aristocracy of the *restauración,*[16] which gave the bankers a great deal of political access and influence. Political power in turn was enshrined in 1921 in a new banking law which officially sanctioned the existing banking cartel through the creation of the Consejo Superior Bancario (CSB), a corporativist institution controlled by the Big Six that was given wide-ranging powers to regulate the sector.[17] The oligopoly was thus institutionalized, creating what would henceforth be referred to in Spain as the banking status quo.[18]

Although it effectively closed entry into the sector, the law of 1921 avoided any form of state discretion over credit allocation. Despite the creation of a number of parapublic credit institutions in the 1920s, these remained heavily circumscribed by the private bankers who controlled their boards.[19] The legislation of 1921 thus established a regulatory regime that combined state-sanctioned oligopoly with laissez-faire for the banking sector. Like granting the monopoly of issue to the Bank of Spain in 1874, sanctioning the banking cartel reflected the political regime's solution to the Treasury's continued indigence through an accommodation with the financial establishment that dominated its political class. As before, the interests of that class stood in the way of fiscal reform. The solution once again therefore implied a symbiotic combination of inflationary finance and monopolistic privileges for the institutions on which the Treasury had come to depend.[20]

The political compromise enshrined in the legislation of 1921 had broad implications for Spanish economic development. At the same

---

[16]   Moya, *Poder económico en España,* pp. 55–91.
[17]   The CSB was empowered to fix the maximum interest rate to be paid on deposits, the minimum capital requirement for the creation of a bank, and other capital ratios, as well as to set the rules of proper business behavior. In 1946, it was authorized to set minimum credit rates and to scrutize any new applications for a banking license. For a full description of the CSB's powers, see Juan Muñoz, *El poder de la banca en España* (Algorta, Vizcaya: Zero, 1970), pp. 167–73.
[18]   Ibid., pp. 60–68.
[19]   Gabriel Tortella and Juan Carlos Jiménez, *Historia del Banco de Crédito Industrial* (Madrid: Alianza, 1986).
[20]   The political class of the Restauración is commonly identified as combining the interests of the landed upper class, the large banks, and protectionist industrial sectors. See Moya, *Poder económico en España;* and Comín, *Hacienda y economía,* pp. 536–41.

time as competition was restricted, the role that the state could play in the economy was checked. One of the clearest illustrations of this was the private bankers' ability to maintain control over the Banco de Crédito Industrial, a parapublic institution chartered in 1921 to compensate for the private banks' failure to extend long-term credit.[21] Another was the fate of the dictatorship of Miguel Primo de Rivera (1923–1929), whose downfall is often attributed to loss of support from the financial establishment, which opposed its protostatist economic orientation.[22] This effective veto by private interests of a more assertive state role persevered throughout the Second Republic (1930–1936), whose leaders are said to have had an attitude of "reverential respect" toward the banks.[23] Juan Velarde observes that the single most important attempt at socialization under the Republic, the agrarian reform effort, was "sentenced to death" when the Supreme Banking Council managed to halt the creation of the National Agrarian Bank. "The resistance of Big Spanish Capital [to any expansion of the public sphere] was so strong," he writes, that "one can observe a clear abandonment of any programmatic plan to socialize key economic sectors in the program of the Popular Front of 1936."[24]

State action to promote industrialization was blocked by the political ascendancy of the financial establishment. Yet, the political elites of both the *restauración* and of the liberal Second Republic also lacked the kind of imperative that motivated state-led industrialization in other European late-comers. As Rosa Vacarro writes in seeking to explain the inverting trends in Spanish and Italian economic development at the turn of the century, "both the resources and the political energy devoted by the Spanish ruling classes to industrial development were much less than in Italy."[25] This lack of ideological thrust was related to

[21]   Tortella and Jiménez, *Historia del Banco de Credito Industrial*, pp. 130–35.
[22]   Juan Velarde, *Política económica de la dictadura* (Madrid: Guadiana, 1968).
[23]   Juan Velarde, "Prólogo," in Muñoz, *Poder de la banca*, p. 5.
[24]   Juan Velarde, "La empresa pública en una encrucijada," in *La empresa pública en España* (Madrid: Instituto de Estudios Fiscales, 1972), p. 66.
[25]   Vacarro, "Industrialization in Spain and Italy," pp. 736–37. Vacarro points out that the trend between 1861 and 1881, when industrial production in Spain grew faster than in Italy, was sharply reversed between 1881 and 1911. Along with the ideological motivations of the political class, she emphasizes the different roles played by the banks, which "in Italy were agents of a powerful macroimpulse, while in Spain they were not" (p. 722). By contrast to the Bank of Spain, the Bank of Italy lent less to the state and more to the national economy during this period, as did the other private Italian banks that were established with German capital after 1893.

Spain's peculiar circumstances as a fallen colonial power at the beginning of the century. Neither territorial unification nor militarism such as drove state promotion of industrialization in Germany or in Italy offered themselves as motives in Spain. Having irreparably lost its international position, the political elite of the *restauración* rather turned its sight inward after 1898; an orientation that persevered in the Second Republic, whose governments, as Charles W. Anderson writes, were "preoccupied with agrarian and educational reform" and thus "did not recognize industrialization as a privileged problem."[26]

The opposition of private economic interests together with the inward orientation of political elites thus failed to provide the political impetus for "catch-up" industrialization. In this context, the inflationary model of industrial finance through indirect monetization of the public debt served only to restart a moribund process of industrial investment and to strengthen the existing structure of economic power. In the absence of a stronger political imperative, neither the state nor the banks took on the role of a "functional equivalent" (in the Gerschenkronian sense) that would have allowed Spain to recover the loss of timing experienced in the latter part of the nineteenth century and catch up with its neighbors to the north.[27] Up until the mid-1930s, Spain's economic development thus appeared limited to the pace that a financial aristocracy with heavy links to Spain's agricultural past would allow. This developmental impasse ended only with the civil war.

The upheaval and economic destruction of the Spanish Civil War of 1936–1939, and the emerging regime's imperative of economic reconstruction in the context of a hostile international environment for the first time created the political circumstances for a more assertive industrialization effort in Spain. Breaking with the complacent attitudes of prewar elites, the new regime espoused economic self-sufficiency early on as its prime objective and adopted a stance of unequivocal economic nationalism to achieve it. The political change was articulated by one of

[26] Charles W. Anderson, *The Political Economy of Modern Spain: Policy-Making in an Authoritarian System* (Madison: University of Wisconsin Press, 1970), p. 38.
[27] In *Economic Backwardness in Historical Perspective* (Cambridge: Harvard University Press, 1962), Alexander Gerschenkron argued that late or "catch-up" industrialization required some institutional mechanism of capital concentration to finance the rapid and large-scale capital investments required to compete with earlier industrializers. He identified the banks and the state as the two most likely agents to fulfill this function. The point with reference to Spain is taken up by Comín in *Hacienda y economía*, p. 540.

the regime's most prominent economic strategists, Antonio Robert, who in a booklet titled *A National Problem: The Necessary Industrialization* expounded an international conspiracy theory of Spanish economic backwardness, placing the blame on four groups: "the exporters of the few agricultural products that Spain can sell in the external market," "traders dedicated to imports," "other world powers interested in retarding our progress," and intellectuals "stupefied . . . by the doctrines of Adam Smith and the propagandist discourses of Cobden, who when he visited the peninsula did so on behalf of British producers."[28] Robert's "necessary industrialization" thesis became the rallying cry for the rigidly inward-looking, capital-intensive industrialization drive pursued by the Franco regime during its first two decades. This period, generally referred to by Spanish historians as the *autarquía,* represents a watershed in Spanish economic history, for, as one critic of the regime admits, "though it is an irritating fact for many, [Spain] industrialized basically between 1939 and 1959."[29]

Two sets of circumstances coincided to explain the adoption of such an inward-looking industrialization strategy. The first was the inauspicious international environment in which the Franco regime had to face the task of reconstruction. The end of war in Europe was followed almost immediately by the United Nations' imposition of a boycott on Spain, which lasted until 1955. Isolation reduced the regime's policy options, as reflected most clearly in Spain's exclusion from the Marshall Plan. A number of observers thus conclude that the *autarquía* was the result of necessity rather than ideological preference.[30]

A second, less often noted, factor was the sharp internal conflict between two broad factions in the coalition that supported Franco's insurgency against the Republic.[31] As Velarde writes, "two partly con-

---

28 Quoted in Velarde, "Banca e industrialización: La etapa autárquica," in Antonio Torrero, ed., *Banca e industrialización en España: Pasado, presente, y futuro* (Madrid: Banesto, 1988), p. 38.
29 Angel Rojo, quoted in Salvador Paniker, *Conversaciones en Madrid* (Barcelona: Kairos, 1969), p. 159. The biggest spurt occurred between 1951 and 1957, when the share of agriculture in national product declined from 41 to 25%. See Jacint Ros Hombravella et al., *Capitalismo español: De la autarquía a la estabilización, 1939–1959* (Madrid: Edicusa, 1978), p. 219.
30 Ros Hombravella et al., *Capitalismo español,* pp. 74–85; Anderson, *Political Economy of Modern Spain,* p. 27.
31 The coexistence of these factions under the Franco regime may be seen as one dimension of the "limited pluralism" model proposed by Juan J. Linz to describe the regime in "An Authoritarian Regime: The Case of Spain," in Erik Allardt and Stein

tradictory messages were represented under the victorious flags of April first, 1939." On one hand "national syndicalism, with its then very modern utopian content," on the other hand "representatives of traditional, right-wing Spanish nationalism . . . , who believed that the time had come to make Spain an important economic power that would be capable of standing side by side other European nations," and who were inspired by "the economic progress experienced by Italy under fascism." The first faction "believed that it would be possible to establish immediately a revolutionary process that required three things: a syndical reorganization of the economy involving a new role for workers in the firm, a very radical agrarian reform, and the abandonment of a liberal—or market—orientation in economic policy; that orientation would be replaced by a growing presence of the state, which was to have a socializing role." The second faction "backed the construction of a strong military industry that would allow greater influence in the Mediterranean, in Africa, and of course in Europe, where fascism had come to an accommodation with local capitalism years earlier," but "heavy-handedly sought to repress any socializing tendencies."[32]

The conflict between proto-leftist national syndicalists ensconced in the Falange and individuals representing the main economic powers that had backed the regime (i.e., landed oligarchy, bankers, and industrialists) was a significant challenge for the regime, because of the role that national syndicalism played in its legitimizing discourse. As an ideology, national syndicalism "presented itself as highly suited to the task of recruiting a large part of the working-class militants who had subscribed to socialism and the CNT."[33] Velarde's analysis suggests

Rokkan, eds., *Mass Politics; Studies in Political Sociology* (New York: Free Press, 1979), or of Amando de Miguel's model of coexisting "political families," in *Sociología del franquismo* (Madrid: Euros, 1975), p. 154. However, the conflict between national syndicalists and conservatives represents a particularly sharp division among these "families" of supporters. For a discussion of the controversy raised by Linz's and de Miguel's characterization of the Franco regime and the positions of some of their critics, see José Félix Tezanos, *Estructura de clases y conflictos de poder en la España postfranquista* (Madrid: Edicusa, 1978), pp. 83–113.

[32] Velarde, "Banca e industrialización," pp. 36–37. Velarde notes that Robert's autarkic industrialization strategy was not the only one entertained at the end of the Civil War. The economist Ramón Carande, for example, advocated a light industrialization model, premised on agricultural modernization, open external economic relations, and progressive tax reform.

[33] Ibid. The CNT (Confederación Nacional del Trabajo) was the main anarchist trade union before the war.

that economic nationalism served as a minimum common denominator under which these conflicting factions could be rallied and by which the national syndicalist wing of the regime could be coaxed into postponing its agenda of radical, socializing reform in favor of promoting national capital. As another set of authors write, the word *autarky* possessed virtues that served to "firm the forces of the fatherland" and to "define political attitudes"—an effect captured in the following exposition by a prominent Falangist member of the regime:

> Autarky and syndicalization form the two columns upon which stands the new economic policy of Spain. . . . To systematically criticize the policy of controls and self-sufficiency or the purpose of achieving an organic and syndical structure of the Spanish economy is equivalent to being an enemy of the independence and freedom of Spain and a promoter of the spread of social anarchy and class conflict among us.[34]

The autarkic industrialization drive involved a dramatic expansion of state interventionism, including extensive price and quantity controls, the establishment of a highly protectionist regime for industry, sharp import restrictions, and strong limitations on foreign investment.[35] At the same time, investment in industry was bolstered by wage repression, which kept labor costs well below prewar levels through 1956 and created opportunities for very high profits.[36] From the standpoint of the present discussion, however, the most significant change was the 1941 creation of the Instituto Nacional de Industria (INI), whose charter explicitly expounded on the inadequacy of private bank initiative to the task of industrialization in Spain and stated the need for "an agency that is endowed with the economic capacity and legal character needed to realize and give form to the great programs of industrial resurgence of our nation."[37]

The creation of the INI appeared to represent a deliberate effort to embark on a statist model of development in which the initiative of private financial capital would be supplanted by that of the state. This vindicated at least in form some of the national syndicalist agenda to use the public sector to break the retarding tendencies that a monopo-

---

[34] José María Areilza, quoted in Ros Hombravella, et al., *Capitalismo español*, p. 80.
[35] For a discussion of economic legislation during this time, see Ros Hombravella et al., *Capitalismo español*, pp. 86–117.
[36] Ibid., p. 257.
[37] Law of September 25, 1941, *Boletín Oficial del Estado*, no. 280 (October 7, 1941).

listic private banking sector was seen to promote. In its initial phase, one of the functions thus ascribed to the INI was to exert a competitive pressure in otherwise oligopolistic sectors.[38]

Despite the political momentum behind its creation, however, the model of development that the INI embodied never took hold under the *autarquía*. Although its military architects had intended the institute to play the role of a large financial holding company modeled on the Italian Istituto per la Ricostruzione Industriale (IRI) and giving the state a significant market presence in the financial sector, the INI's activities were restricted early on to the sphere of production in three basic industrial inputs (coal, steel, and power.)[39] Thus, as Charles Anderson writes, it "did not preempt much industrial terrain from the private sector." At an average of 15 percent from 1943 through 1960, the "INI's participation in total industrial investment was quite modest when compared to public industrial investment elsewhere in Europe . . . 47% of total industrial investment in Austria, 45% in Turkey, 32% in the United Kingdom, 31% in France, 25% in Holland, and 20% in Belgium for approximately the same period." "Almost all the tools of conventional public policy," Anderson notes, "were geared to the advantage of the domestic private industrial investor."[40]

Even more important in limiting the role that the public sector would come to play in the autarkic industrialization process, however, were two sets of measures in the area of monetary and financial regulation that were taken as the INI was being launched. First, and in sharp contradiction of the Falange's prewar call for nationalization of the banking sector,[41] the Franco regime sanctioned the status quo (i.e., the existing cartel) in the sector in 1939, officially closing access to the profession of "banker" and precluding the creation of any new banks, and reestablished the CSB in the banking law of 1946. Though the CSB was now chaired by a government representative (the Minister of Finance), it continued to function, just as it had done before the war, as the executive committee of what was now the Big Seven (Banesto,

---

[38]   Pedro Schwartz and Manuel Jesús González, *Una historia del Instituto Nacional de Industria, 1941–1976* (Madrid: Tecnos, 1978).
[39]   Velarde, "Banca e industrialización," pp. 44–45.
[40]   Anderson, *Political Economy of Modern Spain,* p. 40.
[41]   The Falange's founder, José Antonio Primo de Rivera, who was killed during the Civil War, had made nationalization of the banking sector and agrarian reform the centerpieces of his platform; these reforms, he said, were the fundamental precepts for adherence to his party. Velarde, "Empresa pública en una encrucijada," p. 71.

Central, Hispano-Americano, Bilbao, Vizcaya, Santander, and Popular). One of the clearest indications of this is the anachronistic mode of interest rate regulation that was adopted during this period, which made deposit rates subject to a maximum, and credit rates subject to a minimum.[42] This seemingly contradictory move from the standpoint of promoting industrial investment served the sole purpose of sustaining the banking cartel's cohesiveness in an environment of high liquidity by preventing individual banks from lowering their credit rates below a floor, ensuring the banks a high interest margin. The main difference from the prewar period was that the cartel's decisions now bore the official stamp of approval of the state.

Along with the old framework of banking regulation, the new regime also reestablished the old mode of monetary regulation. After unblocking the banking system by converting the pool of Republican pesetas into national ones according to a regressing scale,[43] the new authorities reestablished the *pignoración automática,* thus recreating the prewar pattern whereby the banks could expand their assets through the purchase of public debt. Indeed, the leeway for this process of indirect monetization was expanded by the regime's decision to abandon the prewar metallic standard in favor of an unbacked fiduciary standard for the peseta and to abolish all legal limits on Bank of Spain lending to the Treasury.[44]

The re-creation of the *pignoración* in the context of a fully sanctioned banking cartel placed the banks in an unsurmountable position to benefit from the large profit opportunities that the autarkic industrialization drive created. It allowed them to monetize their purchases of assets in the economy through their purchases of public debt, supplying them with such an ample guarantee of cheap liquidity as to make it virtually risk-free and costless to expand their industrial holdings and

---

[42] Vicente Galbis, "Negligencia de la política de los tipos de interés en la posguerra," *Revista Española de Economía* 7, no. 3 (1977): 84–85.
[43] During the war, two separate currencies had existed, and on both sides a great part of the cost of the war was financed through monetization. See Comín, "Perfil histórico de la deuda pública española," p. 89; Velarde, "Banca e industrialización," pp. 40–42.
[44] Exchange rate operations were charged to a new Instituto Español de Moneda Extranjera (IEME), which was placed under the authority of the Ministry of Industry. For discussion of this separation of exchange and monetary policy, see "Pérez de Armiñán, "Autoridad financiera y la regulación monetaria"; Ros Hombravella et al., *Capitalismo español,* pp. 86–91; and Mariano Rubio, "La organización de la autoridad monetaria," *Moneda y Crédito,* no. 104, 1968.

lending. As a consequence, the first two decades of the Franco regime saw a new process of concentration in the sector, which reduced the total number of existing banks in Spain from 200 in 1940 to 107 in 1962. Virtually all of the absorptions were carried out by the Big Seven, which were able to increase their share of total bank deposits to 72 percent in 1957.[45] Because the inflationary mode of public finance also stifled the role of the stock market, the dependence of Spanish firms on bank credit also increased substantially during this period. The share of bank credit in the external financing of the private sector rose from an average of 30 percent during the prewar decade to an average of more than 60 percent for the two decades from 1941 to 1959.[46] Through its effect on both the banks' industrial holdings and their increased control of the economy's financial resources, the *pignoración* thus allowed the Big Seven to consolidate their dominant position within Spanish capital during the *autarquía*.

Far from the statist model heralded in the creation of the INI, the mode of industrial finance that drove autarkic industrialization during the first two decades of the Franco regime was a vast expansion of private bank credit and asset purchases by the banks, fueled by the issuance and monetization of public debt.[47] Yet, once again, monetary expansion was not accompanied by state discretion. As one author puts it, the financial legislation of the 1940s was so concerned with freezing the institutional structure of the sector that the government "declined to intervene even in the distribution of credit and financing."[48] This absence of selectivity in the way credit was extended not only precluded state direction over the way financial resources were allocated but also "made any attempt at even minimal control of monetary magnitudes impossible."[49] "The expansion of the money supply was not in the hands of the Bank of Spain or the Ministry of Finance, but rather, by

[45] See Arturo López Muñoz, *Capitalismo español: Una etapa decisiva* (Algorta, Vizcaya: Zero, 1970), p. 246; Ramón Tamames, *La lucha contra los monopolios* (Madrid: Tecnos, 1966), p. 327; and Antonio Torrero, "La evolución del sistema financiero," *Boletín de Estudios Económicos,* no. 96, 1976, p. 860.

[46] Mariano Navarro Rubio, *Mis memorias* (Barcelona: Plaza y Janés, 1991), p. 518.

[47] The inflationary thrust of this setup was justified in the early years of the regime with reference to the successful National Socialist experiment of inflationary war finance in Germany. Ros Hombravella et al., *Capitalismo español,* p. 180.

[48] Raimundo Poveda, "Política monetaria y financiera," in Luis Gamir, ed., *Política económica de España* (Madrid: Alianza Universitaria, 1980), p. 72.

[49] Torrero, "Evolución del sistema financiero," p. 858.

virtue of the mechanism of *pignoración automática* of public debt, in the hands of the private banks."[50]

The choice to forgo state discretion over credit allocation during the *autarquía* gave monetary policy a virtually untamed character as the banks could choose when to trade in their swollen public debt port-folios for credit. This situation contrasts radically with the heavy-handedness of state regulation over almost every other sector of the economy. The banking sector's widely noted influence with the leader-ship of the Franco regime undoubtedly played a role in bringing about this hands-off stance. Yet the lack of regulation of bank credit expan-sion was also uniquely suited to the political needs of the regime's conservative leadership, because it served to consolidate the role of private capital in the Spanish economy and to limit that of the public sector in a politically opaque but highly effective way, subverting the radical agenda of the national syndicalist wing.

The reinstitution of the *pignoración* and of the banking status quo under the *autarquía* simply raised the prewar pattern of inflationary public and industrial finance to a higher power. The viability of such an inflationary process, however, was premised on a relatively insulated and closed economy that was not yet subject to a strong balance of payments constraint in the form of import requirements. It was there-fore inherently self-limiting as a model of industrialization for as small an economy as the Spanish. The experience of German inflationary finance was, in the words of another prominent national syndicalist economist, inapplicable to Spain, where various structural bottlenecks meant that a rampant monetary expansion would eventually produce a "pure inflation."[51]

The most important of these bottlenecks inevitably turned out to be the economy's foreign exchange gap. A first balance of payments crisis in 1951 led the regime to seek foreign assistance and to moderate its autarkic stance in favor of a more traditional import substitution re-gime. In 1953 it signed a series of "secret agreements" allowing the United States to establish military bases on Spanish soil in return for a package of military and economic aid and American efforts to lift the U.N. boycott on Spain. American assistance provided the foreign ex-change that allowed for higher import levels and a rapid rise in indus-

---

[50] Ros Hombravella et al., *Capitalismo español*, p. 158.
[51] Higinio París Eguilaz, *Diez años de política económica en España, 1939–1949* (Madrid: CSIC, 1946), p. 126.

trial production after 1951. Yet it was insufficient to keep up with the inflationary dynamic of the *pignoración*.

The critical point came in 1957, when two drastic wage increases decreed by the national syndicalist Minister of Labor, José A. Girón, led to a sharp increase in credit demand from businesses. Despite a restrictive fiscal stance and a sharp reduction in the amount of public debt issued during 1957 and 1958, the process of monetary expansion could not be halted, because the banks, which sought to take advantage of the surge in demand, could not be stopped from trading in their swollen portfolios of "pignorable" debt for credit at the Bank of Spain.[52] Once the level of net reserves at the Bank of Spain turned negative in early June of 1959, the process became unsustainable.

The economic crisis of 1957–1959 had a profound effect on the evolving political life of the regime. The government's first attempts at stabilization led to a sharp increase in the cost of living, which set off a wave of strikes in the industrial north. Coming on the heels of clashes between Falangist and traditionalist student groups in Madrid a year earlier, the strikes increased the hostility between national syndicalists and conservatives and heightened the sense of a mounting political crisis. After the establishment of Atlantic convertibility and of the French stabilization plan of 1958, the sense of urgency was compounded by the growing perception that the balance of payments situation left no alternative to external economic liberalization other than "an intolerable decline in the standard of living, perhaps accompanied by a drastic harshening of the political regime."[53] The result was the appointment of a new cabinet in 1957, in which neoliberal technocrats were placed firmly in charge of economic policy, permanently displacing the regime's national syndicalist wing.[54] This decisive political shift opened the way for a radical policy reversal that was augured by the stabilization plan of July 1959.[55]

---

[52] Manuel Jesús González, *La economía política del franquismo* (Madrid: Tecnos, 1979), pp. 74–82.

[53] Ibid., p. 114.

[54] This group is sometimes referred to as the Opus Dei technocracy, because of the large incidence of membership in that lay Catholic organization among its leading figures. See Anderson, *Political Economy of Modern Spain,* pp. 103–8, 168–69.

[55] Both the political and economic shifts were strongly encouraged by France's decision to devalue the franc in 1958 and by the onset of Atlantic currency convertibility at the end of that year, which created in Spain "a sense of danger and distancing" (González, *Economía política del franquismo,* p. 166).

The stabilization plan of 1959 represents another hiatus in the course of Spanish economic policy. To this day, it is regarded by Spanish economic historians as the end of a long inward-looking period in Spanish economic development that started at the turn of the century. The plan itself centered on the imposition of a ceiling on bank lending that served to guarantee a large IMF-organized package of foreign lending. But it also marked the abandonment of the autarkic industrialization strategy in favor of an outward-oriented development strategy premised on the intention of "integrating Spain into world markets."[56] The "new economic framework" (*nueva ordenación*) that was adopted as a corollary of the plan resulted in a rapid and substantial liberalization process from 1959 to 1962 that included the deregulation of internal prices, a sharp reduction in tariff levels, the adoption of a single, convertible exchange rate, and the liberalization of inward foreign investment.

The reorientation in the regime's development strategy meant that henceforth monetary policy would have to be kept in line with the new requirement of peseta convertibility.[57] One of the centerpieces of the plan was therefore an irreversible commitment on the part of the government to end the *pignoración* and with it the mechanism that had served as the motor of both Spanish industrialization and the private banks' stupendous expansion of assets during the preceding decades. The stage was now set for a change in the character of financial regulation—an end to the passive role of the state in the allocation of the financial sector's resources. The ensuing turn toward interventionism, however, was strongly conditioned by the legacy of inflationary finance and the resulting pattern of accommodation between political elites and the domestic financial sector that had taken hold at the turn of the century. The apparently radical changes in domestic financial regulation that were to follow the stabilization plan thus masked important elements of continuity in the objectives that financial regulation was made to serve. This continuity is critical to an understanding of both the political character of financial interventionism in Spain and the politics of later-day financial reform.

---

[56] Enrique Fuentes Quintana, "El plan de estabilización," *Información Comercial Española,* nos. 612–613, 1984.

[57] With Spain's entry into the IMF the same month that the stabilization plan was implemented, the system of multiple exchange rates developed in 1950 was abandoned, the peseta was devalued, and a single exchange rate was set at 60 pesetas to the dollar.

3

Cheap Credit and the Politics of Interventionism

The Stabilization Plan of 1959 marked the abandonment of autarky in favor of a development strategy that sought to integrate Spain into world markets and to unequivocally establish the primacy of private initiative over that of the state. In the years following the plan, the Spanish economy was transformed by a rapid and substantial liberalization of domestic product markets, international trade, and inward capital flows.[1] Because the success of this new development strategy was premised on a convertible currency, and hence required the abandonment of the unorthodox mode of monetary expansion that had driven Spanish industrialization (the *pignoracíon*), the stage was also set for a significant change in the regulation of the domestic financial system. Yet, contrary to the liberal thrust of the *nueva ordenación* in the regulation of product markets and external trade relations, its effect on the financial system involved the creation of a highly interventionist framework of credit regulation that, for the first time in Spanish history, gave state officials a direct say over how

---

[1] The evolution of effective tariff levels is discussed in Manuel Jesús González, *La economía política del franquismo, 1940–1970: Dirigismo, mercados, planificación* (Madrid: Tecnos, 1979), pp. 324–30. González's discussion emphasizes the curtailment of tariff reductions after 1966. Nevertheless, the liberalization that took place from 1959 to 1962 was very significant.

the financial sector's resources would be allocated. This apparent paradox is an important key to understanding the politics of financial interventionism in Spain.

Financial interventionism has traditionally been interpreted by political scientists in one of two ways, both of which center on the juxtaposition of state and market and on the notion of a balance between public and private power. The state-centric literature, always with an eye on questions of international political economy, has tended to interpret a state's ability to direct credit allocation as an important element of state strength, and more specifically, of a state's capacity to achieve its economic objectives despite possible opposition from social actors.[2] Other authors, by contrast, portray interventionism as essentially clientelistic in nature, and in this sense, as typical of "weak" rather than "strong" states.[3] The Spanish financial interventionism of the 1960s fits neither of these interpretations very well. Its introduction was driven by specific economic policy choices that were linked to the legacy of inflationary finance in Spanish development and involved fundamental (rather than particularistic) political objectives on the part of the regime's new technocratic elite. Financial interventionism was instituted to manage conflicting aspects of the regime's new economic strategy. It was also offered to private actors as an alternative to other, more intrusive forms of state control. Rather than a change in the balance between public and private power, interventionism in Spain is best understood as an attempt to reconcile economic liberalization with domestic political stability, and as entailing a new accommodation between public officials and the private banks in a changing domestic political economy.

Interventionism and the *Nueva Ordenación*

In the 1940s and 1950s, the political life of the Franco regime had been defined by the uneasy coexistence of national syndicalists and their opponents. The years following the events of 1957–59 (which

---

[2] For example, John Zysman, *Governments, Markets, and Growth: Financial Systems and the Politics of Industrial Change* (Ithaca: Cornell University Press, 1983); Chalmers Johnson, "Political Institutions and Economic Performance: The Government–Business Relationship in Japan, South Korea, and Taiwan," in Frederic C. Deyo, ed., *The Political Economy of the New Asian Industrialism* (Ithaca: Cornell University Press, 1987).

[3] For example, Jorge de Esteban and Luis López Guerra, *La crisis del estado franquista* (Barcelona: Labor, 1977); Arvid J. Lukauskas, "The Political Economy of Financial Restriction: The Case of Spain," *Comparative Politics*, no. 1, 1994.

effectively marginalized the former), brought to the fore other cleavages among the regime's supporters and within its policymaking elite. One notable example was the early displacement of the neoliberal academic economists who had participated in the drafting of the IMF-sponsored stabilization plan by a more politically minded group of technocrats closely associated with the Catholic lay organization Opus Dei who spearheaded the introduction of French-style planning in Spain.[4] Under the leadership of Laureano López Rodó, a professor of public administration and prominent Opus Dei member who had been named general technical secretary to the office of the presidency in 1957, the Planning Commission was established in 1962, and a little over a year later, the first of four Spanish economic development plans came into effect. Over the following years, the Planning Commission quickly acquired the status of a virtual economic superbureaucracy[5] that gained its cohesiveness from the pro-business, managerial philosophy forged by Opus Dei members in opposition to radical national syndicalism during the previous decade. The central objectives of that philosophy, as articulated by López Rodó, were to advance the role of private initiative in Spain's economic development and to supplant the antiquated corporativism that characterized economic regulation with the principle of "administrative rationalization."[6]

The process of bureaucratic reforms initiated by the Opus Dei planners included an ambitious attempt to change the legal framework of banking regulation. The most important piece of legislation in this regard was a banking law passed in 1962 that departed from the regulatory framework established in 1921 and 1946 in four principal ways. First, it nationalized the Bank of Spain and the parapublic credit institutions (henceforth called official credit institutions, or EOCs), whose private status was rejected as a vestige of the old economic corporativism. Second, it established a complex institutional structure, in which

---

[4] The principal figures in the first group were the economists Juan Sardá, head of the Bank of Spain's research service, and, among others, Enrique Fuentes Quintana and Angel Rojo, whose later-day role is discussed in chapters 4 and 5. González refers to this group when he highlights the role of the "technical team" of "efficient functionaries" involved in the negotiations with the international bodies in 1957–59: *Economía política del franquismo*, pp. 29, 33.

[5] Richard Gunther, *Public Policy in a No-Party State: Spanish Planning and Budgeting in the Twilight of the Franquist Era* (Berkeley: University of California Press, 1980).

[6] See the discussions of López Rodó in Carlos Moya, *El poder económico en España* (Madrid: Tucar, 1975), p. 91; and Charles Anderson, *The Political Economy of Modern Spain* (Madison: University of Wisconsin Press, 1970), pp. 103–18.

regulatory authority over the financial sector was allocated to three public agencies (the Bank of Spain which was charged with overseeing the private banks, a new Savings Bank Credit Institute which was given regulatory authority over the Savings banks, and a new Medium- and Long-Term Credit Institute which was created to coordinate and oversee the newly nationalized official credit institutions and to regulate medium- and long-term credit extended by the banking sector). Third, the law professed the intention to end the legally sanctioned status quo in the banking sector by imposing a regime of banking "specialization" (separation of commercial and industrial banking) and opening the door to the creation of new "industrial banks." Finally, the law set the legal basis for a regime of state-directed credit allocation by defining the credit system as an "instrument" of the Planning Commission.[7]

The new regulatory framework instituted in 1962 gave rise to two broad conduits of privileged financing (referred to as "privileged financing circuits") that allowed state officials to direct a significant portion of the financial sector's resources to specific users and productive activities. The first circuit involved credit channeled through the now nationalized EOCs and financed through a compulsory public debt ratio that was imposed on both commercial and savings banks. The burden of this coercive constraint was carried disproportionally by the savings banks, which were forced to allot as much as 80 percent of their resources to state-designated investments, compared to a ratio of just 10 percent imposed on the commercial banks. Selective credit allocation was, however, also achieved through a second, less coercive mechanism: so-called special rediscount lines that allowed the commercial banks to rediscount credits extended to state-specified users with the Bank of Spain. The special rediscount lines also served to replace the *pignoración* as the mechanism whereby liquidity was injected into the financial sector. They were first introduced as a special rediscount for long- and medium-term credit in 1960, in the throes of a severe recession that followed the implementation of the stabilization plan, and vastly expanded over the following decade to cover an ever-larger number of sectors and economic activities.[8] Together, the two "priv-

---

[7] "Ley 2/1962 sobre bases de ordenación del crédito y de la banca," *Boletín Oficial del Estado,* April 14, 1962.

[8] It allowed the authorities a greater measure of control over the rate of monetary expansion than the pignoración, however, because the banks could no longer hoard public debt that they could trade in when the authorities tried to impose stabilization measures.

ileged financing circuits" grew rapidly over the 1960s, accounting for 49 percent of private sector financing by 1970.[9]

The technocratic ideology that justified the new regulatory framework asserted objectives (administrative rationalization and economic modernization) that coincide with the transformative or developmental agenda emphasized in the statist view of interventionism. Spanish observers, however, tend to associate the interventionist past with the authoritarianism of the Franco regime rather than state autonomy or strength, and to attribute it to the clientelistic relationships that could be fostered through selective credit regulation.[10] Such a "rent-seeking" explanation of interventionism, however, fails to consider the fact that very similar forms of financial regulation were adopted in countries with political regimes as fundamentally different from the Spanish as those not just of France, but also of Norway or Sweden. It also overlooks the fact that political patronage could be applied equally, if not more, effectively through alternate, less circuitous forms of state control that did not subsume the instruments of monetary policy, as illustrated by the case of Italy. While clientelism and patronage were undoubtedly part of the consequence of financial interventionism in Spain, they thus do not represent a compelling explanation for its introduction in the first place.

A different explanation of why financial interventionism was introduced in Spain at the same time that the rest of the economy was liberalized has been offered by Charles Anderson, who has argued that many of the technocrats' actions were based on a direct and almost unqualified importation of regulatory institutions from Spain's immediate neighbor to the north, France.[11] In its complexity and detail, the edifice of privileged finance established in Spain in the early 1960s indeed bore a remarkable resemblance to the system developed in France over the 1940s and 1950s, and this degree of similarity is partly accounted for by the fact that France served as the model that the

---

[9] On the privileged financing circuits, see Raimundo Poveda, "Política monetaria y financiera," in Luis Gamir, ed., *Política económica de España*" (Madrid: Alianza Universidad, 1980); idem, *La creación de dinero en España, 1956–1970: Análisis y crítica* (Madrid: IEF, 1972).

[10] Enrique Fuentes Quintana, "Prólogo," in Rafael Termes, *Desde la banca* (Madrid: Rialp, 1991), p. liv; Lukauskas, "Political Economy of Financial Restriction."

[11] Anderson, *Political Economy of Modern Spain*, pp. 164–67.

Spanish technocrats were seeking to imitate.[12] Yet the parallelism between French and Spanish regulatory institutions during this period
was not just a matter of simple institutional mimickry. Rather, the
wholesale adoption of the French model of financial regulation in Spain
reflected fundamental choices in the area of economic policy strategy
on the part of the regime's new technocratic elite, which had little to do
with the regulatory framework itself but virtually compelled its adoption. As in France, interventionism was intended to reconcile two conflicting elements in the economic policy strategy pursued by the Spanish technocrats: an open trade regime and a relatively relaxed flow of
cheap central bank credit to the economy.

Many features of the regulatory framework imported from France in
the early 1960s are consistent with the Spanish technocrats' stated
objective of "rationalizing" the character of public administration, and
particularly the relationship between state and private actors in the
economy. The nationalization of the monetary authority, the segmentation of financial operations, and even the principle of state-directed
credit allocation all seem to conform to this idea, and in this sense
support a statist interpretation of the adoption of interventionism (i.e.,
one that gives primacy to the transformative agenda of state elites).
Other aspects of the new interventionism, however, are not so easily
explained. The two-tiered structure of the privileged financing circuits
and the integration into these circuits of the central bank's main monetary policy instruments are not clearly linked to any industrial policy
imperatives and even seem to constrain state capacity by compromising
the independence of monetary policy. Both measures, however, were
necessary corollaries of another type of choice by the technocrats: to
maintain cheap credit as a central element in economic policy, even as
the economy was opened to international product markets. In the

---

[12] The regime of banking specialization and the regulatory segmentation of the credit
market with separate authorities to oversee commercial, industrial, and savings banks
were directly modeled on French banking regulation. The dual structure of the privileged
financing circuits in Spain was also an almost exact replica of the French privileged
financing circuits, which involved a Treasury circuit (similar to the Spanish Official Credit
circuit) and the more "indicative" use of selective rediscounting. The use of these circuits
by state authorities is often described as the backbone of postwar industrial policy in
France. See Stephen Cohen, *Modern Capitalist Planning: The French Model* (Berkeley:
University of California Press, 1977); Zysman, *Governments, Markets, and Growth;*
Stephen S. Cohen, James Galbraith, and John Zysman, "Rehabbing the Labyrinth," in
Cohen and Peter A. Gourevitch, eds., *France in the Troubled World Economy* (London:
Butterworth, 1982).

words of one critic, the planners in the 1980s chose, "explicitly or implicitly, to completely subordinate monetary and financial policy to what we might term an economic policy of 'production.'"[13] The evident external referent for this choice of relative continuity with the past in Spain was the French postwar policy-strategy, which has been variously described as driven by the imperatives of "creating an economy in which capital was both abundant and cheap," and of "of stimulating investment above all else."[14]

In choosing to maintain a cheap credit policy stance, Spanish planners were opting, as their French counterparts had done before them, to eschew the alternative strategy of export-led growth, which was followed by a number of other European countries in the postwar period, most prominently West Germany, and also, up to the mid-1960s Italy.[15] In both of those countries, long-term growth was premised on domestic price stability and an undervalued currency that bolstered exports and domestic savings and discouraged imports and consumption.[16] By contrast, the Spanish industrialization of the 1960s was based on a continuous expansion of bank credit supplied to producers at low, administratively set interest rates and instrumented principally through special rediscount lines.[17] The clearest evidence of this choice is the high level of central bank rediscounting that was maintained in the years following the stabilization plan (see in Table 13 the relatively high level of claims on banks and savings bank as a percentage of

---

[13] Luis Angel Rojo, "Política monetaria," in *España: Perspectiva 1968* (Madrid: Guadiana, 1968), p. 63. For a discussion of Spanish interest rate policy during the 1960s, see Christopher Browne and Leo van Houtven, "The Evolution of Monetary Instruments and Policy in Spain," *IMF Staff Papers* 21, no. 1 (March 1974); and Vicente Galbis, "Negligencia de la política de tipos de interés en la posguerra," *Revista Española de Economía*, no. 3, 1977.

[14] Michael Loriaux, *France after Hegemony: International Change and Financial Reform* (Ithaca: Cornell University Press, 1991), p. 113; Peter A. Hall, *Governing the Economy: The Politics of State Intervention in Britain and France* (New York: Oxford University Press, 1986), p. 244.

[15] Sofía A. Pérez, "'Strong' States and 'Cheap Credit': Economic Policy Strategy and Financial Regulation in France and Spain," in Douglas J. Forsyth and Ton Notermans, eds., *Regime Changes: Macroeconomic Policy Regimes and Financial Regulation in Europe from the 1930s to the 1990s* (Oxford: Berghan, 1997).

[16] In a fixed exchange rate system, a lower-than-average domestic inflation rate leads to an undervalued currency, encouraging exports and punishing imports, whereas a higher-than-average inflation rate implies an overvalued currency, encouraging imports and hurting exports, and leading to balance of payments shortfalls where the current account is not covered by the capital account.

[17] Galbis, "Negligencia de la política."

Table 13. Claims on commercial and savings banks in four countries, 1955–1965 (percent of total central bank assets)

Year	Italy	FRG	France	Spain
1955	3%	10%	24%	21%
1960	1	2	27	12
1965	3	5	19	14

Source: Computed from IMF financial statistics.

Table 14. Average inflation in four countries, 1950s and 1960s

Years	Italy	FRG	France	Spain
1950–1959	2.8%	1.2%	6.2%	5.8%
1960–1969	3.4	2.4	3.9	5.8

Source: Computed from IMF financial statistics.

central bank assets in Spain and France, compared to Germany and Italy). And its most important consequence was the continuation of relatively high levels of inflation in Spain during the 1960s (see Table 14).

The choice of cheap credit growth strategy can be linked to the adoption of indicative planning and the French/Spanish mode of financial interventionism in at least two ways. First, the idea that monetary expansion could be used as a forcing mechanism on the rate of growth required that such monetary expansion be channeled into those types of productive investments that would maximize productivity growth over the medium term and minimize the damage of domestic inflation to the economy's competitiveness. As Michael Loriaux writes for the French case, the cheap credit strategy was based on the government's "ability to accelerate economic reconstruction and to respond to the demand that excess liquidity generated by hastening the production of a commensurate supply of goods," so as to "bypass the need for monetary stabilization."[18] This strategic imperative served as an important rationale for the adoption of both indicative planning and selective credit regulation. Second, as John Zysman notes, the institutionalization of a cheap credit strategy in the form of administratively set credit rates also created a more immediate, technical need for instruments of selective credit regulation to make the strategy compatible with the

[18]   Loriaux, *France after Hegemony,* p. 106.

maintenance of open trade relations and a convertible currency. Administratively set credit rates implied excess demand for credit over supply for credit at those points when the rates were below market-clearing levels; that is, when monetary expansion needed to be restricted to elude or address a balance-of-payments crisis. To maintain low credit rates at those times, state authorities needed some way of selectively allocating credit to address the imbalance between credit demand and supply.[19]

These links lie behind the parallelism between the Spanish and French modes of financial interventionism and explain why financial interventionism was adopted in Spain as a corollary of trade liberalization. They also fit the manner in which interventionism evolved in France, where guidelines for selective credit allocation were first instituted following de Gaulle's decision to forgo a radical stabilization of the inflated wartime currency pool and in response to balance of payments problems during the late 1940s,[20] and in Spain, where selective rediscounting was first instituted in 1960 as part of a decision to restart the process of credit expansion in order to end the severe economic inactivity that had been caused by the stabilization plan.[21] In both countries, regulatory decisions that allowed public authorities to impose selectivity in credit allocation closely followed more fundamental decisions to eschew a "price stability"–oriented policy course, such as was adopted in Germany and Italy after the war. Financial interventionism in France and Spain may thus be largely understood as an attempt to rationalize a decision by state elites to pursue an expansionary policy rather than price stability.

If interventionism was the necessary corollary of such an expansionary policy strategy, the underlying policy choice itself is best understood in political terms. The pursuit of a cheap credit strategy was endowed with a certain economic logic based in Keynesian theory (that of maximizing the internal use of financial resources and of avoiding the liquidity trap that caused the interwar economic crisis). However, the extent to which price stability was subordinated to growth in both France and Spain carried clear risks for export competitiveness. The failure to

---

[19]   For discussion of this relationship between cheap credit and selectivity in the French case, see also Pierre Patat and Michel Lutfalla, *A Monetary History of France in the Twentieth Century* (New York: St. Martin's Press, 1990), pp. 124–25.
[20]   Loriaux, *France after Hegemony,* pp. 114–15.
[21]   Anderson, *Political Economy of Modern Spain,* pp. 114–52.

conform to Keynesian precepts in other ways (e.g., the limited role attributed to fiscal policy in both countries), moreover, suggests that economic ideas alone do not offer a sufficient explanation for the choice of policy strategy.[22] However, the rejection by French and Spanish planners of an economic strategy premised on domestic price stability does seem consistent with a tendency to use monetary expansion instead of expanding the state's tax base, which had a strong historical legacy in both countries.[23] In the case of France, it has been argued, the postwar strategy grew out of a decision in 1945 to reject radical monetary reform and to place political stabilization ahead of economic stabilization to defeat the political threat posed by the left.[24] Despite the very different political regime, an analogous set of reasons explains why the Franco regime's new technocrats opted for the French, rather than the German or Italian, policy course as they sought to integrate Spain into the world economy.

The technocrats' actions, including both their economic liberalization program and their regulatory reforms, must ultimately be understood in terms of their overarching objective of sustaining the existing social and political order in Spain. As Charles Anderson writes, "the prime policy objectives—growth with economic stability, improved foreign trade, and centralized political order in society—remained consistent."[25] The choice to tie Spain to a booming world economy was meant to commit the regime to a private capital–friendly policy course and to dispel any future chance of a turn toward the socializing agenda of radical national-syndicalism. Yet it was also meant to ensure a sufficient rate of economic growth to sustain the political regime and to mitigate the latent crisis of legitimacy posed by its nonparticipatory character and its peculiar situation as an authoritarian regime in postwar Western Europe.

---

[22]   Fiscal policy in France was modestly expansionary through most of the planning period, but remained heavily dominated by monetary policy. See Hall, *Governing the Economy,* pp. 244–45. In Spain, fiscal policy under the Franco regime remained extremely rigid and was restricted by the limited tax base and by a steady effort to cut the public debt after 1952. See Gunther, *Public Policy in a No-Party State,* chap. 1.

[23]   On France, see Charles S. Maier, "The Politics of Inflation in the Twentieth Century," in Fred Hirsch and John H. Goldthorpe, eds., *The Political Economy of Inflation* (Cambridge: Harvard University Press, 1978), pp. 55–60.

[24]   Richard F. Kuisel, *Capitalism and the State in Modern France* (Cambridge: Cambridge University Press, 1981), pp. 192–202, 267–68; Cohen, *Modern Capitalist Planning,* pp. 91–97.

[25]   Anderson, *Political Economy of Modern Spain,* p. 141.

The regime's underlying political precariousness became patent in the large-scale industrial strike wave of the late 1950s, which had been one of the factors precipitating the technocrats' rise within the regime. However, trade liberalization promised to create its own stresses. The first round of tariff reductions over 1959–1962 placed severe strain on the technologically outmoded steel and coal-mining sectors, both of which entered a stage of irreversible crisis in the early 1960s.[26] At the same time, the regime's ability to repress growing wage pressure (resulting from large rates of emigration of rural labor to other European countries during the 1950s) was constrained by the technocrats' decision to seek EEC associate status for Spain in 1962.[27]

All these circumstances strongly advised against the use of orthodox methods of price stabilization to control wage pressure and thus also against the adoption of a strategy of export-led growth based on the imposition of domestic price stability. Once taken, this path perpetuated itself. Over the course of 1959–62, the new government depenalized strike activity and legalized collective bargaining, seeking to preempt a more severe political crisis. The result was a veritable "explosion of collective bargains" and a rise in working-class militancy[28] that translated into a significant rise in nominal wages over the 1960s, threatening the economic growth process by which the technocrats sought to sustain the political order.[29] These developments became an increasingly important motive in economic policy. The government's response to growing labor demands was to rely on cheap credit and monetary illusion to diffuse the cost of nominal wage increases and restore profitability. As one critic of the planners described it, "One day the workers salaries are increased and the next day the

[26] Arturo López Muñoz and José Luis García Delgado, *Crecimiento y crisis del capitalismo español* (Madrid: Cuadernos para el Diálogo, 1968), pp. 189–212.

[27] Anderson, *Political Economy*, pp. 113–18, 190–94; González, *Economía política del franquismo*, pp. 165–71. Attainment of EEC associate status was considered critical to the success of trade liberalization, but it was denied. In 1970, however, the EC granted the regime a preferential trade agreement.

[28] José Maravall, *Dictatorship and Political Dissent: Workers and Students in Franco's Spain* (London: Tavistock, 1978), p. 28; idem, *El desarollo económico y la clase obrera* (Madrid: Ariel, 1970), pp. 93–100. Maravall notes that in 1959, 179 collective agreements were met, covering 427,636 jobs, and by the end of 1964 as many as 4,772 collective bargains had been negotiated, covering close to two million workers. The collective bargaining process was accompanied by a rapid rise in strikes and worker stoppages, which in 1962 alone involved 659,360 workers.

[29] Manuel Román, *The Limits of Economic Growth in Spain* (New York: Praeger, 1971).

employer is given a special credit line, so that he won't go bankrupt as a consequence of the wage increase. This way, the wage increase is destroyed via prices . . . [and] tension is defused. But the instrument of such a policy is that of inflation . . . which serves as the palliative of social conflict."[30]

The economic logic of pursuing a cheap credit strategy thus shrouded a political strategy of diffusing the cost of economic transformation and thus defusing social conflict through monetary expansion. Financial interventionism, however crudely applied, was intended to reconcile such an inflationary domestic dynamic with a more open trade regime and with the planners' objective of linking Spain to a booming world economy. The motivations for such a strategy cannot be simply reduced to the clientelistic character of the Franco regime. It entailed a real formula for counteracting the ability of labor and of traditional sectors, particularly agriculture, to limit the process of accumulation and investment that the planners viewed as essential to the regime's survival.[31] Nor can it be simply ascribed, as the planners themselves would have it, to the actions of a more rational and purposive state. It was the regime's underlying political precariousness, rather than its strength, that called for such a regulatory solution.

Interventionism and Reciprocal Consent

The introduction of selective credit regulation constituted an attempt by the technocrats to reconcile the integration of Spain into the world economy with a domestic policy strategy of relative continuity with the inflationary past. However, the imposition of an interventionist regulatory framework on a private financial sector that by almost all accounts was one of the regime's *poderes fácticos* (de facto powers) also raises a question of historical discontinuity that requires attention: the implica-

---

[30] Luis Angel Rojo, interviewed by Salvador Paniker in *Conversaciones en Madrid* (Barcelona: Kairos, 1969), p. 162.
[31] More specifically, credit expansion and the resulting diffusion of costs through inflation served to address two tasks. The first was to facilitate the shift of resources from some sectors into others. In this sense, the discussion of the strategic value of demand-shift inflation in France by Zysman in *Governments, Markets, and Growth*, pp. 138–44, is fully applicable to the Spanish case. Second, cheap credit to industry, the cost of which was diffused through inflation, also served to offset nominal wage increases and rising agricultural prices that were the result of labor migration. On the latter, see Román, *Limits of Economic Growth*.

tions of interventionism for the relationship between public and private power in Spain.[32] Two sets of literature are relevant to this question: the state-centric literature in comparative and international political economy, and the "financial oligarchy" thesis advanced by a number of Spanish social scientists in the 1960s.

Instruments that allow state officials to direct capital flows to specific users are commonly interpreted by political scientists as an important element of a state's "capacity" to shape comparative advantage and impose its objectives on social actors in the political economy. In this light, the creation of an interventionist framework in Spain in the early 1960s might be interpreted as a shift in the balance between private and public power in favor of the latter. However, although undoubtedly the technocrats' ascent increased the state's ability to direct the allocation of credit by private economic actors, the "strong state" interpretation of interventionism is contradicted by several aspects of the Spanish experience. The first is the banking sector's reaction to the sudden extension of state discretion over its activities. With very minor exceptions, there is no evidence that the banking sector raised real opposition to the expansion of state controls during these years,[33] even though the new financial interventionism was instituted as part of a "new economic order" that in every other way centered on market-oriented liberalization. Indeed, the banking sector itself participated in the design of this new economic framework,[34] and the new banking regulation was drafted at a time when the banks were increasingly represented in policymaking organs.[35]

One way of understanding the banks' apparent acquiescence in the

[32] José Félix Tezanos points out that there is almost complete unanimity among analysts of the Franco regime in identifying the heads of the Spanish banks as the power "nucleus" of the economy, thus attributing them a great deal of political influence within the regime. *Estructura de clases y conflictos de poder en la España postfranquista* (Madrid: Edicusa, 1978), p. 70. Even those analysts who ascribe to Juan Linz's less class-based "limited pluralism" model of the regime, place the banks at the center of the regime's influence circle. See, for example, Armando de Miguel, *Sociología del franquismo* (Barcelona: Euros, 1975), p. 46; Anderson, *Political Economy of Modern Spain*, p. 76.

[33] The only significant exception was the CSB's pro forma opposition to the nationalization of the Bank of Spain. The annual reports of the large banks were conspicuously devoid of criticism of the new regulatory system.

[34] Much of the *nueva ordenación* was first articulated in a report by the Research Service of the Banco Urquijo, an industrial bank linked to the Banco Hispano Americano, titled *La economía española, 1954–1955* (Madrid: Banco Urquijo, 1956).

[35] For bank board members in high public office, see list C-1 in Ramón Tamames, *La oligarquía financiera en España* (Madrid: Planeta, 1977), pp. 218–27.

extension of state controls is offered in the work of a group of Spanish economists and sociologists who in the 1960s sparked a heated public debate about the power of the financial cartel.[36] Documenting the vast pattern of holdings by the banks in large industrial firms as well as the extensive presence of their board members in the high echelons of the bureaucracy, the work of these economists supports the thesis that the state was so in thrall to the bankers that public policy could be made to serve the banks' interests whether the regulatory framework was interventionist or not. These authors offer compelling evidence of the banking sector's ubiquitous influence under the Franco regime. And there is much to support their argument that the banks were able to have their needs met in a multiplicity of ways. However, the singular focus on documenting the "bank power" thesis means that this work is geared almost exclusively toward explaining away the significance of interventionism. It therefore overlooks some important subtleties in how the interests of public officials and the private banks were reconciled in interventionism.

The relationship between public authority and the private banking sector at the heart of the new regulatory regime must be viewed in the light of the broader shift in economic orientation of which financial interventionism was part, and of the perceived alternatives to it. Although the banks had been the most important beneficiaries of the autarkic industrialization experience, the limitations of this economic model had become apparent to all by the late 1950s. As the most important investors in the Spanish economy, the banks also stood to profit from a shift in economic policy that would tie the Spanish economy to the booming postwar world economy. Moreover, the economic and political crisis of the 1950s had shaken the existing political balance within the regime, raising the possibility that future social unrest

---

[36]   The most prominent examples of this literature are Juan Muñoz, *El poder de la banca en España* (Algorta, Vizcaya: Zero, 1970); Ramón Tamames, *La lucha contra los monopolios* (Madrid: Tecnos, 1961); and a series of articles published under the pseudonym Arturo López Muñoz in *Triunfo* and *Cuadernos para el Diálogo* by José Luis García Delgado, Juan Muñoz, and Santiago Roldán. Their arguments revolved around a "financial oligarchy" view of the Franco regime that was broadly analogous to the "power elite" arguments made by American political scientists at the time. The publication of this work encouraged national syndicalists to renew their calls for nationalization of the banking sector and prompted a law that made it a conflict of interest for an individual to be simultaneously on the board of one of the official credit institutions and a private bank. See Muñoz, *Poder de la banca*, pp. 184–85; Velarde, *Sobre la decadencia*, pp. 657–60; and the ongoing debate in the 1968 issues of *Cuadernos para el Diálogo*.

might bolster the influence of radical national syndicalists, whose calls for socialization of the economy had until then been checked by private capital.

The support of the private banks for both the program and political leadership of the technocrats must thus be understood in terms of their support for an economically viable growth strategy that maintained the primary position of private as opposed to public initiative in the Spanish economy. Such a growth strategy was best pursued by engaging in some measure of external liberalization and by tying Spain to the West's major international economic institutions. The regime's perceived political inability to pursue a noninflationary growth strategy virtually compelled the financial sector to accept some mechanism of selective credit allocation that could be used to reconcile monetary expansion with the external constraints of a convertible currency.

There is ample evidence that, in the Spanish political context of the time, financial interventionism was viewed as an alternative to a more aggressive role by the state in the Spanish economy. The first World Bank report on Spain, for example, prescribed an increased role for public credit institutions at the same time that it attacked the privileged role that the Instituto Nacional de Industria (INI) had been given during the *autarquía* and called for limitations on the activities of the public sector.[37] This view of financial interventionism as an alternative to a powerful public sector is reflected as well in the actions of the technocrats who sharply downgraded the INI's role at the same time that the "privileged financing circuits" were being instituted.[38] A similar trade-off underpinned the compulsory public debt ratio. Given the limited fiscal capacity of the state and the existing retrograde tax structure, the imposition of a ratio on the banks must be understood as an alternative to more progressive tax reform, from which the banks, as the largest investors in the Spanish economy, stood to lose far more.

In these various ways, the Spanish banks' acceptance of the new

---

[37] International Bank for Reconstruction and Development, *Economic Development of Spain* (Washington, D.C., 1962).

[38] The INI's role was redefined from serving the goal of economic self-sufficiency to playing a subsidiary role to private capital and initiative. In 1963 the INI was subordinated to the planning authority, which radically reduced its role in public investment outside of the energy sector and redirected the institute's activities toward supporting the investment needs of private firms and taking over failing firms for restructuring. See Pablo Martín Aceña and Francisco Comín, *INI:50 años de industrialización en España* (Madrid: Espasa-Calpe, 1991), chap. 4.

interventionist framework is congruous with Richard Samuels's observation that "although credit allocation is an effective tool of the strong state, the creditor or guarantor state may well be the least threatening, and hence the most acceptable to private interests."[39] Indeed, much of the relationship between the Spanish banks and the Franco regime's technocrats is captured by Samuels's concept of "reciprocal consent" between state and market actors and by his distinction between "jurisdiction" and "control" in the relationship between business and the state in Japan. "Jurisdiction," Samuels writes "is the territory within which authority can be exercised and control is the exercise of that authority. By consent I imply that both public and private jurisdiction in markets are negotiated and draw attention to the interdependence of public and private power. Market-jurisdiction is not monopolized by states or private firms. Likewise control, defined in terms of leadership and authority, is something better discovered than attributed."[40]

The interventionist regulatory regime in Spain conformed to Samuels's concept of a compact in which private actors, in this case the banks, traded jurisdiction (over credit allocation) for control (over the financial system). In the Spanish case, this compact was strongly premised on two conditions that protected the banks' profits and existing position in the economy: (1) the de facto continuation of the banking cartel's status quo; and (2) the continued (if now more controlled) provision to the banks of ample central bank refinancing. The first of these conditions was the sine qua non of the compact. While a significant degree of discretion over credit flows was granted to the planning authorities, those aspects of the new legislation that challenged the banks' control over the financial sector and the economy at large were carefully calibrated so as to contain the competitive impact on the sector.

By requiring the banks to specialize in either commercial or industrial banking and by legalizing the creation of new "industrial banks," the Banking Law of 1962 purported to end the regulatory status quo in the sector and its control over Spanish industry. The technocrats' attempt to shift from a "universal" to a "specialized" banking system was, however, always beset by a lack of purposive clarity. The text of the law suggested that the regime of specialization was meant to address a

39 Richard Samuels, *The Business of the Japanese State: Energy Markets in Comparative and Historical Perspective* (Ithaca: Cornell University Press, 1987), pp. 13–14.
40 Ibid., pp. 8–9.

massive "mismatching" in industrial finance that had developed during the *autarquía,* whereby long-term industrial investment projects were financed by rolled-over ninety-day credits.[41] But it also referred to the objective of "disengaging the banks from the life of industry."[42] Unlike the economic mismatch rationale, this second argument was of a political nature. It was meant to address the increasingly widespread perception created by the rapid expansion of the banks' industrial holdings during the *autarquía* and seized upon by the "financial oligarchy" theorists that the banks' economic power made the Franco regime captive to private interests. The preamble to the law thus stated that the "preeminent position that the commercial banks [had] acquired in the financial system was favored by the so-called banking status quo and by a process of concentration in large organizations that, far from encouraging the specialization of the banks, turned them into multi-functional institutions. . . . This situation increased the influence of the banks over private business" and had to be "confronted decisively," the preamble stated.[43]

Despite these political vows, the status quo was never effectively broken, as a result of adroit adjustments in the application of the law. The newly chartered industrial banks were given the significant privilege of being the sole institutions allowed to issue long-term certificates of deposits, but they were prevented from effectively competing with the commercial banks by being allowed to operate only three offices. The regulatory regime for the creation of new industrial banks was, moreover, "cautious to the point of mistrust." It set very high capital requirement for the establishment of new industrial banks and left authorization of new banks to the discretion of the Ministry of Finance. It also set no limitations to the control of industrial banks by commercial banks. Nine of the fifteen industrial banks approved between 1962 and 1972 thus were chartered by the existing commercial banks, which were quick to set up their own industrial subsidiaries to take advantage

---

[41] José Miguel Andreu and Carmen Arasa, *Banca universal vs. banca especializada: Un análisis prospectivo* (Madrid: Ministerio de Hacienda, IEP, 1990), pp. 267–68. The law classified private banking institutions in two categories: commercial banks, whose business was to be limited to ordinary commercial credit lines and deposit taking, and industrial banks (or merchant banks), whose function would be to finance industrial investment and to promote industrial companies.
[42] Poveda, "Politica monetaria y financiera," p. 78.
[43] Quoted in Antonio Torrero, "La evolución del sistema financiero," *Boletín de Estudios Económicos* 30, no. 96 (1976): 859.

of the privileges granted to this category of institutions. Hence, although quantitative measures show a significant decline in the degree of concentration in the sector from 1959 to 1973 when banks are considered as individual entities, they show no significant change when the sector is analyzed in terms of banking groups (i.e., the groups controlled by the Big Seven along with two smaller groups, RUMASA and Grupo Catalana).[44] Independent industrial banks controlled only 2.5 percent of the banking sector's deposits by 1975 and hence never attained the weight "needed to offer any noticeable competition to the large mixed banks."[45]

Other aspects of the implementation of the Banking Law compounded this failure of the industrial bank experiment. Even without the use of their new industrial subsidiaries, the commercial banks were able to keep virtually all of their industrial holdings by simply issuing new stock, because the only actual limit imposed was that a commercial bank's portfolios could not exceed the sum of its capital and reserves.[46] Ultimately, the specialization attempt thus produced only an artificial separation of activities, rather than any real change of the banking system's structure.[47] As one observer notes, "the specialization experiment failed because it had very little chance in the institutional framework in which it was attempted. [The authorities] tried to impose the idea in the context of a structure in which the initiative would have had to come . . . from those who held economic power and experience in the banking system."[48]

Competition continued to be restricted in other ways as well. A 1962 decree announcing the legalization of foreign bank entry was never implemented. The external liberalization of the economy thus never extended to the financial sector, making the latter an island of protec-

[44]   Oscar Fanjul and Fernando Maravall, *La eficiencia del sistema bancario español* (Madrid: Alianza Universidad, 1985), chap. 2, in particular pp. 73–76. RUMASA and Catalana, two groups created under the new legal framework, both failed in the early 1980s (see chapter 6).

[45]   Torrero, "Evolución del sistema financiero," p. 863, and Andreu and Arasa, *Banca universal,* pp. 271–73. See also Muñoz, *Poder de la banca,* pp. 98–100; and Poveda, "Política monetaria y financiera," p. 79.

[46]   As a consequence, new stock issue, which had grown at an annual rate of 8.2% from 1955 to 1962, grew at a rate of 31.7% between 1963 and 1966. See Poveda, "Política monetaria y financiera," n. 17.

[47]   Practically all of the independent industrial banks were involved in the real estate and tourism sectors, and failed during the 1970s when these sectors were hit hard by the oil crisis. See Andreu and Arasa, *Banca universal,* p. 287.

[48]   Torrero, "Evolución del sistema financiero," p. 867.

tionism at a time when most other sectors of the economy were opened to foreign competition. Most of the foreign investment that followed the liberalization of inward capital flows in 1959 was mediated by the Big Seven, providing the latter with a large new source of profits. A provision in the legislation of 1962 that made authorization of branch network expansions a function of a banks' total capital also supported the position within the sector of the Big Seven, "which were the ones that got branch expansions approved according to this criterion."[49] Unfavorable tax treatment of the financing that firms raised on the capital markets; the discriminatory regulatory treatment of the savings banks;[50] an anachronistic system of interest rate regulation, which subjected deposit rates to a maximum and credit rates to a minimum; and the continued operation of the Consejo Superior Bancario (CSB)— all contributed to an oligopolistic financial market structure in the 1960s.

The trade-off between jurisdiction and control, however, is perhaps best seen in the way competition was indirectly limited through the imposition of the compulsory public debt ratio. I have noted that from the standpoint of the banks, this ratio represented a relatively benign alternative to more radical tax reform. But its establishment also entailed an important implicit bargain. The public debt ratio served to finance the newly nationalized official credit institutions and thereby kept these institutions from acquiring a commercial market presence. Indeed, the financing circuit established with the creation of the compulsory ratio reduced the EOCs to mere administrative bodies that simply allotted a share of the banks' resources to users selected by the planning authorities rather than compete with the Big Seven in the capture of deposits. This limitation made the expansion of official credit compatible with the existing financial market structure. It also meant that the state directly underwrote those credits that carried the highest risks (in many instances to companies in declining sectors in which the banks themselves had invested), exempting the banks from this role without taking on a competitive presence in the financial

---

[49] Ibid., p. 860.

[50] Ibid., p. 871. The savings banks were forced to allocate 80% of their resources to compulsory investments (65% of which was earmarked to financing the INI), did not have access to the Bank of Spain's special rediscount lines, and were prevented from issuing long-term certificates of deposits, as the commercial banks were able to do through their industrial subsidiaries.

market.[51] The aspect of interventionism that appeared to be the most coercive and heavy-handed (the compulsory ratio) was thus an oblique means of supporting the existing structure of the financial sector. In this sense, the surrender of jurisdiction served to legitimize the de facto maintenance of the banking cartel.

The interventionist framework instituted in the early 1960s to reconcile conflicting aspects of the technocrats' growth strategy was thus made acceptable to the banks through the continued restriction of competition. The banks gave up jurisdiction over the allocation of a portion of their resources, but they maintained their oligopolistic position of control over the Spanish financial market. The accommodation between the technocrats and the banking cartel, however, also involved a second aspect of the way selective credit regulation was instituted: the continuation of cheap liquidity from the central bank. The "special" rediscount lines, which allowed the banks to rediscount those credits that they granted to qualifying sectors, were almost continuously expanded over the 1960s to include an ever greater number of specified borrowers and uses.[52] Interventionism thus imposed few constraints, for money was so cheaply and readily available to the banks that they were generously compensated for any opportunity costs entailed by the compulsory ratio. Such monetary expansion also reconciled the technocrats' objective of providing cheap credit to industry while maintaining an oligopoly in the banking sector, because it allowed the banks to charge low rates on their credits to industry while enjoying oligopolistic interest and profit margins. This suppression of the latent conflict between the financial cartel and producer groups was a critical characteristic of the interventionist regime.

The upshot of these arrangements was that the Big Seven protected and in some ways even strengthened their position in the financial sector, in spite of the avowed intention to end the status quo in the 1962 law. Rapid economic growth allowed the savings banks and new industrial banks to increase their share of deposits at the expense of the commercial banks. Between 1962 and 1974, the savings banks' share increased from 24 percent to 28 percent, and the industrial banks

---

[51]   See Gabriel Tortella and Juan Carlos Jiménez, *Historia del Banco de Crédito Industrial* (Madrid: Alianza, 1986), pp. 142–45; Muñoz, *Poder de la banca,* pp. 180–81. The credits extended by the EOCs to the steel and coal mining concerns are prime examples. See chapter 4.

[52]   Poveda, "Política monetaria y financiera," pp. 93–95.

Table 15. Index of basic figures for Big Seven private banks and national income, 1965–1974 (1960 = 100)

	1965	1970	1974
Capital and reserves	200	625	1,180
Deposits	230	473	975
Profits	166	477	1,210
National income	211	378	733

Source: Adapted from Antonio Torrero, "La evolución del sistema financiero," *Boletín de Estudios Económicos* 30, no. 96 (1976): 868.

acquired just above 8 percent (although, as noted, most of the latter were controlled by the Big Seven). The commercial banks, however, nonetheless increased their share in the financing of the private sector from 57 percent to 60 percent over the same period.[53] Within the commercial bank category, the Big Seven's share of deposits declined only minimally, from 72.7 percent in 1952 to 70.2 percent in 1972. Moreover, the Big Seven capital and reserves grew by sixfold and their profits by fivefold in the 1960s (see Table 15). This steady accumulation of assets in the large commercial banks became a particularly critical factor in the following decades, when most of the industrial banks failed, leading to renewed concentration in the sector.

Rather than a shift in the balance between public and private power, financial interventionism in Spain thus reflects an accommodation between an elite of technocratic planners, who sought to sustain the existing political order by outwardly liberalizing the economy while continuing a relaxed rate of monetary expansion, and the private banking cartel, which was interested in the profit opportunities that such a policy turn could bring and also in preempting an alternative policy turn that might have involved expanding the public sector's presence in the market or its fiscal capacity. This regulatory accommodation allowed the technocrats to implement a cheap credit–driven growth strategy as they opened the Spanish economy to international trade and capital flows, while preserving the banks' dominance in the Spanish financial system.

Protection and continued liquidity were the bases of this relationship of reciprocal consent. The question remains, however, why the planners sought such a relationship in drafting the new regulatory framework,

[53] Torrero, "Evolución del sistema financiero," p. 856.

in particular since it conflicted with some of the political objectives addressed by the text of the 1962 law.

One answer is offered by the financial oligarchy theorists, for whom the position of economic control acquired by the large banks in the preceding decades translated automatically into control of the political regime. Such an interpretation, however, gives excessively short shrift to the technocrats' relative independence of purpose, and in particular to the important role of political objectives in their agenda. To be sure, the banks controlled a very significant share of the Spanish economy through their asset portfolios and their webs of interlocking directorships. Most political analysts of the Franco regime also attribute to them a very great amount of direct political influence with Franco, thanks largely to their support of the nationalist cause during the war. An even more compelling fact, however, is that by the late 1950s the cartel stood out as the sole clearly organized representative of national private capital in Spain. The banks' cohesiveness—their leadership met on a regular basis and was represented on the boards of almost all large enterprises in Spain—stood in sharp contrast to the virtual absence of any alternative coordinated economic elite. This scenario made it difficult for any group that opposed a stronger state presence in the economy to forgo the political partnership of the bankers. As we shall see, the central bank reformers who set out to dismantle the interventionist framework in the 1970s made a calculation very similar to that of the Franco regime's technocratic planners. In both instances, however, it was the political objectives and ideological agenda of an incoming elite of policymakers, rather than the banks' economic clout, that made the bargain necessary.

4

Shift within the State

T he 1960s was the decade in which Spain experienced its own "economic miracle." From 1959 to 1966, real output grew at an annual average of 7.5 percent, and industrial production rose at an average 11 percent. Meanwhile, the percentage of the work force employed in agriculture fell from 49 percent in 1960 to 29 percent in 1970. Although this transformation had begun under the *autarquía* and would continue at an even faster pace in the early 1970s, in the minds of many Spaniards the 1960s marked an end to the backwardness and marginalization that the country had experienced since the turn of the nineteenth century. The arrival of American multinationals and of hoards of Northern European tourists are popular symbols of this belated accession to the club of Western industrialized nations. Foreign investment and the tourism boom, along with the liberalization of trade relations initiated in 1959, also feature prominently in stylized accounts of the Spanish economic miracle. Folklore and standard economic accounts, however, tend to neglect the role of another factor behind the rapid transformation: the continued supply of ample and cheap credit to the Spanish economy. Tourism revenues (mainly) and foreign direct investment (to a lesser extent) did ease the foreign exchange constraint on the Spanish economy, but cheap bank credit continued to be the principal motor of investment during the 1960s.[1]

The flow of cheap credit was a central element in the growth strategy of the technocratic planners who were given control over Spanish economic policy after 1959, because it defused social conflict and suppressed the latent conflict between an oligopolistic financial sector and other sectors in the Spanish economy. The success of such an expansionary policy orientation, however, hinged on a particular set of economic circumstances that involved aspects in both the international environment and the domestic political economy. The cessation of this context in the late 1960s created new problems for Spanish policymakers that would set the stage for a second major regulatory shift. This outcome, however, depended on the changing configuration of conflict and identities among different groups in the state's policymaking elite.

From a comparative standpoint, the initiation of the shift away from interventionism and in favor of market-oriented reform occurred at an early point in Spain, so early, in fact, that the international changes to which liberalizing reforms are commonly attributed had yet to acquire a compelling character. Growing economic constraints did not determine the decision to abandon interventionism, but abetted a shift within the policymaking elite in which the regime's technocratic planners were displaced by a group of central bank reformers who were committed to the dismantling of selective credit allocation for essentially ideological reasons. The existence of this group of reformers and the nature of their reform agenda were the consequences of a long-running domestic political dynamic. They formed in reaction to the legacy of inflationary finance in Spain and in direct opposition to the planning bureaucracy's ascendance during the 1960s. Changing economic conditions did not so much cause the move away from interventionism as they were seized upon to forward a domestically incubated reform agenda that was driven as much by ideological antagonism as by economic realities. Moreover, those changing conditions did not just involve a changing external context; they also reflected the internal

---

[1] Gross foreign exchange receipts rose from $600 million in 1960 to $2.2 billion in 1966. Close to $1.3 billion were tourism revenues; another $420 million were transfers, almost entirely worker remittances. See OECD, *Economic Surveys: Spain* (Paris, 1969); and Ramón Tamames, *Estructura económica de España* (Madrid: Guadiana, 1974), 2:479, 547, 561.

exhaustion of a political strategy of using monetary expansion to facilitate economic change.

This chapter describes the origins of the financial reform process in Spain, linking it to this second, more subtle shift within the policymaking bureaucracy under the Franco regime. It is important to point out that this shift, and the regulatory turn, began well before the political regime transition, though it would later be strongly expedited by that transition. Moreover, as in the early 1960s when the technocratic planners had gained preeminence and instituted the interventionist framework of credit regulation, change was accompanied by continuity. The new central bank reformers felt it necessary to establish a working alliance with the banking sector. From its inception, the financial reform process was therefore conditioned by the second-order objective of forging a new compact with the banks that would be compatible with the reformers' agenda. This combination of change within the policymaking elite and continuity in the compactual character of reform is critical to understanding why domestic financial deregulation was initiated at such an early point in Spain, yet at the same time followed a very drawn-out and skewed course.

A New Relay within the State

Signs that the technocrats' economic growth formula might not be sustainable indefinitely first became clear with a sharp deterioration in domestic economic activity during the last quarter of 1967. After seven years of rapid productivity growth, industrial production came to an abrupt halt, leaving consumption to take up the whole increment in domestic demand by the end of the year. At the same time, outflows of short-term capital rose to such a level as to turn what would have been a $75 million basic surplus in the balance of payments into a net overall deficit of $140 million. The government's first response was an attempt to restore the economy's external balance without significantly altering the existing policy strategy. In November, it took advantage of a 14.3 percent devaluation in the pound sterling to devalue the peseta by the same ratio (and for the first time since 1959), accompanying this move by a package of stop-gap stabilization measures.[2] Contrary to 1959,

---

[2] These measures included a freeze on public salaries and pensions, price and wage

when devaluation had successfully underpinned the restoration of the external balance, the 1967–1968 measures failed to bring domestic demand into line with production. As they had done in the late 1950s, the banks drastically reduced their liquidity levels to meet credit demand, leading to a new surge in private credit growth. The economy thus experienced a new boom starting in late 1968, leading again to a sharp deterioration of the current account in 1969.[3]

The failure to restore the economy's external balance through devaluation in 1968–1969 challenged the cheap credit–driven growth model by which the planners had sought to maintain the political regime's viability. The sharp rise in capital outflows indicated that the policy of simply fitting interest rates to the growth objectives set out in the plan was untenable in the face of higher international inflation and interest rates and of changes in the domestic political economy that made it harder to repress wage demands. However, the consequences that these new economic constraints were to have on the course of financial regulation in Spain were entirely dependent on the particular configuration of conflict and identities within the policymaking elite to which the regulatory shift of 1959 had given rise. They were also cloaked by internal controversy in the Franco regime and by the effects of political scandal.

The new balance of payments problems in 1969 coincided with revelations that Spain's largest export firm, MATESA, the recipient of more than half of all the privileged export credit granted by the Banco de Crédito Industrial (BCI), one of the official credit institutes, was defaulting on a large amount of its official debt, leaving the Treasury with massive losses. The scandal broke in an already very tense political situation that involved factional conflict within the cabinet over Franco's July 1969 decision to name Prince Juan Carlos as his successor (a move backed by the Opus Dei faction but strongly opposed by other ministers). MATESA thus became the "the sole great politico-economic scandal in forty years of the Franco dictatorship."[4] And it did so pre-

---

controls, a rise in the rediscount rate for commercial paper and in the rate on time deposits, and depreciation allowances to stimulate investment. See OECD, *Economic Survey: Spain*, 1969, p. 17.

[3] Ibid.; OECD, *The Capital Market, International Capital Movements, and Restrictions on Capital Operations in Spain* (Paris, 1971).

[4] Gabriel Tortella and Juan Carlos Jiménez, *Historia del Banco de Crédito Industrial* (Madrid: Alianza, 1986), p. 188.

cisely by connecting a growing public perception of corruption within the regime with the privileged financing circuits that had been the prime instrument of the planners' growth strategy. As two observers write, the scandal "cast doubt on the central elements of the economic policy · followed after the Stabilization Plan of 1959, and in particular the organization of official credit as it was set forth in the Law of 1962. But it also undermined the individuals who had directed and inspired the economic policy of the sixties, and whose common link was assumed to be their membership in Opus Dei, an organization to which MATESA's management was also said to belong."[5]

The MATESA scandal resulted in a major cabinet shakeup in 1969 that appeared to vindicate the "technocratic orientation" of López Rodó by including almost no one who was not a member of Opus Dei and by upgrading the position of planning commissioner to the ministerial level.[6] This apparent victory, however, proved to be a pyrrhic one, masking the rapid decline of the planners' influence over economic policy at the end of the 1960s, a development that was confirmed by López Rodó's move to the Foreign Ministry three years later. Filling the void was the less public but easily documented rise in policy leadership of a group of reformers connected with the central bank, an institution whose annual reports had begun to call for financial liberalization as early as 1966, yet whose influence had remained strongly checked by that of the planning bureaucracy.[7]

The central bank's campaign to promote financial reform bore its first fruits in the summer of 1969; that is, at the very same time that the failure of the 1967 stabilization measures were becoming apparent and that the MATESA scandal erupted into an open political crisis. The new pressure on the Spanish current account allowed the central bankers to push through a significant change in the way interest rates were fixed. Until then, maximum rates on bank deposits and minimum rates for lending operations had been officially set by the Ministry of Finance. The 1969 reform linked all bank rates to the central bank's rediscount

[5] Ibid., p. 156.
[6] The broader political crisis surrounding the cabinet shakeup is discussed in Raymond Carr and Juan Pablo Fusi, *Spain, Dictatorship to Democracy* (London: George Allen & Unwin, 1981), pp. 189–94.
[7] OECD, *Economic Surveys: Spain*, 1966; OECD, *Capital Market*, p. 44; and the following annual reports of the Bank of Spain: 1967, p. 19; 1968, pp. 107, 138; 1969, pp. 111–15.

rate by way of fixed differentials and made lending rates subject to a ceiling rather than a floor.[8]

The spectacular turnaround in the country's external balance during the following year seemed amply to confirm the adequacy of this "flexibilization."[9] Yet the 1969 measures made no link between the loosening of interest rates and the overall rate of monetary expansion. Indeed, despite the global rise in rates that the July 1969 measures produced, the fast rate of monetary expansion in 1969 was not significantly reversed until September, when an 18 percent ceiling on credit expansion was imposed.[10] To stop the outward flow of short-term capital, the credit ceiling had to be supplemented by the imposition of a six-month prior deposit of 20 percent on the value of imports, a measure that produced a sharp monetary contraction though it did little to reduce imports.[11] Together these measures reduced the expansion of credit to the private sector from 25 percent in 1969 to 10 percent in 1970. Yet, once the initial six-month deposits began to be released in the summer of 1970, the government's ability to reign in monetary expansion came to an end, leading to a new acceleration of credit growth during the second half of the year.

Underlying the resilience in credit growth was the planning bureaucracy's continued institutional influence over the financial system, in particular its indirect authority over the central bank's rediscount window. "Special" rediscount lines were sharply expanded after the cut in ordinary rediscount lines in 1969, reflecting a growing standoff between the reformers and the planners at the end of the 1960s.[12] The

---

[8] The rediscount rate was raised by 1% to 5.5%. In addition, time deposits with industrial banks carrying a maturity of more than two years, lending operations with a maturity of more than three years, and deposits in foreign currency or convertible pesetas were liberalized, and preferential rates for the banks' principal customers were authorized. None of these measures had much significance, however, because they affected only a very small proportion of bank operations in Spain. See OECD, *Capital Market*, pp. 44–45.

[9] Ibid., p. 45.

[10] Given the fast rate of credit expansion reached in September, the ceiling implied a reduction of the (seasonally adjusted) rate of growth of bank credit in the last months of the year to about half the rate prevailing in the period up to September. See OECD, *Economic Surveys: Spain*, 1970, p. 34.

[11] OECD, *Economic Surveys: Spain*, 1971, p. 13.

[12] In the fall of 1969, for the first time the central bank instructed the commercial banks to keep a minimum cash ratio that had been on the books since the Law of 1962 yet never applied. It would, however, prove inadequate as a tool to stop the renewed credit expansion because it left "out of account" a number of "easily moneyable assets," such as

planning bureaucracy, in essence, was able to evade the limits imposed through global monetary policy decisions by expanding the number of sectors and uses eligible for automatic rediscounting. In doing so, it had negated the effect on credit growth of the interest rate increases and the reduction of ordinary rediscount lines imposed in 1969.

The planners' ability to resist nonetheless soon fell victim to the growing influence gained by the reformers as a result of the MATESA scandal, which forced the resignation of the Bank of Spain's governor and brought a new, more resolute leadership to the central bank. Two appointments were particularly important in this regard: that of Enrique Fuentes Quintana to the Bank of Spain's board of governors in 1970, and that of Luis Angel Rojo as head of the bank's Research Service in 1971. Often referred to as the guru of the liberalization drive by public officials involved in the process, Fuentes Quintana epitomized a precursor generation of academic economists who had spearheaded the creation of economic faculties in Spanish universities during the 1940s and 1950s, and adhered strongly to a neoliberal, market-oriented economic philosophy.[13] His prestige and influence were expanded by his extensive mentoring of a generation of younger economists, many of whom went on to the Bank of Spain's Research Service. With this network of disciples and colleagues, Fuentes's appointment to the board paved the way for a major transformation of the central bank's role in Spanish economic policymaking.

A critical step in this process was the appointment of Fuentes's academic colleague Luis Angel Rojo to head the bank's Research Service in 1971. According to Fuentes's own account, the Research Service in the early 1970s remained an enclave within a wider "technostructure" that limited the reformers' influence in the bank. The position of governor, for example, had been held by prominent regime politicians rather than economic experts. Under Fuentes's sponsorship, Rojo set out to transform this technostructure in a way that would allow the bank to take a central role in economic policy over the next years. Rojo intensified the

"effects rediscountable in special lines and unused margins of ordinary rediscount lines": OECD, *Economic Surveys: Spain*, 1971, p. 29, n. 1.

[13] For discussion of the positions held by Fuentes under the Franco regime, see Anderson, *Political Economy of Modern Spain*, pp. 99–107, and Richard Gunther, *Public Policy in a No-Party State: Spanish Planning and Budgeting in the Twilight of the Franquist Era* (Berkeley: University of California Press, 1980), pp. 91–95. As Anderson notes, the regime tolerated a wide spectrum of orientations among academic economists as long as they did not refer openly to the political order.

Research Service's recruitment of academic brainpower, turning it into a springboard for high-ranking administrative positions in the bank. As one later-day reformer described it, the common experience in the Research Service—which often included advanced graduate study in leading American economics departments—produced a high degree of affinity in economic ideas even among members of very different political orientations. A decade later the head of the service (a post that Rojo retained until his appointment as governor in 1992) was indisputably regarded as the second-ranking official in the bank.[14]

In the early 1970s, Fuentes and Rojo set in motion a process of reforms that focused on redressing two key obstacles to the central bank's control over monetary policy: (1) the special rediscount lines that were outside of the central bank's authority; and (2) the absence of a money market through which the monetary authority could control the level of liquidity in the financial system in a routine and discretionary fashion. Both of these obstacles were related to the interventionist regulatory framework created by the planners. Yet, although the central bank's agenda was defined in terms of its ideological opposition to that framework, the institutional battle against the planners did not turn out to be the most important obstacle for the reformers.

The planning bureaucracy's influence over the general course of economic policy in Spain was decidedly limited by a bill passed in 1971, which originally had been drafted to reform the official credit institutes in the aftermath of the MATESA scandal. The reformers were able to attach a number of "additional provisions" to the legislation; the most important was the elimination of the special rediscount lines, and their replacement by a compulsory investment ratio that obliged the banks to allocate a given proportion of their deposits as credits to specified users.[15] This move effectively ended the planners' ability to manipulate the expansion of bank lending and thus placed much stronger constraints on them.[16] In line with the reformers' agenda, the 1971 law

---

[14] Interviews, Madrid, 1991.
[15] Within this ratio, which was not to exceed 25% of the banks' liabilities, the Ministry of Finance set a percentage that had to be covered with purchases of public bonds, while the rest was to be covered with credits and loans to users that were previously eligible for special rediscount. The ratio was initially set at 22% for commercial banks and at 7% for industrial banks. The minimum public bond ratio, which was imposed only on commercial banks and served to finance the loans granted by the official credit institutions, was set at 15%. See OECD, *Capital Market*, p. 67.
[16] Though the monetization of excess lending by the official credit institutions remained

also shifted a large number of regulatory functions to the Bank of Spain, among them control of the Institute for Exchange and Foreign Currency (IEME) (formerly under the control of the Ministry of Industry) and authority over both the savings banks (formerly under the Institute for Savings Banks Credit, ICCA) and the industrial banks (formerly under the Institute for Medium- and Long-Term Credit, ICMLP). The last two regulatory bodies were abolished, and the supervision of the official credit institutions was passed to a new downgraded Institute for Official Credit (ICO).[17] The 1971 reform thus had three important consequences: (1) it ended the planners' ability to interfere with the central bank's rediscount policy; (2) it dismantled the segmented regulatory structure that had served the planners' policies; and (3) it gave the Bank of Spain authority over all private institutions in the credit market.[18]

Interpreting the Initiation of Reform

Before going on to describe the subsequent course of reform in Spain, it is worth considering the developments just discussed in light of general arguments about the politics of liberalization in formerly interventionist states. As discussed in chapter 1, the prevalent tendency is to attribute such domestic regulatory reform (at least as pertains to secondary economies) to changes in the international economic environment. Two kinds of systemic changes receive particular attention in the literature. The first involves changes in the international monetary order, starting with the rise in global inflation and international monetary instability caused by the changing policy stance of the United States in the mid-1960s, and resulting eventually in the collapse of the Bretton Woods order. The second is the emergence and rapid growth of off-

---

an unresolved issue for the reformers for a decade to come, the coup to the special rediscount lines in 1971 had the virtue of requiring explicit government authorization for any such monetization of credit.

[17] The law also authorized the Ministry of Finance to delegate its authority over "collective investment" institutions, such as pension funds, to the monetary authority.

[18] Because they did not operate as real banks in the sense of intermediating savings in the economy, the official credit institutions did not create money. They therefore did not interfere with the reformers' policy objective of controlling monetary expansion in an operational sense, but only to the extent that the central bank was forced to monetize official credit under political pressure.

shore financial markets during the 1960s (a result largely of regulatory decisions that accompanied the changing policy stance in the United States). The increased level of capital mobility that the growth of off-shore markets is generally purported to entail lies at the heart of the prevalent market-driven view of liberalization, according to which internationalization undermined the segmentation of national financial markets that had allowed for relative policy autonomy under Bretton Woods, as well as the ability of governments to regulate domestic credit flows, thus negating the practical value of selective credit regulation while strengthening the political leverage of social actors who stood to benefit from liberalization. In both of these ways, the growth of international financial markets is said to have compelled governments to abandon interventionism.

The initiation of regulatory reform in Spain was undoubtedly influenced by the international developments emphasized in the literature. But it also highlights the extent to which the domestic effect commonly attributed to those systemic developments (i.e., the move away from interventionism and toward market-oriented reform of the financial system) depended on a set of domestic conditions that are quite different from those commonly stipulated in the literature yet would have strong implications for the course of reform in Spain. The rise in global interest rates, combined with a previously unseen dynamism in short-term capital movements, was indeed the immediate problem that needed to be addressed to restore the current account balance after 1967. Yet these problems could be solved technically by a rise in Spanish interest rates and a commensurate restriction of credit growth, coupled with an expansion of capital controls. They did not compel the abandonment of selective credit regulation. What was required was that the rate of credit expansion be uncoupled from the way state officials imposed their criteria for credit allocation, not the abandonment of dirigisme.

The experience of France, which in the second half of the 1970s effectively pursued such a change, coming just as close to meeting the government's monetary targets as the German Bundesbank, offers evidence that such a regulatory adjustment was possible, at least from a technical standpoint.[19] So does the case of Spain itself, where, once the flexibilization of interest rates of 1969 was supplemented by new capital controls in 1970 and by the abolition of the special rediscount lines

---

[19] See OECD, *Economic Surveys: France,* 1983, p. 40; *Economic Surveys: Germany,* 1984, p. 30.

in 1971, the current account was very quickly and effectively turned around in the early 1970s. There is also no evidence of any substantial positive sectoral pressure on the Spanish government to initiate a full-fledged process of anti-interventionist reform outside of the policymaking elite.[20] The changing economic context of the late 1960s thus may have contributed to the shift in the ideological orientation of Spanish financial regulation, but it did not compel such a shift. The magnitude of the balance-of-payments problem experienced before the OPEC oil shocks was simply not great enough. Something else was required to turn a necessary monetary policy adjustment into the categorical redirection of financial regulation that began in Spain in 1971.

It might be argued in response that international market pressures are sufficient to explain the political shift in favor of anti-interventionist reformers even if they did not compel such a change from a technical standpoint, and hence that the market-driven view of liberalization does in fact account for the early regulatory turn in Spain. Despite its appeal, however, such an interpretation fails to recognize two other aspects of the Spanish experience that are not captured in standard systemic arguments yet played a crucial role in bringing about the regulatory turn and determining the subsequent course of reform. The first comprises the sources of constraint on the technocrats' economic policy strategy. The second was the prior existence of a contending network of policymakers in the central bank, who defined themselves by their shared ideological opposition to the interventionist practices of the regime's planning bureaucracy and who were determined to push forth a program of financial liberalization.

A key consideration in understanding the shift in policy leadership that took place at the end of the 1960s concerns the differing rates of success of the attempts to achieve stabilization through devaluation of 1959 and 1967–69. A standard market-driven account of liberalization would attribute this difference to the greater mobility of international capital flows at the end of the 1960s. This factor, along with the changing character of the international monetary order, surely played a role in the balance-of-payments problems encountered by Spanish authorities at the time. However, a closer look at the evolution of the domestic political economy during the 1960s reveals that the technocrats' cheap credit growth strategy was experiencing clear signs of

---

[20] The IMF and the OECD backed such reforms. Yet the 1969 crisis was resolved without substantial assistance from international monetary institutions.

internal exhaustion by late 1967. The sources of this internal exhaustion had both an economic and a sociopolitical component. The first derived from the substantial structural transformation that the Spanish economy had experienced in the years up to 1967. As John Zysman has argued for the French and Japanese experiences, the completion of the basic stage of transformation from a predominantly rural economy to an industrial economy limited the productivity gains that could be achieved by selectively expanding the money supply.[21] In the Spanish case, this problem was compounded by the limited attention paid for decades to the modernization of the agricultural sector and by high rates of labor emigration. By 1967, this trend had produced a declining rate of agricultural productivity (given the labor-intensive character of much of the sector) and a rise of industrial wages that "sustained an inflationary process that ultimately halted expansion."[22]

The second component lay in the declining utility of cheap credit as a political mechanism for defusing social conflict while keeping real labor costs down. The economic effects of having substantially exhausted the productivity gains to be had from simply shifting labor from agriculture to industry played itself out in the context of rapidly changing industrial relations in Spain. During the *autarquía,* the Franco regime's labor legislation had been highly repressive, making virtually any kind of collective action on the part of workers impossible. The organizing principle of labor market regulation during that period was compulsory affiliation with state-sponsored vertical syndicates that officially represented both workers and management by economic sector. Wages were set by the Labor Ministry. The official syndicate became the main institutional bastion of the national syndicalist faction of the regime. Yet by the late 1950s it was failing miserably as an instrument of state control. According to José María Maravall,

> The labour market began to operate increasingly independent of governmental controls. Managerial strategies of linking productivity with wage increases resulted in a progressive gap between real and official wages, in a period where productivity and competition became the main concern for important sections of management. Wage drifting

[21] John Zysman, "Inflation and the Politics of Supply," in Leon N. Lindberg and Charles S. Maier, eds., *The Politics of Inflation and Economic Stagnation* (Washington, D.C.: Brookings Institution, 1985), pp. 140–71.
[22] Manuel Román, *The Limits of Economic Growth in Spain* (New York: Praeger, 1971), p. 4.

was especially acute in Spain in the mid 1950s and contributed to the inflationary process. From a capitalist point of view, anti-inflationary policies required strict wage controls and work conditions and productivity more flexible than the official norms of the Ministry of Labour.[23]

The growing economic drawbacks of the repressive framework of labor market regulation and the political failure to avert widespread labor unrest in the late 1950s led to the legalization of collective bargaining between elected works councils and management after the cabinet reshuffle of 1957. Although the law continued to recognize only the official syndicate as a legal trade union organization, it set the stage for the emergence of a clandestine trade union movement in the 1960s. The main protagonist of this movement hailed from neither of the historical Spanish unions (the Socialist UGT and anarchist CNT) but rather from a new organization: the Workers Commissions (Comisiones Obreras, or CC.OO.). Sponsored by the Spanish Communist Party (PCE), the CC.OO. gradually managed to infiltrate the official trade union and gain control of the works councils, successfully undermining the control of the syndicate in the bargaining process.[24]

The explosion in collective bargaining that followed these changes led to substantial growth in nominal wages, the cost of which was diffused only through continuing high rates of inflation during the first half of the 1960s. It was also accompanied, however, by a dramatic rise in worker militancy and strike activity, which intensified in 1966, after shop-floor elections that placed the CC.OO. in firm control of works councils. These developments placed clear limits on the extent to which workers could be made to accept nominal wage increases that were subsequently eroded by inflation. Thus, although real wage growth in 1965 had been successfully reduced to 2.3 percent through a 13.2 percent inflation rate, it rose to 11.2 percent in 1966 and to 8.9 percent in 1967.[25] This wage dynamic and the rise in worker militancy represented a very substantial new constraint on the uses of inflation to promote growth and were a prime factor behind the balance-of-

[23] José María Maravall, *Dictatorship and Political Dissent: Workers and Students in Franco's Spain* (New York: St. Martin's Press, 1977), p. 23.

[24] The historical unions were weakened by the political repression suffered during the preceding decades, but also because of their stance of open opposition to the official syndicates (ibid., pp. 30–31).

[25] Based on hourly labor costs in manufacturing and consumer price index data; OECD, *Economic Surveys: Spain,* 1969 and 1971.

payments difficulties of 1967–69. Yet they constituted a dynamic that was produced by the technocrats' growth strategy independently of changes in the international context. The growing constraints on the uses of monetary expansion in Spain in the late 1960s were thus largely endogenous and political rather than simply determined by external market forces.

A primarily systemic interpretation of the shift toward market-oriented reform in Spain also fails to recognize the extent to which the qualitative shift in policy leadership at the end of the 1960s was dependent on the preexistence of a network of reformers that were poised to seize the opportunity afforded by the changing economic context. The inception of the central bank reformers as a contending policy network espousing an alternative policy agenda had its origins in 1959, when the Bank of Spain's Research Service began to be staffed by a generation of neoliberal academic economists whose influence over economic policy had remained checked by that of the planning bureaucracy. Instrumental in this process was Mariano Navarro Rubio, who, although a member of Opus Dei, had close connections to the academic community, in particular to its leading neoliberal members. Named Minister of Finance in the 1957 reshuffle, Navarro Rubio had been a key advocate of the IMF-backed stabilization plan of 1959 and had recruited the support of academic economists on the technical staffs of the ministries of Finance and Commerce in this effort. After he was dismissed from the cabinet in 1965 (according to most accounts because of his growing antagonism to Planning Commissioner López Rodó), he became governor of the Bank of Spain, where he set in motion the transformation that Angel Rojo would later complete. Several years before the arrival of Fuentes and Rojo, Navarro had placed the Research Service in the hands of young economists who shared his opposition to the planning bureaucracy's policy orientations,[26] a change reflected in the bank's annual reports which criticized the policy orientation laid out in the development plans and called for financial reform as early as 1966.[27]

---

[26] A first-hand account of this shift is offered by the then-governor Mariano Navarro Rubio, in *Mis memorias* (Barcelona: Plaza y Janés, 1991), pp. 300–310. Some of the economists brought into the Servicio de Estudios at this time were Angel Madroñero, Antonio Sánchez Pedreño, and Mariano Rubio Jiménez, who would become governor under the Socialist government in the 1980s.

[27] Bank of Spain, *Annual Report*, 1967, p. 19, *Annual Report*, 1968, pp. 107, 138; and

The emergence of a contending policy network in the central bank thus began well before the change in the international context at the end of the 1960s had become apparent. The reformers' motivations, moreover, had roots even further back, in the legacy of inflationary finance of the past. Fuentes and Rojo's bid to transform the central bank grew out of an economic perspective that clashed directly not only with the developmentalism of the planners but with the inflationary tendency in Spanish economic development. The group of individuals that they represented had its brief heyday during the design of the Stabilization Plan in 1959, only to be displaced by the establishment of the planning bureaucracy. Their agenda for institutional reform responded directly to this experience, to a historical view of Spanish development that placed the Stabilization Plan of 1959 opposite the development plans of the 1960s, and to the notion that "there had existed no monetary policy at all in Spain up to this point."[28] Strengthening the central bank's role in economic policymaking and providing it with the instruments to control liquidity in the financial sector, the reformers believed, would give them a lever on economic policy. Cutting off the access of politicians to cheap credit was the philosophical imperative that informed their agenda for reform.[29]

These considerations belie the validity of a market-driven interpretation of reform in Spain. Indeed, they illustrate how the a priori acceptance of a powerful systemic explanation can obfuscate the more subtle endogenous dynamics driving the turn toward market-oriented reform in interventionist states. The failed experience of restoring the external balance through devaluation in 1967–69 may indeed have been experienced as an increase in external constraint because of the novelty of

---

Annual Report, 1969, pp. 111–15. These calls were seconded in the OECD publications during the same period, reflecting the reformers' strong ties to this organization. See OECD, Economic Surveys: Spain, 1966, and Capital Market, p. 44. The concentration of expertise that took place under Navarro Rubio also explains why, despite its subordination to the Ministry of Finance, the central bank was fully responsible for relations with the IMF. See Joaquín Muns, Historia de las relaciones entre España y el Fondo Monetario Internacional, 1958–1982: 25 años de economía española (Barcelona, 1984).
[28] This view was repeated emphatically by several officials who participated in the reform process of later years, whom I interviewed in Madrid in 1991–92. It is captured in an oft-quoted remark: "The Stabilization Plan developed us, while the development plans destabilized us."
[29] For two personal testimonies, see the interview with Angel Rojo in Salvador Paniker, Conversaciones en Madrid (Barcelona: Kairos, 1969), and Enrique Fuentes, "Prólogo," in Rafael Termes, Desde la banca (Madrid: Rialp, 1991).

sharper short-term capital movements, but that failure was largely predetermined by changes in the domestic political economy. The role played by international market developments was not autonomous or generic. It did not compel the state to abandon interventionism, but rather fostered the rise within the policymaking bureaucracy of a contending network of reformers, whose existence and motivations for promoting change were rooted in domestic experiences. These origins account for the early initiation of a regulatory shift in Spain. But they also had other important consequences for the course of reform during the 1970s and 1980s.

The Reemergence of Accommodation

The reformers' growing influence at the beginning of the 1970s allowed them to undermine the planning bureaucracy's control over economic policy by abolishing the special rediscount lines in 1971. In 1973 they scored another major achievement when the Bank of Spain became one of the first central banks to adopt a policy of targeting monetary aggregates after the breakdown of the Smithsonian Agreement. To gain an effective lever on economic policy, however, they also needed to create the institutional structure that would allow the central bank to exercise control over monetary policy. The key prerequisite here was the creation of a real money market in which the monetary authority could operate in a routine fashion to control short-term liquidity fluctuations.

In this second objective, however, the reformers' policy agenda came into direct conflict with the interests of the private banks. The end of lax central bank rediscounting in 1971 radically altered one of the principal elements of the compact that had underpinned credit regulation in the 1960s. If the banks accepted this change, they did so because the other major pillar of that compact (protection from both domestic and foreign competition) was still intact. With the growing threat of competition from international financial markets, bankers had increasingly come to view protection as resting on a rigid framework of interest rate regulation that ensured their ability to maintain a pricing cartel. This regulatory framework, however, was precisely what stood in the way of the creation of a money market. The course of financial reform in the following years thus reflected the competing pressures of the monetary authorities' attempts to gain a handle on monetary policy and the banking sector's ability to resist significant changes in the regulatory regime.[30]

The conflict became apparent in 1973, when the oil shock played havoc with Spanish price levels. In pursuing its new policy of monetary aggregate targeting, the central bank tried to use existing government bond issues to control liquidity in the credit markets. The long-term nature of these issues, however, rendered them a very rigid instrument, leading interbank interest rates to soar dramatically in response to the bank's tightening, and to drop sharply in early 1974 when the bank attempted to rectify its first intervention. The principal problem for the reformers thus became the central bank's inability to "inject liquidity into the economy in a regular fashion" so as to meet its new policy objective.[31] In response, two measures were carried out in 1974: the creation of central bank credits to the banking system with a very short (usually one-week) term, and a modification of the commercial banks' liquidity ratio (from a daily ratio to a ratio averaged over ten days). These measures, it was hoped, would lead the banks to create a money market where they could place their day-to-day cash surpluses, and in which the central bank could intervene to regulate liquidity.[32]

The reformers' efforts to create such a market, however, did not bear fruit for over a decade.[33] This failure, which limited the success of their monetary targeting during the 1970s, was due to the banks' ability to resist any alteration in the regulatory framework that might undermine their oligopolistic modus vivendi. No money market was created in response to the offering of short-term central bank credits because these credits were allocated to the banks in rigid proportion to their deposits rather than by public auction, so that any element of competition over the capture of funds was absent. Given the lack of price

---

[30] The changes of 1971 made possible a significant turnaround in the balance of payments. Thus, from late 1971 through 1973 a substantial surplus in current accounts despite an increase in domestic demand allowed the authorities to support a strong upswing in economic activity by relaxing their monetary stance.

[31] OECD, *Economic Surveys: Spain,* 1975, p. 25.

[32] Ibid., p. 29.

[33] As we shall see, a real money market came into existence only after foreign banks, which were allowed to enter the domestic market at the end of the 1970s, provided the necessary impulse.

competition in the sector, the banks felt very little compulsion to maximize their operating margins by creating a money market for their cash surpluses.[34]

Having successfully undercut the planning bureaucracy's capability for obstruction, the reformers thus came to face a much firmer obstacle in the resistance of the national banking cartel. Interviews of some of the principal reformers during this period clearly convey the sense that their task after 1971 became one of maneuvering around the veto power of an economic sector that seemingly comprised the regime's only untouchables. The banks' resistance to the reformers' agenda, however, differed from that of the planners not only because of their greater political staying power but also because they were the principal institutional clients of the central bank, in which the reformers were anchored. They were also the most important representatives of private capital in Spain. For both reasons, the financial sector could hardly be forgone as a political partner in a neoliberal agenda for institutional reform. Thus, even though the banks' determination to preserve the framework of the Consejo Superior Bancario (CSB) conflicted with the reformers' aspiration to expand the policy influence of the central bank, any real confrontation was precluded by the necessary institutional connection between the two groups.

It is thus hardly surprising that the reformers responded by seeking the banks' active partnership. The critical task was to find the basis for a new compact that would be compatible with the central bankers' monetary policy objectives. The strategy adopted by the reformers was to make their monetary policy agenda part of a broadly defined project of "financial liberalization." This broadening of the agenda served at least two purposes. One was to strengthen the general political appeal of their reform agenda by shifting the focus of future public debate from the politically divisive issue of monetary discipline to a "public interest" argument about the "allocative efficiency" gains that could be derived from liberalization. This conceptual transformation of the reformers' agenda was particularly important because it tapped into the easily made association between interventionism and authoritarianism and into the corresponding association between economic and political liberalism in the Spanish context of the 1970s. By presenting their

---

[34] Interbank money market rates therefore continued to fluctuate widely and monetary policy took on a pronounced stop–go character over the following years. See OECD, *Economic Surveys: Spain*, 1977, pp. 26–29.

agenda for institutional reform in this light, the reformers made it more difficult for the banks to sustain an overtly antireformist stance in the long run.

Second, and more immediately, by broadening the reform agenda the reformers could present their objectives as part of a package of measures that could be fashioned to entice the banks' support. This strategy of co-optation can clearly be seen in the course that financial reform took in the years leading up to the political transition. The first critical measure in this regard was the liberalization of commissions charged by the banks on their lending activities in 1972. In the context of an unaltered pricing cartel, this measure could have only a perverse effect on the economy, because it effectively deregulated the price of credit without making it subject to competition. In a very concrete way, however, it served to compensate the banks for the imposition of the compulsory investment ratio in 1971 and created a putative link between their interests and the reformers' liberalization project. The liberalization of commissions was followed by the liberalization of bank branches in 1974. This measure, which was also taken without any accompanying measures to alter the oligopolistic structure of the Spanish financial market, led to a dramatic expansion of bank branches after 1974 which sharply increased the banking sector's costs of operation. Given that commissions had been deregulated, the banks had little trouble passing on these cost increases on to their increasingly vulnerable clients.

The particular pattern of deregulation instituted in the mid-1970s made little economic sense. Yet it served to compensate the banks for the loss of cheap liquidity and, more important, got them implicitly to buy into the liberalization agenda. From the reformers' standpoint, this early stage of the reform process was therefore not fruitless because it sowed the seeds that would eventually strengthen the more reformist elements among the bankers. For the Spanish economy, however, it had a highly perverse impact because it bolstered the banks' ability to exploit their oligopolistic position precisely at the moment that industry was hit by the world recession. The full extent of these consequences, however, can be understood only in terms of the changing relationship between the banks and their industrial clients during the 1960s and 1970s.

It should also be noted that, although little progress was made in the creation of a money market in the years preceding the regime transition, the reformers did gain further institutional ground in 1974 in two other ways. The first was the liberalization of interest rates on bank activities (lending and deposits) with terms of more than two years. Although the economic impact of this measure was marginal (very few deposits and loans had terms of more than six months) and was therefore not opposed by the banks, it did create an expectation that such liberalization would be progressively extended to shorter-term operations. The second advance was the regulatory "equalization," or "harmonization," of the different types of credit institutions now regulated by the Bank of Spain, which ended the experiment of "specialization" that had served as one of the organizing principles of selective credit regulation.[35] By simplifying the structure of credit regulation, this move served as another preliminary step toward the reformers' ultimate objective of placing the central bank in control of monetary policy. Even though the reformers were prevented by the banks from achieving their main aims during the last years of the Franco regime, they thus managed nonetheless to enact reform measures that, although secondary or even perverse from the economy's standpoint, facilitated the future success of their agenda in one of two ways: either by eroding the institutional framework that had given the planning bureaucracy influence over financial flows or by involving the private banks in partial measures that imbued the broader liberalization agenda with a measure of de facto validity.

Industrial Crisis: The Economic Backdrop

As we saw in chapter 2, the Spanish banking sector developed in the early part of the twentieth century along the lines of the universal banking model, financing industrial ventures through both lending and direct investment in industrial firms. In contrast to Germany, however, where such an institutional model led banks to become heavily involved in the competitive strategies of their clients and where bank-led industrialization was linked early on to export promotion, in Spain the

---

[35] Between 1973 and 1974, all legal distinctions between industrial and commercial banks were abolished, and the latter were allowed to accept long-term interest-bearing deposits, a privilege previously granted only to the industrial banks. At the same time, the investment ratio of the savings banks was reduced, bringing it closer to that of the commercial banks and somewhat mitigating the institutional discrimination that these institutions had been subjected to.

banks' involvement in industry took hold in the context of a highly protectionist and inward-oriented policy regime and was driven by their involvement in inflationary public finance, which enabled them to acquire industrial assets at very little cost and risk. All of these tendencies were accentuated during the *autarquía,* when the banks' involvement in industry became so thoroughly premised on the availability of extraordinary profit opportunities that it acquired a highly speculative character. Coupled with the institutionalization of a banking cartel and the complete suppression of competition in the sector, this tenuous relationship of the banks to their industrial clients produced a latent conflict of interests between industry and finance, which was suppressed only by cheap central bank rediscounting.

The abandonment of cheap credit in the early 1970s and the changing economic fortunes of Spanish industry in the 1960s brought this conflict to the fore. The precariousness in bank–industry relations can be observed in three aspects of the banks' behavior, starting in the early 1960s: (1) the banks' response to industrial crisis in sectors in which they were heavily invested; (2) their overall investment behavior once the generalized industrial recession of the 1970s set in; and (3) their lending behavior once cheap rediscounting was discontinued.

One of the most graphic illustrations of the underlying character of the banks' relationship with industry is offered by their response to economic crisis in two sectors in which they were heavily invested: steel and coal. Both sectors entered a stage of profound crisis after the first stage of import liberalization in 1962. Their weight in Spain's late industrialization was due largely to a pattern of investment in capital-intensive industry in which the banks had heavily participated during the autarkic period and which was to render the Spanish economy particularly vulnerable to the economic crisis of the 1970s. The banks' response in both cases contrasts sharply with that of their German "universal bank" counterparts, which in the postwar period took on the role of "insulating government from difficult and complex corporate problems" by taking the lead in organizing rescue operations of large industrial conglomerates.[36] The Spanish banks from the very beginning backed away from troubled industrial firms, leaving the public sector to engage in a massive socialization of losses.

[36] Kenneth Dyson, "The State, Banks, and Industry: The West German Case," in Andrew Cox, ed., *State, Finance, and Industry: A Comparative Analysis of Post-War Trends in Six Advanced Industrial Economies* (Brighton: Wheatsheaf, 1986), p. 137.

Steel was the first large sector to succumb to this fate. After a decade of significant expansion during the 1950s, the private companies in this sector were hit by heavy losses after the liberalization of imports in 1962.[37] Under the *autarquía,* the banks had acquired a central position in the sector through a dense network of overlapping board memberships that included all of the main companies and extended through the coal-mining sector (which was vertically integrated with steel), so that they could act as an "authentic coordinating pivot of monopolistic interests."[38] As investors and creditors, they had enjoyed very large returns on their investments in the sector despite a conspicuous failure to innovate. As a result, most private companies in the sector remained specialized in processing iron ore and were incapable of supporting integrated production or continuous casting. Only ENSIDESA, the public steel conglomerate created by the Instituto Nacional de Industria (INI) in 1950, had the scale and technology to compete in world markets. The lifting of tariffs on steel imports in 1962 therefore had an immediate and dramatic effect on profits. The banks' first reaction was to press for renewed tariff protection, which led to a moratorium in the planned tariff reduction schedule in 1963. When this measure failed to reverse the sector's trend, a program of "concerted action" was agreed on a year later between the state and UNINSA, a consortium of northern mining companies that had been formed in 1961 to challenge EN-SIDESA's lead in integrated steel production. UNINSA was granted 30 billion pesetas of privileged financing along with an extensive package of tax breaks.

Remarkably, given their heavy involvement in the sector and the fact that they were the main creditors of the failing firms, the private banks did not participate in the financing of the investment program that UNINSA was to carry out under the agreement. The 30 billion pesetas received by the consortium were furnished instead and in roughly equal

[37] The crisis of the steel sector is discussed in Arturo López Muñoz and José L. García Delgado, *Crecimiento y crisis del capitalismo español* (Madrid: Edicusa, 1968), pp. 207–19; Arturo López Muñoz, *Capitalismo español: Una etapa decisiva* (Algorta, Vizcaya: Zero, 1970), pp. 73–93; and Francisco Comín and Pablo Martín Aceña, *INI: 50 años de industrialización* (Madrid: Espasa-Calpe, 1991), pp. 381–85. The banks' links to individual companies and central involvement in the sector through an extensive network of overlapping board members that also includes the coal mining sector is discussed in Ramón Tamames, *La lucha contra los monopolios,* 2d ed. (Madrid: Tecnos, 1966), pp. 381–84, and detailed in López Muñoz and García Delgado, *Capitalismo español,* pp. 205–7 and graphs 2, 3, 6, and 7.

[38] López Muñoz and García Delgado, *Crecimiento y crisis,* p. 207.

parts by the INI, the Banco de Crédito Industrial (BCI, one of the official credit institutions), and a number of foreign banks.[39] As one team of observers reported, "the concerted action" program seemed to have been invented "for the exclusive purpose of avoiding the nationalization" of companies that, "given their links to the banks, should have access to other means of financing."[40] Despite the massive injection of public funds, UNINSA's creditors requested a new refloatation scheme in 1971 to cover continued losses. The INI eventually agreed to provide 80 percent of the new capital needed. Yet, when the moment came, the banks refused to subscribe to any part of the new stock. The conglomerate was thus nationalized after all, and the INI ended up with duplicate integrated steel production facilities that made little sense from an international competitive perspective.

The retreat of the banks and the massive socialization of losses that occurred in steel were repeated in 1966 when the coal-mining sector was threatened with massive default. Whereas they had initially opposed nationalization in steel, the banks in this case opted almost immediately to forgo their stakes in favor of the state. The high profits that this sector had yielded in previous decades had been "based fundamentally on the low cost of the labor factor and on a level of tariff protection that had made any modernization of the works unnecessary for its beneficiaries."[41] In the early 1960s the sector was therefore characterized by "atomization, old plants, obsolete machinery, underinvestment, low product quality, and low profits."[42] Though coal had also been the beneficiary of a "concerted action" program under the First Development Plan, the program was abandoned only a year after the failing companies had received the second of two large aid packages in 1966. In its stead, eight of the largest mining concerns of the north were merged into a single company, HUNOSA, 70 percent of which was taken on by the INI.[43] Within three years HUNOSA had absorbed vir-

---

[39]   López Muñoz, *Capitalismo español*, p. 92. In the case of the foreign banks, the loans were guaranteed by either the Treasury or the INI.
[40]   Ibid., p. 77.
[41]   Ibid., p. 106.
[42]   Comín and Martín Aceña, *INI*, p. 375.
[43]   Of the 2.6 billion pesetas of new capital provided by the INI, 65% was earmarked for the payment of bank credits. The remaining 907 million was paid to the old owners to cover assets that were estimated to be worth 780 million pesetas. See ibid., pp. 375–81, and López Muñoz, *Capitalismo español*, pp. 105–19. According to most accounts, the appraisal grossly exaggerated the companies' real worth, which explains why HUNOSA's

tually all of the remaining mining concerns in Spain, accumulating over 8 billion pesetas in losses by 1970 (i.e., more than twice the capital with which it had started). A new capital restructuring in 1971 finally led the INI to become the conglomerate's sole shareholder. As with steel, the banks were conspicuously absent from the sources of external financing on HUNOSA's balance sheet during the years leading up to the INI's forced takeover.[44]

The contrast between the response of the Spanish banks to these industrial crises and that of the German universal banks in the 1960s and 1970s, illustrates the extent to which the effects of particular institutional arrangements, such as "universal banking," are contingent on the broader structural and political context within which they develop.[45] Given the Spanish banks' well-established historical links to the coal and steel sectors, their abandonment of these sectors once they ceased to be sources of extraordinary profits was remarkably rapid and unqualified. A broadly similar story can be told for the shipbuilding sector, in which the INI's share rose from 40 percent to over 90 percent between 1966 and 1977.[46] Certainly, all three of these sectors were

---

former creditors not only gave their blessing to the nationalization but were its principal promoters. See Juan Velarde, *España ante la socialización económica* (Madrid: Zero, 1970), p. 70, quoting *YA*, July 25, 1967. Moreover, the old proprietors never transferred all of the assets, keeping the most valuable parts of the old companies' fixed capital. See Comín and Martín Aceña, *INI*, p. 379.

[44] The structure of HUNOSA's financing mirrored that of UNINSA, with the INI and the official credit institutions furnishing the bulk of the funds, supplemented in this case by a smaller financing package from two foreign banks. The contribution of the official credit institutions amounted to a direct bailout. When the INI subscribed 92.5 million in a HUNOSA equity extension in 1969, the amount was not cashed out by the public holding, but simply subtracted from the debt owed to the BCI. See López Muñoz, *Capitalismo español*, p. 114, and HUNOSA balance sheet on p. 118. See also Pedro Schwartz and Manuel Jesús González, *Una historia del Instituto Nacional de Industria, 1941–1976* (Madrid: Tecnos, 1978), pp. 109–16.

[45] The solidity of the bank–industry relationship in Germany is sometimes overstated, as a number of authors have argued. See, for example, Kenneth Dyson, "The Politics of Corporate Crisis in West Germany," *West European Politics* 7, no. 1 (1984), and John R. Griffin, "Investment and Ownership in a Volatile Economy: Big Banks and the Case of the East German Economic Transition," *Politics and Society* 22, no. 3 (1994). Nonetheless, the response to industrial crisis by the German banking sector as described by Dyson involved a level of support to the restructuring effort that contrasts starkly with that of the Spanish banks. Griffin's analysis on the other hand, illustrates the extent to which even the postwar relationships between banks and industrial firms in Germany was dependent on other institutional and structural conditions.

[46] Schwartz and González, *Historia del INI*, p. 133, and Comín and Martín Aceña, *INI*, pp. 396–400.

particularly vulnerable to international market conditions in the 1960s, and the socialization of losses that occurred in them was not unique to Spain. What is exceptional about the Spanish case is that, after having played a major role in promoting the hothouse investment strategies pursued in these sectors during the autarkic period, the banks not only divested but refused even to participate in the financing needed for their restructuring.

The banks' behavior in these early industrial crises foreshadowed their more general reaction to the recession in the 1970s. At the time of their retreat from steel and coal in the 1960s, the banks were increasing their investment in other sectors. Their holdings in nonfinancial firms expanded significantly throughout the first half of the 1970s, peaking at 33 percent of their total portfolios and 4.2 percent of their total assets in 1975 (see Table 16).[47] Thereafter, however, the banks began a steady divestment that continued unabated for more than a decade, leading these two ratios to decline to 12.8 percent and 1.5 percent respectively by 1986. The banks undertook a significant return to industry only in 1988, at the height of the economic boom of the late 1980s, only to sell off large packages of industrial stocks in the early 1990s, when the Spanish economy was once more hit by recession.[48] This strongly pro-cyclical investment behavior reveals the extent to which their relation to Spanish industry lacked the kind of long-term orientation typically associated with "patient capital" or with a universal banking system. It supports one observer's contention that Spanish bankers, unlike their German counterparts, regarded their industrial holdings principally as a source of extraordinary profits, or as assets that were easily sold to boost profits.[49] They also served to capture clientele and, in the late 1980s, became a means of protection against the threat of hostile takeovers.[50]

The banks' divestment from industry during the 1970s and 1980s illustrates the precarious character that bank–industry relations had

[47] The continued rise in 1974 is explained by the fact that the impact of the first oil shock on Spanish industry was deferred by a domestic oil price freeze.
[48] Jordi Blanch, Antoni Garrido, and Esteve Sanromá, "Las relaciones banca-industria y su incidencia sobre la eficiencia bancaria," *Economía Industrial,* no. 272, 1990, p. 91.
[49] Peter Bruce, *Financial Times* correspondent, interviewed in Madrid, spring 1991.
[50] The primacy of these motives and the absence of the kind of long-term strategic involvement in industry were also reflected in the atomized nature of the banks' industrial holdings across sectors. Blanch et al., "Relaciones banca-industria"; Carlos Chuliá, "Relaciones banca-industria," *Papeles de Economía Española,* no. 44, 1990.

Table 16. Nonfinancial firm holdings of Spanish banks, 1972–1988

Year	Percent of total bank portfolios	Percent of total bank assets
1972	21.1%	3.2%
1973	25.7	3.5
1974	29.8	3.8
1975	32.9	4.2
1976	27.8	3.4
1977	27.7	3.1
1978	25.3	3.1
1979	23.1	2.6
1980	20.7	2.1
1981	19.9	2.0
1982	17.7	1.6
1983	22.1	2.0
1984	15.7	1.7
1985	14.3	1.5
1986	12.8	1.5
1987	13.7	1.4
1988	21.9	2.1

Source: Adapted from Jordi Blanch, Antoni Garrido, and Esteve Sanromá, "Las relaciones banca-industria y su incidencia sobre la eficiencia bancaria," *Economía Industrial,* no. 272, 1990, p. 90.

taken in the course of Spanish industrialization. In quantitative terms, however, this direct investment behavior was less consequential for the Spanish economy than the manner in which the banks altered their behavior as financial intermediaries in response to the tightening of central bank rediscounting. After the elimination of the special rediscount lines in 1971, the banks increased their profits by switching from a strategy of earning a steady interest margin on an ample supply of cheap credit to one of using their "market power to shift costs from the financial to the productive sector."[51] This change in their business strategy was supported by the peculiar pattern of financial deregulation instituted in the early 1970s. The liberalization of commissions in 1972 allowed the banks to pass on the increased cost of their resources to their borrowers through the operation of a price cartel that was institutionalized in the form of a monthly luncheon at which the heads of the Big Seven met to agree on a common business course (a practice that continued until the end of the 1980s). The banks were thus able to increase their gross earning margins from 3.97 percent of average assets

[51] Alvaro Cuervo, "Banca, industria y crisis bancaria," *Economía Industrial,* no. 272, 1990, p. 68.

in 1974 to 6.15 percent in 1980, when all other sectors were seeing their profits plummet.

This shift in burden of adjustment from the financial sector to industry was magnified by the liberalization of bank branches in 1974, which was ensued by a phenomenal race among the Big Seven to expand their branch networks. The oligopolistic process of nonprice competition "made growth the fundamental objective [for the banks], since it was assumed that profitability was a given."[52] The number of bank offices increased from 5,628 in 1974 to 12,238 by 1979, giving Spain the highest bank branch per capita ratio in Europe and sharply increasing the banks' operating costs (see table 7 in chapter 1). The peculiar pattern of deregulation carried out in Spain in the early 1970s thus "made it perfectly possible that an increase in the domestic level of competition degenerated into an increase in global inefficiency, without provoking . . . the disappearance of the more inefficient units."[53] The price of this rising cost inefficiency was borne almost wholly by borrowers. By 1976, the average return on capital of Spanish industry had sunk to 3.5 percent, while that of the Spanish banking sector remained above 12 percent.[54]

The banks' massive branch expansion at a time when all other sectors of the Spanish economy were hit by a severe economic crisis lays bare the extraordinary level of protection afforded to the sector. Perversely, the banks' ability to pass on their rising costs was buttressed by the economic crisis itself. "The whole scheme rested," writes one observer, "on the [dissipating] capacity for resistance offered by the productive sectors of a progressively deteriorating economy" and on the "complete defenselessness of Spanish industrial firms in the financial arena."[55] One of the most telling measures of this defenselessness was the debt-to-equity ratio of Spanish firms, which according to one estimate rose from an average of 60 percent between 1965 and 1975 to over 300 percent by 1979.[56] Spanish industry thus was made to bear

---

[52]   Antonio Torrero, *Tendencias del sistema financiero español* (Madrid: H. Blume, 1982), p. 25.
[53]   Cuervo, "Banca, industria y crisis bancaria," p. 69.
[54]   *El País,* August 5, 1979. Torrero estimates that the banks passed on as much as 82 percent of the sharp rise in their costs to borrowers from 1974 to 1979 (*Tendencias,* p. 53).
[55]   Ibid., pp. 55, 44.
[56]   Manuel A. Espitia, "Política financiera y resultados de la empresa industrial española (1964–1988)," *Economía Industrial,* no. 272, 1990, p. 96.

extraordinary financial costs precisely when it had to absorb the two external oil shocks. As another observer notes, this situation set in motion a self-feeding cycle in which high financial costs raised the number of defaults on bank loans, which increased the banks' costs, and these additional costs where passed back to industry through even higher borrowing costs, further increasing the number of failures in the industrial sector.[57]

Eventually, as we shall see, this process would spill over into the banking sector itself. The crucial point here is that the manner in which liberalization was carried out in the early 1970s supported the banks' changing business behavior and had consequences for the Spanish economy that far outlasted the first phase of the reform process. Among these consequences was the absorption of a large number of unprofitable private firms by the INI in the 1970s and early 1980s. After 1974, the INI's socialization of losses, begun in steel, coal, and shipbuilding during the 1960s, was generalized to a much larger number of sectors, a process abetted by both the banks' divestment and the heightened financial burden placed on Spanish firms. By the early 1980s, the Spanish public sector, although still modest by European standards at just 8 percent of GDP, had grown considerably and was one of the least profitable among OECD members. Annual state transfers to cover losses at public companies rose by almost 1.3 billion pesetas between 1975 and 1984 and accounted for more than 15 percent of the state's budget in 1982.[58] The relationship between an indigent and defeated colonial state and its domestic creditors at the turn of the twentieth century thus came full circle in the 1970s, with a public treasury that was saddled by massive losses at precisely the time of the political transition. The burden on public finances would in turn play a role in the politics of accommodation between the banks' and Spain's posttransition governments, continuing to condition the process of financial reform in the 1980s.

Changes in the economic context did play a role in bringing about domestic financial liberalization in Spain. Yet this relationship was not a simple one. It required a particular domestic political configuration, and it did not determine the shape that reform was to take. Interna-

---

[57] Cuervo, "Banca, industria y crisis bancaria."

[58] Olga Ruiz Cañete, "Empresa pública y transferencias estatales," *Papeles de Economía*, no. 38, 1989; Alvaro Cuervo García, "La empresa pública y el déficit," *Papeles de Economía Española*, no. 23, 1985.

tional conditions fostered domestic change but had little impact on the shape of that change. Their effect was contingent on the existence of an elite of reformers set on dismantling the apparatus of financial interventionism and was overdetermined by the internal dynamics of the Spanish political economy in the 1960s. Stated differently, international and domestic economic conditions helped to bring about the shift to liberalization because they fed into a cleavage within the Spanish policymaking elite. Change in the economic context accelerated a shift in the leadership over Spanish economic policymaking in which the planning bureaucracy was displaced by central bank reformers. Yet the course of reform was thoroughly determined by the internal struggle and historically defined agenda of these reformers, which came to center on the objective of strengthening the central bank's influence over economic policy and establishing its exclusive jurisdiction over the financial system.

Change in the character of financial regulation also was accompanied by continuity in the compactual politics of regulation. To advance their principal objective of restructuring authority within the state, the reformers were willing to institute some deregulation measures without taking complementary steps that would have increased the level of competition in the financial system. In the early 1970s, this tactic produced an embryonic liberalization process that was clearly punitive for the rest of the Spanish economy. Given the precarious commitment of the banks to their industrial clients, the pattern of deregulation that was implemented allowed the banks to increase their oligopolistic profits in the face of tighter liquidity by expanding their income margins and passing the costs on to their borrowers. It also gave rise to a massive expansion of the banks' branch networks, which sharply raised the banks' operating costs, thus adding to the financial burden placed on industry.

The shift within the Spanish policymaking bureaucracy that led to an early espousal of liberalization thus also shifted the burden of adjustment disproportionally to Spanish producers, the vast majority of whom did not have access to international financing. To be sure, the economic incoherence of the early reform process was in large measure due to the reformers' still-limited room for maneuver under the old political regime. As we shall see, the political transition strongly bolstered the reformers' position. Yet it also strengthened the politics of reciprocal consent between state elites and private bankers.

5

Financial Reform and
the Political Transition

The most important reform measures in the financial liberalization process initiated in Spain in the early 1970s were passed as two executive orders by the first democratically elected government in over four decades, just days after it took office in July 1977. This link in the timing of political democratization and anti-interventionist reform was reasserted in the Pactos de la Moncloa, which were signed by all of the major parliamentary parties in October 1977 and are commonly considered a cornerstone of the regime transition. The centerpiece of the Pactos was an incomes policy agreement that limited wage increases to 20 percent and monetary growth to 17 percent. Yet this agreement was accompanied by a statement of intent on a variety of economic reforms that were meant to reconcile the democratization process with the widely recognized need for economic adjustment. Reform of the financial system appeared here side by side with tax reform and the creation of a democratic welfare state.

Two contextual factors might explain the prominent place accorded to financial reform in the democratization process. One was the dire financial situation of a large number of Spanish firms and the investment crisis that the country began to experience after Franco's death in November 1975. The cost of credit became the focus of a public controversy in the press which struck directly at the privileged position of the Spanish banking sector. The debate lent urgency to the idea of reforming the financial system. The second factor was the salient voice gained in Spanish political circles by foreign bankers during the critical years 1976–78. Like the acute financial situation of Spanish businesses, the efforts of foreign (principally American) banks to secure permission to operate in Spain appeared to add an element of direct political pressure in favor of "liberalization." That pressure gained its significance less from the size of the foreign financial support (which at $13 billion in 1977 was relatively modest in relation to the almost $6 billion that the Bank of Spain continued to hold in existing reserves) than from its symbolic value in preempting a crisis of confidence in the Spanish economy at a moment when the domestic banks' backing for the transition government's economic program was all but clear.[1] The foreign bankers' cooperation in the face of the domestic banks' recalcitrance seemed to place them in an unprecedented position to press for an opening of the Spanish financial market. Even the left-leaning daily *El País* argued that traditional "sovereignty" arguments against opening the financial market to foreign participation had little relevance when many of the largest Spanish industrial firms relied on foreign lending and some of the most technologically advanced sectors of industry (including chemicals and electronics) were already controlled by foreign capital.[2] The key, the newspaper noted, was to ensure that the foreigners came to compete by assertively liberalizing the domestic financial system at the same time that the foreign banks were let in.

Given the position of privilege that the Francoist regulatory framework had given the banks while Spanish producer groups were being asked to accept the heavy burden of adjustment to a post-OPEC economic order, there was thus an obvious link to be made between financial liberalization and political democratization. Such a link was also stipulated in the statements of the reformers anchored in the Bank of Spain, who began to refer openly to the need for increased competition in the financial system to ameliorate the terms of financing for Spanish

---

[1]   Most of the foreign loans were syndicated by American banking giants and used, along with the reserves accumulated from 1971 through 1973, to finance the current account deficit caused by the oil shock–induced decline in competitiveness during the mid-1970s. See OECD, *Economic Surveys: Spain,* 1978, p. 16; Sima Lieberman, *The Contemporary Spanish Economy* (London: George Allen & Unwin, 1982), p. 287.
[2]   *El País,* May 24, 1977. See also the editorial in the issue of May 12.

firms.[3] However, both the timing and the content of the financial reform package of July 1977 reflect the primacy of the original agenda
that had been fashioned in the central bank during the years leading up
to the transition: strengthening the central bank's ability to control
liquidity in the credit market and its institutional position vis-à-vis
other state actors. This objective required a working alliance with the
private banks in the transition period which would lead the reformers
to sacrifice many of the aspects of liberalization involved in the putative
link between financial reform and democratization.

The agenda for institutional reform incubated in the central bank
during the early 1970s was dramatically boosted by the influence that
the reformers attained in the transition process. One key development
was the appointment by Adolfo Suárez (the prime minister appointed
by the king in 1976 to oversee the transition to free elections) of
Enrique Fuentes Quintana (the principal sponsor of Angel Rojo's mission in the Bank of Spain) as economics minister, and his reappointment as vice president for economic affairs after Suárez's Unión de
Centro Democrático (UCD) won the first free elections in June 1977.
From these two posts, Fuentes was able to define the economic program of the transition including the content of the financial reform. He
was also able to move other members of the reformers' network into
key positions in the policymaking bureaucracy, ensuring that the
central bank's agenda would have strong advocates at the center of
executive power long after his own premature departure from office in
1978.

Fuentes's appointment and the position that the reformers gained in
the Spanish regime transition were the result of several factors. One
was the transition government's immediate imperative to curb the uncertainty created by Franco's death in the period leading up to the
elections and to raise enough foreign financing to stave off speculation
against the peseta during that period. While Suárez set out to secure the
political transition by negotiating with the Socialist opposition at
home, he went on a personal campaign to raise sovereign loans from
American banks and the IMF in 1976 and early 1977.[4] The reformers'
connections through the central bank to the IMF, which organized and
matched most foreign debt that Spain raised in the 1976–78 period,

---

[3] See, for example, L. Angel Rojo, "La reforma del sistema financiero español," in *VI
Jornadas de Mercado Monetario* (Madrid: Intermoney, 1978).
[4] *El País*, May 10, 1977.

clearly was an asset in this context. By placing Fuentes in charge of economic policy, Suárez could reassure foreign creditors that the neo-liberal orientation represented by the central bankers would carry the day in the transition process.

Such external constraints contributed to the reformers' ascent during the immediate transition period, but foreign creditors had very limited influence over the actual course of financial reform. Other factors played a more determinant role in establishing the reformers' influence over economic policy. The concentration of economic expertise that had developed in the central bank over the preceding decades and the reformers' cohesiveness as a network of policymakers with a clearly defined agenda are among the most important ones. The absence of an alternative network of economic experts was compounded by the rapid delegitimization suffered by the planning bureaucracy as a result of its close association with the authoritarian past, and by the precarious state of the public enterprise sector as a result of the INI's massive absorption of failing firms.

The effect of this concentration of purpose and expertise in the central bank was magnified by the fact that individuals such as Fuentes and Rojo, even though having held important policymaking positions under the Franco regime, enjoyed reputations for independence from the political past, thanks to their antagonism to the regime's planning bureaucracy. Fuentes was also known for having fought (and lost) a battle to give the state a wider and more progressive tax base (a goal he achieved after the elections). This background gave him significant moral authority in political circles during the transition period.[5] Last (and foreshadowing the course that events would take in Eastern Europe), the reformers' ascent was facilitated also by the easy ideological association between any form of economic interventionism and the political authoritarianism of the past.

The reformers' decision to launch a major financial reform initiative when the political transition had hardly overcome its moment of crisis is explained by their calculation of the risks and opportunities that the transition entailed. The economic context of the late 1970s brought the reformers' agenda to the forefront of public debate in a manner that

---

[5] Fuentes's 1973 tax reform bid is discussed in Richard Gunther, *Public Policy in a No-Party State: Spanish Planning and Budgeting in the Twilight of the Franquist Era* (Berkeley: University of California Press, 1980), pp. 91–95. On Rojo's trajectory, see *Institutional Investor*, May 31, 1994.

highlighted the more political and conflictual elements of financial regulation, especially the way the existing framework had sanctioned the
operation of the banking cartel through the powers conferred on the
Consejo Superior Bancario (CSB). Democratization thus did not just
challenge the existing framework; it did so in a manner that emphasized the conflict of interest between the banks and other sectors of the
Spanish economy rather than the issue of monetary control. The reformers thus suddenly found their program at the heart of a hot political debate over economic privilege in a free society. In Fuentes's first-
hand account of the reform process, he explains how this threat
induced him to seek to pass the principal package of liberalizing legislation at the earliest politically feasible point:

> It was a question of visibly accelerating the liberalization process so as
> to demonstrate a political resolve to play the financial reform card.
> This objective . . . had already been attempted in the measures of
> August 1974.[6] Yet the financial system continued to respond to an
> interventionist framework. . . . The measures of 1977 addressed these
> [remaining problems]. They were intended to catapult the financial
> reform process so far that the advance would be irreversible. From
> then on, the timing of subsequent steps toward greater freedom and
> competition could be debated, but it would be impossible to take a
> step backward without incurring a very high cost and highly criticiz-
> able contradictions. This would inhibit any attempt to turn back the
> clock. . . .
>   The measures adopted in 1977 had, beyond their defects and limita-
> tions, two very important virtues: that of affirming publicly and politi-
> cally the economic logic of financial reform and that of setting its
> future course, even if this was to be achieved with short steps spaced
> out in time. After 1977 [this] economic logic of financial reform . . .
> held complete sway as a source of inspiration for economic policy.
> Nobody, absolutely nobody, was able to articulate a valid alternative
> to the reform criteria that the Bank of Spain had developed and begun
> to apply to the country's economic policy.[7]

---

[6] The reference is to the creation of short-term central bank credits.
[7] Enrique Fuentes Quintana, "Prólogo," in Rafael Termes, *Desde la banca* (Madrid:
Rialp, 1991), pp. lx–lxii.

The timing of the 1977 reform package (which, Fuentes acknowledges, carried substantial risks) was thus determined neither by the pressure of foreign bankers nor by the short-lived rise in dependence on foreign debt but by the unique opportunity and threat that the reformers saw in the political transition. This political calculus is also reflected in the inclusion of financial reform in the Pactos de la Moncloa, which established a direct link between the central bankers' agenda and the democratization process. As Fuentes's account makes explicit, the agenda being advanced in this way had been drafted in the central bank during previous years. The reformers took the risk of launching such a substantive package such a short time after the election to undermine the political chances of any alternative vision of financial reform before the incipient parliamentary process had gathered steam. Opposition came, according to Fuentes, from the "beneficiaries of the traditional financial system," including the "traditional" bankers who were opposed to any changes in the rigid structure of credit regulation that supported their cartel, industrial firms receiving privileged credit, and politicians who enjoyed the "enlightened financial despotism of the concession of discretional credit."[8] Yet there are strong reasons to believe that the reformers' main concerns in implementing the reform package before the opening of the legislative process lay elsewhere.

As Fuentes's statement intimates, the political transition carried the threat that other political actors would gain control of a reform process that up to now the central bank had managed to direct. The introduction of the 1977 reform measures by executive orders served to preempt greater political and parliamentary involvement, at a time when the main opposition party of the left (the Spanish Socialist Workers' Party, or PSOE) still endorsed nationalization of the banking sector. The reformers' choice to pursue the liberalization agenda at the high point of the transition, moreover, rendered the reform initiative hostage to the imperative of securing the banks' support for the new government's economic program. In the month leading up to the election, the reform package had to be formulated in the course of ongoing negotiations to ensure that the bankers would not try to sabotage the transition process. The timing of the reform initiative therefore placed the re-

---

[8] Ibid., p. liv.

formers in a particularly weak position vis-à-vis the bankers. Fuentes's choice to proceed nonetheless is explained by his desire to forestall a political challenge to the central bank's agenda and by his belief that this agenda required a working alliance with the banking sector. "I was convinced," he writes, "that these liberalization measures were a critical part of the adjustment policies that the country would have to apply to get out of the crisis," and "even more convinced that without the support of the Spanish bankers and the heads of the savings banks, which together accounted for 90 percent of the Spanish financial system at the time, those reforms, no matter how adequate they were, would not become a legal reality or guide the daily practice of the Spanish financial system."[9]

The effort to establish a powerful working alliance with the banks involved at least two tasks. The first was to get the banks to sign on to the basic principle of liberalization and to change the way they operated in the political arena. They would not do so unless the leadership structure in the cartel changed to favor bankers who were more receptive to the idea of shifting away from the corporativistic framework of the CSB toward granting greater authority to the central bank and allowing the latter to act as their mediator vis-à-vis the government. Such a change, along with the adoption of a defensible public position on the issue of liberalization, was essential to make the banks a viable political ally.

The task of "reforming" the bankers was accomplished with the creation in November 1977 of the Spanish Association of Private Bankers (AEB) at Fuentes's behest. His account is again worth quoting at length:

> In my talks . . . with the men who headed the large national banks I soon became convinced . . . of their opposition to the liberal orientation of the reform. Among my memories of the difficult months I spent in charge of the country's economic policy there are few so bitter as that of a luncheon with the heads of the big Spanish banks in the Bank of Spain . . . [where] the [bankers] were informed of the financial reform process that I had in mind, some of which was contained in the already passed measures of July 1977. No comments were forthcoming . . . other than laconic admonitions about the perils of such a

[9] Ibid., p. lxii.

reform agenda, and its untimeliness in an economy that was undergoing a deep crisis and in a society that was attempting to find a constitution that would create a pluralist democracy, capable of sheltering all Spaniards. . . .

Two bankers—only two back then—understood how much was at stake for the financial sector in choosing to play the liberalization card: Rafael Termes and José Angel Sánchez Asiaín. From that day on I was determined that one of them should head the AEB. . . . The appointment by the banking sector's hierarchy, at that time headed 'de facto' by the Banco Español de Crédito, was still to be negotiated. Its chairman, an executive of great authority and long tenure whom I respected and admired, proposed a number of individuals . . . who, however, did not meet the requirements for the reformist objectives that were to orient the financial sector. I insisted on my idea of what the AEB should be and on my candidate for its presidency. He responded with polite forcefulness that I had the wrong mission, and therefore the wrong person in mind. "The AEB's mission is modest and limited, no more than negotiating the collective wage agreements of the banking sector. The rest is fantasy. . . . But let it be as you wish. I'll do everything possible to see that your candidate becomes the first president of the AEB."

Fuentes's candidate, Rafael Termes, was indeed appointed and "understood the role the business association had to play in the process of change of the Spanish banking sector." The AEB could not be simply a "platform for the negotiation of collective bargaining in the banking sector." Rather, in Termes's own words, it would have to be "the institution that would define the image, thinking, and voice of the banks as private enterprises, [able] to relate to the economic and monetary authorities in the government in the matters that affect [the banking sector], and capable of relating to the unions that would be its interlocutors in the industrial relations process, as well as to public opinion so that its positions would be well known and understood."[10] Unlike the CSB, where the big banks had exercised public powers behind closed doors, the AEB was meant to operate as a conventional lobbying organization that would orient the banking sector's position on policy issues and represent it in public. Breaking with the bankers' initial

10   Quoted ibid., p. lxiv.

opposition, the new organization declared the banking sector's endorsement of financial liberalization and launched a campaign to refute the accusation that the high cost of credit to Spanish firms was linked to the banks' extraordinary profit margins by pointing the finger instead at the heavy hand of the state in the financial system. Parting with the corporativist rhetoric of the past, the new AEB president thus took it upon himself to defend the banks in the language of neoclassical economics, a practice that was soon emulated by other bankers.

However, if the bankers were willing to adopt a democratic demeanor and to endorse the principle of liberalization, their support was based on the premise that liberalization would be carried out in a way that protected their interests. The second task for the reformers was therefore to reach a compact with the banks over the manner in which reform was carried out. The deregulation process had been molded so as to make it acceptable to the banks even before the transition. If the reformers were now in a stronger political position to impose some of their agenda on the bankers, their desire for the bankers' support meant that reform would nonetheless continue to be driven by the search for mutual accommodation.

The new regulatory compact is clearly discernible in the content of the reform package designed by Fuentes's team in the months leading up to the elections and passed in July 1977. The package centered on measures that advanced the main objectives of the reformers' original agenda: giving greater technical control over the banking system's liquid assets to the monetary authority and dismantling the institutional structure that had given other actors in the state a say in financial policy. The most important measure regarding the first objective was the establishment of an auction system to allocate the short-term bonds and credits through which the central bank was seeking to routinize liquidity control. This measure, vetoed by the banks in 1974 when the credits were first created, promised to be a big step forward in the central bank's effort to create a money market.[11] Nevertheless, access to the auctions continued to be restricted to the banks, which were able to coordinate their bidding, and the development of a real money market therefore did not take hold until well into the 1980s.

Other measures included in the July 1977 package also were meant

---

[11] As discussed in chapter 4, the existing system of proportional allocation of public debt to the banks curtailed the emergence of a money market.

to fulfill the central bank's original agenda. One of these was the deregulation of interest rates. According to officials, this measure could be expected to improve the financing available to firms with good investment prospects, because regulated credit rates subsidized inefficient users of capital at the expense of more efficient users. A more immediate concern behind it, however, was the central bank's desire to create a financial environment in which economic actors would be malleable to its interventions. Market-determined interest rates were a key requirement for the attainment of this goal. Opposition from the banks (which were particularly averse to paying higher interest rates on deposits) nevertheless was so intense that only rates on credit and deposits with terms of more than one year were included in the original package; rates on shorter-term deposits and credits were only gradually liberalized over the following years.[12]

The third main component of the July 1977 package focused on eliminating the institutional bases of selective credit regulation. It included the immediate abolishment of the Junta de Inversions, a Ministry of Finance committee that had decided which sectors and activities were eligible for privileged financing during the indicative planning years, and a schedule to dismantle the compulsory investment ratio. The authority to decide which sectors qualified for the investment ratio while it was being dismantled was raised to the ministerial level, and supervision of the banks' compliance with the ratio was shifted to the Bank of Spain.[13] As with the liberalization of interest rates, the reformers argued that dismantling the ratio should help to reduce the financial burden on efficient firms, because the banks needed to charge higher rates on the portion of their credit that fell outside of the ratio to compensate for the low return on the credits they granted to comply with it. Undeniably, however, the same measures also served to give the coup de grace to the institutional framework that had given state actors outside of the central bank control over the financial system, offering one more illustration of how aggregate welfare arguments used to justify a reform process that was driven by the monetary policy concerns of the reformers.

The reform package of July 1977 thus salvaged as much of the origi-

---

[12] *El País*, May 15, 1977.
[13] The number of sectors that could qualify was also radically cut. See Raimundo Poveda, "Las financiaciones privilegiadas de las entidades de depósito," *Papeles de Economía Española, Suplementos sobre el sistema financiero,* no. 11, 1985.

nal Bank of Spain agenda as was compatible with the reformers' corollary objective of establishing a partnership with the banks. By contrast, it conspicuously failed to reform the structure of the Spanish credit market to allow some measure of competition. Though credit deregulation and the dismantling of the compulsory investment ratio shifted a greater proportion of the credit system's resources into the market, the oligopolistic structure of that market remained virtually unchanged. The accommodation between central and private bankers therefore came entirely at the expense of other economic sectors, continuing the pattern established in the early 1970s.

The failure to reform the structure of the Spanish financial market is particularly evident in three areas, the first of which was the entry of foreign banks. Some of the largest Spanish industrial firms were able to resort to the Euromarkets in the transition period,[14] but most enterprises lacked access to these markets. Foreign borrowing thus could not significantly alter the costs imposed by the banking cartel on the majority of domestic producers. Opening the domestic financial market to foreign banks therefore offered a powerful opportunity for the government to alter the Big Seven's collusive behavior in the credit market. There was, moreover, a compelling legal precedent for such a move, as the intention to allow foreign banks in had been on the books since a 1962 decree that had never been implemented. In addition, the minister of finance in the first post-Franco government (prior to Suárez's appointment) had promised foreign bankers access when he negotiated a $1 billion loan in 1976. All the same, the measure was first delayed and then implemented in such a way as to ensure that the foreigners would not undermine the Big Seven's ability to act as a cartel.

The issue was dealt with in the months leading up to the election amid growing friction between some members of the government, including Suárez, and the bankers. The prime minister and some of his close associates apparently viewed the rising cost of credit as a sign of "disloyalty" to the government and as an attempt by the banks to extract concessions in exchange for their support of the government's transition program.[15] In the spring of 1977, Suárez began negotiations with the heads of several American banks, independently of Fuentes.[16]

---

[14] For figures and details of loans, see Reyes Fernández Durán, "La segunda entrada de la banca extranjera en España," *Información Comercial Española*, no. 545, 1979.
[15] *El País*, August 3, 1977; January 18 and June 1, 1978.
[16] *El País*, May 10, 1977.

In April the rumor spread that he had reached an agreement with several American banks to allow their entry in return for a large package of credits.[17] *El País* reported that its sources in the banking sector denied the possibility of such an agreement, arguing that it would be political suicide for the prime minister to take such an action unilaterally. The next day, however, the paper reported that Suárez had reached a deal with the head of Citibank, whereby five American banks would grant an IMF-matched loan of $500 million to Spain in return for a promise that they, along with a small number of European and Japanese banks, would be allowed to set up operations in Spain by the end of the year. Yet only three days later, just as several Spanish firms were signing new loan agreements with foreign banks, Ministry of Finance officials announced that foreign banks would not be allowed to establish offices in Spain in 1977 after all.[18]

The disjointed manner in which the entry of foreign banks was handled in the months before the election reflected a growing split between the so-called politicians in the government and the central bank reformers. Suárez's eventual retreat demonstrates the reformers' ultimate ability to maintain control over the reform process, in a manner consistent with their objective of enlisting the domestic banks as partners. When a decree authorizing the entry of foreign banks was finally passed in the summer of 1978, it imposed such heavy restrictions on their operations that it made it impossible for them to exert the competitive pressure that would have tangibly changed the credit conditions faced by Spanish businesses. The entry of foreign banks was made subject to discretional authorization by the government upon the advice of the Bank of Spain and the still operative CSB. Those institutions that did receive authorization were allowed to open only three offices, including the head office, and the amount of financing that they were allowed to raise in the Spanish market was limited to 40 percent of their lending to Spanish firms, excepting funds raised on the Spanish interbank market. The decree also included other significant restrictions on the invest-

---

[17]   A month earlier, officials had launched a campaign to raise international financing for the public sector in Japan and the United States, including a trip by the king to Saudi Arabia. The director general for financial policy announced on his return that foreign banks would be allowed to operate in Spain in 1978. See *El País*, March 15, 1977.
[18]   *El País*, April 1, May 7, May 8, May 11, May 12, 1977. Shortly thereafter, Telefónica signed a $25 million loan headed by Chase. See *El País*, May 15, 1977.

ment activities of foreigners, limiting their ability to invest directly in Spanish firms.[19]

These restrictions effectively curtailed the ability of foreign entrants to engage in retail banking and forced them to raise a large part of their resources on the interbank money market, over which the Big Seven exercised control.[20] Attempts by foreign banks to assert competitive downward pressure on credit rates in the early 1980s were thwarted by the Big Seven's manipulation of rates in the interbank money market.[21] This situation led in the late 1980s to the withdrawal of several American banks, whose comparative advantage rested on their ability to operate under competitive market conditions that did not exist in Spain. Those foreign banks that were more successful made their Spanish operations profitable by assenting to the Big Seven's collusion and exploiting the opportunity for oligopolistic price fixing.[22] This strategy, however, reduced their potential for expansion, and the market presence of foreign banks remained very limited until some of the restrictions were lifted in the early 1990s in compliance with European directives. One important impact that the foreign banks nonetheless had was to boost the role of the interbank market in their efforts to circumvent the 40 percent restriction on deposit taking, thus helping to create a money market during the 1980s.

The objective of infusing a greater degree of competition into the domestic credit market was also compromised in two other areas. The first was a long-announced plan to reform the official credit institutions (the EOCs), which in the 1960s had mediated a significant share of the financial system's resources. In 1971 EOC financing had been tied to the compulsory investment ratio imposed on the banks when the spe-

[19] *El País,* May 31, 1977; Daniel Alvarez Pastor and Fernando Eguidazu, "La banca extranjera en España: Régimen legal," *Información Comercial Española,* no. 545, 1979. Significantly, the Bank of Spain took the most protectionist position, delaying the decree by arguing for a 25% limit. See *El País,* June 9 and July 6, 1978.

[20] The limitation on the capture of domestic deposits was viewed as by far the most important by foreign bankers, as deposits represented the cheapest source of funding for the Spanish credit market (as opposed to raising funding from other intermediaries on the Euromarkets), and the restrictions placed them at a clear disadvantage vis-à-vis the domestic banks. See *El País,* March 8, 1978.

[21] Acting as a cartel, the Big Seven were able to raise interbank money rates whenever a foreign bank announced a cut in credit rates. See, for example, *El País,* August 19 and September 13, 1984, and August 8, 1985.

[22] Interviews, Madrid, 1991.

cial rediscount lines were abolished.[23] This scheme had entailed an implicit bargain whereby the private banks surrendered a part of their deposits to finance the ECOs and the EOCs refrained from competing with the private banks in the capture of available savings. "Thanks to the implicit lack of competition," a high-ranking EOC official writes, "the resources of the private banks were greater than those they could have raised in the face of a more 'aggressive' stance by a public banking sector." Moreover, "the official credit institutions were forced to allocate an important part of their resources to the financing of sectors and firms that were . . . not profitable, thus freeing the private banks from the need to shoulder this burden."[24]

The EOCs were a readily available avenue for the government to inject a measure of competition into the domestic credit market while controlling the speed at which competition occurred. Turning the EOCs into a single institution and allowing it to take deposits in competition with the private banks would have given the government the market presence that might have allowed it to break the Big Seven's collusive behavior without recourse to nationalization and without the risks that the unhindered entry of foreign banks might entail. The feasibility of such a design derived from the instant (and very substantial) deposit base that could be tapped by including the Postal Savings Bank and from the fact that the EOCs had an extensive national network of offices. Although this option was never officially articulated during the years of the centrist government, there is evidence that it was seriously entertained by some of the economic policy officials closest to Suárez.[25] In the end, however, the reform of the EOCs was limited to a

[23] Jaime Requeijo, "Los circuitos privilegiados de financiación y reforma del crédito oficial," *Información Comercial Española*, no. 596, 1983; Luis Tarrafeta, "Evolución del crédito oficial," *Economistas* (Colegio de Madrid), no. 30, 1988; Gabriel Tortella and Juan Carlos Jiménez, *Historia del Banco de Crédito Industrial* (Madrid: Alianza, 1986), p. 200.

[24] Tarrafeta, "Evolución del crédito oficial," p. 11.

[25] In 1978 there were repeated reports in the press that a number of government officials were considering reorganizing the EOCs and using them more aggressively in response to the banks' perceived bullying of the government in the credit markets. See *El País*, June 1 and August 8, 1978. An article in an economic journal put out by the Banco de Bilbao arguing against the EOCs' transformation into a public bank, suggests that this alternative was regarded as a serious possibility in policymaking circles in the early 1980s. See "El crédito oficial y su reforma," *Situación*, no. 2, 1982. Reports of plans for such a reorganization appeared again in 1982, after the government failed to persuade the banks to lower their interest rates. See *Mercado Financiero*, February and December 1982.

change in the way they were financed (a direct corollary of the dismantling of the compulsory investment ratio) and to a commitment to give
their management greater autonomy. The basic character of the institutions as administrative bodies that played a subsidiary role was maintained.[26] A reorganization along the lines just outlined would take
place only a decade and a half later, and then for a different set of
reasons (see chapter 6).

As in the case of foreign bank entry, the centrist government's failure
to use the EOCs to inject greater competition into the credit market
reflects the central bank reformers' ability to maintain control over the
financial reform process. The central role that these institutions had
played in the planners' privileged financing circuits made them a prime
target of the reformers. The transition offered the reformers an opportunity to complete what they had first attempted in 1971. The compulsory ratio had been introduced then as the lesser of two evils in the
struggle against the planners' cheap credit policies. Now the ratio itself
was the target. The minimalist approach to the EOC reform reflects the
reformers' fundamental animosity to the idea of giving other state actors authority in the financial system. But equally important, an aggressive use of the EOCs would have conflicted with the objective of establishing a working alliance with the private banks. The reformers'
decision to constrain the EOCs by forcing them to raise their resources
in the market without equipping them to compete with the banks in the
capture of deposits mirrors the way the entry of foreign banks was
handled. It also shows that both the bankers and the central bank
authorities regarded the private banks' hold over short-term savings as
the cornerstone of their position in the financial system.

The accommodation between the reformers and the banks is also
seen in the stance taken toward the domestic capital markets. The
principal characteristic of the Spanish securities market in the late

---

[26] Tortella and Jiménez, *Historia del Banco de Credito Industrial,* pp. 199–201; Requeijo, "Circuitos privilegiados." The actual reform conformed to that outlined in the Pactos
de la Moncloa and in the government's Programa de Saneamiento y Reforma Económica
of 1977, drafted under Fuentes's direction. It required the EOCs to raise 30% of their
financing in the market so that the compulsory investment ratio could be dismantled. This
objective was stalled for three years because private banks stopped extending long-term
credit after 1977; it was addressed again after the Socialist victory, when the EOCs were
forced to balance their books with limited access to public funding. See Robert Graham,
"Spain Feels Its Way toward a Liberal Financial System," *Banker,* January 1981; Tarrafeta, "Evolución del crédito oficial."

1970s was its extreme narrowness. In contrast to the situation in most other industrialized countries, industrial stocks accounted for only about 10 percent of capitalization, whereas the stock of the banks and public utilities accounted for more than 70 percent. This "bankarization" of the market had become particularly acute after 1974, when, with higher interest rates and economic uncertainty, the stock market had virtually ceased to be a source of long-term industrial finance. As part of the liberalization agenda, a committee of prominent economists was established in 1977 to produce a report on stock market reform. Made public a year later, the report spelled out a basic set of goals: to increase the transparency, flexibility, depth, and competition in these markets, to integrate them electronically, and to alter the form of bidding. It also set out the steps to be taken to move from the Latin capital market model, in which state-licensed *agentes* charging a fixed commission were the primary actors, to the Anglo-Saxon model of "market players and makers."[27] Yet no measures to implement the commission's recommendations were taken until almost a decade later, when the prospect of European financial integration finally led to the Capital Market Reform Law of 1988.

The virtually complete inaction in this area of reform is striking because, in contrast to the official credit institutions, the capital markets were assigned a central role in the liberal market model that conceptually underpinned the reformers' program. In that model, it is precisely the capital market that is intended to be the prime supplier of long-term investment finance for private firms. When asked about this paradox, the officials I interviewed offered two explanations. The first was the opposition of the *agentes,* who under the old law exercised a state-licensed monopoly on trading, charging fixed commissions on transactions while bearing no risks. The second was fear that the "disintermediation" process that would be set in motion with capital market reform would contribute to the problems of banks that were hit by the crisis that started in 1978.

The first of these explanations is contradicted by the fact that when the reform of the capital market was finally carried out a decade later, the *agentes* were quickly sacrificed once their main clients, the banks, had signed on. In hindsight the crisis in the banking sector clearly

[27] This distinction is discussed by Enrique Fuentes Quintana in "La bolsa de valores: Problemas de hoy y soluciones de mañana," *Bolsa de Madrid,* no. 100 (May 1987).

represents a more compelling reason for the delay, but as we shall see in chapter 6, the crisis was circumscribed until late 1982. Up until that point, it affected only the smaller industrial banks that had been created in the 1960s, and they were effectively taken over without a crisis of confidence in the system. The banks' problems, moreover, were driven by the failure of nonfinancial firms, not by competition in the credit market or the availability of alternative sources of financing for industry. Although the large banks had to write off large amounts of bad debt in the late 1970s, they continued to increase both their interest and profit margins through 1981. Thus the banking crisis was surely a very major concern to the authorities, but it is difficult to see why it would have called for complete inaction on capital market reform.

A more likely explanation is the fact that capital market reform threatened to curtail the big banks' control over the Spanish financial market. As two observers write, "the banks were, on the one hand, the most important individual investors [in the market] in terms of the volume of their stockholding. On the other hand, they were also the main institutional investors [trading on behalf of their clients]. In addition, they were the most important issuers of stock. . . . [However,] bringing savings to the markets was a form of increasing their own competition in capturing cheap resources, and taking firms to the stock market meant giving out information, and, in all likelihood, loosing power."[28]

Although there were inherent contradictions in their role in the capital markets, the banks were thus able to resolve them through their extensive control. The traditional institutional structure of the capital markets and the monopoly of the *agentes* guaranteed that control. The opposition of the banks represents a much more congruent explanation of the long delay of stock market reform, and it fits the pattern manifested in other reform areas of postponing any change that might significantly weaken the economic position of the Big Seven. Like the careful calibration of foreign bank entry and the minimalist reform of the official credit institutions, the inaction in the area of capital market reform fitted the reformers' strategic objective of establishing a working alliance with the banks. Measures that would have injected greater competition into the Spanish financial market were postponed in the

[28]   José Manuel García Hermoso and Sebastián Ubirría Zubizarreta, "Reforma y transformación del mercado de valores," *Papeles de Economía Española,* no. 44, 1990, p. 138.

late 1970s in order to get the bankers to accept those changes most important to the central bank's agenda.

There was one exception to this rule in yet another area of the reform process: domestic savings banks. These institutions, which had the character of nonprofit trusts dating back to the nineteenth century and tied to a local regional base, had carried the brunt of the interventionist system, being forced to allocate as much as 80 percent of their savings to the financing of the public sector under the Franco regime. They had also up to this point been barred from a wide range of banking activities (including the discounting of commercial paper, the most common form of bank lending in Spain). The greater part of their free deposits had therefore been deposited with the commercial banks, reducing them to adjuncts of the latter in the financial system. The reform of 1977 included several important alterations to this regulatory subjugation. It cut the compulsory investment ratio of the savings banks from 80 percent to 60 percent and set a schedule for further reductions, and it allowed the savings banks to engage in lending activities. The deregulation of interest rates would also allow the largest of these institutions to act more aggressively over the following decade and to increase their share of deposits at the expense of the commerical banks.[29]

In view of the savings banks' limited political influence in relation to the Big Seven, this regulatory equalization may appear to challenge the political analysis of the reform process advanced here. There are several reasons, however, why this deviation fitted the reformers' agenda and even the accommodation with the Big Seven. First, dismantling the savings banks' compulsory ratio was one more way for the central bank to limit the authority of other state actors over the financial system. This was particularly important in the case of the savings banks because most were ruled by regional governmental authorities. The process of regional devolution that took place during the regime transition confronted the reformers with a new wild card, one that potentially threatened the central bank's authority over the whole financial system. By harmonizing the regulatory treatment of the savings and commercial banks, the reformers were therefore furthering the central bank's objective of maintaining regulatory control over these institutions in the future.

Second, the savings banks were not regarded to be as great a threat to

[29]   Fernández Durán, "Segunda entrada."

the Big Seven as either the foreign or official credit institutions. They therefore represented the one way in which the reformers could address calls for greater competition in the sector that conflicted least with their priority of establishing a working alliance with the Big Seven. This estimation was borne out by the savings banks' behavior in the initial years after the reform, when, despite prodding from government officials, they refused to expand their lending to firms and continued to deposit a high proportion of their resources with the commercial banks.[30] Until 1989, the savings banks' competitive potential also continued to be limited by legal restrictions that kept them from expanding beyond their regional base. As a sector, they did manage to increase their share of deposits at the expense of the commercial banks by 10 percent over the 1980s, and by the early 1990s, the two largest savings banks (Cajamadrid and La Caixa) had acquired a deposit base that placed them in the league of the big commercial banks. However, because their operating costs were even higher than those of the commercial banks and they required high credit margins to cover those costs, the savings banks were not inclined to exert downward pressure on credit rates in the 1980s. They continued to allocate their credits overwhelmingly to households rather than enterprises, intensifying rather than mitigating the effects of the commercial banks' reallocation of credit from productive activities to sheltered sectors (see Table 5 in chapter 1), and they did not place any significant pressure on the commercial banks to cut their operating costs or credit margins (as reflected in Table 7, chapter 1).[31]

The way the 1977 reform was carried out thus meant that credit deregulation took place in an essentially unaltered oligopolistic market structure. The result was a significant deterioration in the financial costs and terms faced by Spanish firms when the second oil shock struck them. As a result of the reduction in the compulsory investment ratio, the availability of term credit declined dramatically within a year.[32] And contrary to the reformers' argument that the reduction in

---

[30] See *El País,* March 1 and June 1, 1978.

[31] Juan R. Quintas, "Cajas de ahorro y financiación de la empresa española," *Economía Industrial,* no. 293, 1993, Table 1 and Fig. 7; Jordi Canals, *Competitive Strategies in European Banking* (New York: Oxford University Press, 1993), p. 119.

[32] Total fixed-interest stock investment in industrial concerns by the banks declined from 40 percent in 1977 to as little as 10 percent just a year later, and term financing for industry practically disappeared. See Graham, "Spain Feels Its Way," p. 105; Antonio Torrero, *Tendencias del sistema financiero español* (Madrid: H. Blume, 1982), p. 127.

the ratio would bring down the cost of credit, the reform was followed by a sharp rise in credit rates from 1976 to 1979. "The cost of credit" to companies, one report of the Spanish Employers Confederation declared, was "prohibitive for all but speculative investments."[33] According to one survey, investment credit was averaging 21 percent in 1980 (representing a real interest rate of over 5 percent in the context of an acute recession) and the head of the AEB admitted to 20 percent.[34] The result was rapid decapitalization accompanied by a sharp rise in firms' indebtedness as they struggled to protect their market share and capital by borrowing to finance reposition investment, even if they had to do so at a negative internal rate of return.[35]

In the Spanish political context of the late 1970s, such economic repercussions proved unsustainable. With the UCD torn by factionalism and by falling popularity, and with an increasingly open stand-off between Suárez and the bankers, Fuentes resigned in 1978. To mitigate the disappearance of term lending, the bimonthly cuts in the compulsory investment ratio had to be interrupted in 1979.[36] During the following year, the government expanded the amount of credit being granted by the official credit institutions and forced the central bank to monetize the increase. The result was a resurgence of inflation in 1980–81. Worse yet for the reformers was a rapid rise in the public deficit, which was to add a whole new dimension to their agenda.

Aggravating the impact of the second oil shock, the accommodation with the banks thus appeared to threaten the principal objectives on the reformers' agenda in the early 1980s. This threat, however, would prove to be temporary, tied to the political precariousness of the centrist government. The reformers' rise to a position of leadership in Spanish policymaking during the transition proved to be far more enduring than the UCD. It would be fully realized precisely with the Socialist victory of 1982. The character of both financial reform and economic policy in Spain during the 1980s therefore continued to be driven as much by a shift within the state elite that began in 1969 as by the political transition of 1977.

[33] Quoted in Torrero, *Tendencias,* p. 120.
[34] Antonio Torrero, "Banca y crisis económica," *Información Comercial Española,* no. 570, 1981, and *Tendencias,* pp. 36–37, 108.
[35] Alvaro Cuervo, "Análisis económico-financiero de la empresa española," *Papeles de Economía Española,* no. 3, 1980, and Torrero, *Tendencias,* pp. 123–25.
[36] The cuts were later resumed, but at a significantly reduced rate.

6

Socialist Victory and Regulatory Accommodation

The neoliberally inspired process of financial reform initiated in the early 1970s and advanced forcefully by central bank reformers during the political transition deregulated credit without significantly altering the highly oligopolistic structure of the Spanish financial market. It therefore exacerbated rather than mitigated the rise in financial costs that Spanish industrial firms experienced as a result of the centrist government's efforts to fight inflation through monetary restraint. After the second oil shock, and with the increasingly precarious hold on office of the Unión de Centro Democrático (UCD), the economic repercussions of this pattern of liberalization seemed to threaten the prospects of neoliberal reform itself.

The elections of 1982, however, decisively altered this situation by giving an ample absolute majority to the Spanish Socialist Workers' Party (PSOE). The Socialist victory served to consolidate the central bank's leadership, and with it the shift in the Spanish policymaking bureaucracy that had begun in 1969. In the first half of this chapter, I discuss the reasons for this outcome, and its consequences for the reform process during the mid-1980s. I also discuss the impact of the "banking crisis" of this period, suggesting that it did not, as is often argued by government officials, represent a hardy economic reason for delaying a more fundamental reform of the Spanish financial market,

136

but that it played an important role in shaping the relationship between central and private bankers within the Spanish policymaking community.

After 1982, the reform process came increasingly to center on the reformers' new imperative of finding a way of financing growing budget deficits without compromising the central bank's room for maneuver. However, it also continued to be constrained by the reformers' determination to sustain a close working relationship with the private banks. The result was a new accommodation that allowed the reformers to finance the growing budget deficit without recourse to monetization, while preserving the banks' dominant position as financial intermediaries in the economy. This accommodation was to have important implications for the development of the Spanish public debt market, the financial costs born by the Treasury, and, by extension, those faced by Spanish firms.

In the second part of the chapter, I cover the reform process after Spain entered the European Community (EC) in 1986. The prospect of European financial integration added an important exogenous dimension to the reformers' agenda in the late 1980s because it threatened the "national" character of the large Spanish banks and with it the relationship on which the central bankers had staked their position. The focus of the reform process shifted, forcing advances in some areas that had been neglected (such as the stock market), but also heightening concern for the banking sector. The result in the late 1980s was the adoption of a distinctly nationalistic stance toward the financial sector that belied the reformers' anti-interventionist philosophy and contrasts with the central bank–inspired strategy of encouraging foreign investment in other sectors.

The Consolidation of Central Bank Policy Leadership

As befits any electoral victory by an untested left-wing party, the PSOE's coming to power in 1982 produced uncertainty and concern in Spanish financial circles. The party's economic program had included an open call for nationalization of the banking sector as late as 1978. Yet, such apprehension turned out to be remarkably short-lived. It was allayed by a series of appointments that clearly established the central bank's position of leadership in economic policy. These included the reappointment of the incumbent Bank of Spain governor and, most important, the appointment of a prominent young Bank of Spain economist, Miguel Boyer, to head a new consolidated superministry of finance, economics, and commerce. Boyer's replacement in 1985, Carlos Solchaga, also was a bank-trained economist and a personal pupil of Angel Rojo (the head of the Bank of Spain's Research Service). Many of the individuals named to the second-tier positions in the new superministry had similar curricula.[1]

The Socialist top appointees represented a younger generation of economists, many of whom belonged to the network that had been sponsored by Fuentes Quintana and Rojo in the 1970s. These appointments not only affirmed the policy leadership of the central bank but established it in a more unequivocal fashion than ever before. They also marked the onset of an increasingly symbiotic relationship between the Bank of Spain and the Ministry of Finance, as the latter came under the control of individuals who had strong personal ties to the central bank's Research Service and who unabashedly accepted that institution's intellectual authority. The identification between these new cadres and the central bank, as numerous interviewed officials described it, was so strong that one can speak of a veritable colonization by that institution of the upper ranks of the economic policy bureaucracy. One manifestation of this was the rapid dissipation of the tension between "politicians" and "reformers" that had persisted in the economic team of the centrist government.[2] The Socialist victory of 1982 thus resulted in the consolidation of a shift within the Spanish economic policy community that had begun as early as 1969.

The consolidation of the central bank's leadership within the policy-making bureaucracy and the new government's unequivocal endorsement of the reformers' policy orientation can again be attributed to a

[1] During the PSOE's first term, the three posts of state secretary in the ministry reflected an attempt to balance the neoliberal orientation of Boyer with the party's left faction headed by Vice President Alfonso Guerra. The Economy post was given to a party member known for his neoliberal orientation, the Finance post to an inspector of finance who was not a party member, and Commerce to a party member who was closer to the party's left. Before his resignation in 1985, Boyer dismissed the second and effectively marginalized the third of these secretaries of state. In 1986, the new minister, Carlos Solchaga, restructured the ministry's second tier in a manner that clearly established the hegemony of the neoliberals. See *El País,* November 9, 26, and 30, 1986, and April 21, 1988.

[2] That tension was replaced by a new kind of rivalry within the PSOE's party leadership, between the populist faction of Alfonso Guerra and the so-called *renovadores* who were placed in control of economic policy. Though the conflict led to Boyer's resignation in 1985, González left economic policy firmly under the control of the neoliberals.

confluence of factors. Two aspects of the economic context in which the Socialists took office supported the central bank's position. One of these was the demonstration effect that the French policy experiment with redistributive Keynesianism in 1981–82 had on the new Socialist leadership. The back-stepping in French Socialist policy in late 1982 seemed to illustrate the impossibility of national Keynesianism in a context in which governments in the other major world economies were imposing monetary and fiscal austerity; a perception that was bolstered by an increase in speculative pressure against the peseta and a fall in foreign reserves in the weeks after the PSOE electoral victory.[3] These circumstances appeared to offer strong arguments in favor of a central bank–chartered policy stance that would send the right signals in international currency markets. As the new prime minister, Felipe González, explained in announcing the government's austerity program, he saw "no room for maneuver."[4] González's choice of economic team may also have been influenced by a domestic development: the intensification of a crisis in the banking sector in late 1982, just as the Socialists were taking office. Like the French demonstration effect, the spector of a financial crisis offered an incentive for González to bolster the authority of the central bank.

These contextual factors gave the central bank a significant voice with the Socialist leadership. But they cannot account for the degree to which that institution's opinions were to dominate economic policy over the following decade without the longer-running developments in the policymaking elite described in earlier chapters. One reflection of those developments was the consistency with which Spanish economists—who had displaced all other professionals within the bureaucracy over the previous decade—believed that the central bank's view reflected virtually unquestionable expertise.[5] Another was the fact that many of the PSOE's own top economic experts, such as Miguel Boyer, either had been trained in the Bank of Spain's Research Service or were closely associated with Rojo's network. The philosophy that was to guide Socialist economic policy in the 1980s—what came to be known as "supply-side socialism"—can thus be traced directly to the changing diagnoses put forth in the Bank of Spain's annual reports in the years leading up to the Socialists' victory and to a series of articles by Rojo

---

[3] *New York Times,* January 4, 1983.
[4] *El País,* December 2, 1982.
[5] This opinion was expressed virtually without exception by the officials I interviewed when I asked them to explain the bank's ascendance after the transition period.

and others that stressed the supply-side nature of Spain's economic crisis and argued that adjustment required a reduction in real wages to compensate for the wage growth that had taken place during the transition.[6]

The position of the reformers in the PSOE was also aided by the programmatic moderation that the party had undergone in the years leading up to its electoral victory.[7] This moderation was accompanied by a conspicuous rapprochement between the party leadership and the Big Seven, who after the transition had become the main providers of electoral financing.[8] In its 1982 electoral program, the party had dropped its earlier commitment to nationalization of the banking sector in favor of a less radical program of financial reform that centered on easing the financial plight of Spanish industry by reorganizing the official credit organizations (EOCs) and by keeping banks that had to be rescued with public funds in public hands, so that the state could exert competitive downward pressure on credit rates. The new program also referred to the need to reach agreements with the large banks, "to restore the banks' role as great investors and promoters in the industrial sector."[9]

Negotiated Deficit Financing: 1983–1987

The prominent position afforded to the reformers in the first Socialist cabinet ensured that the central bank's policy preferences would be given the highest priority under the PSOE's rule. Inspired by the view that macroeconomic policy could do little to address rising unemploy-

---

[6]   See Antón Comesaña and José María Serrano Sanz, "Problemas escogidos y olvidados de la política económica española," in *Diez ensayos sobre economía española* (Madrid: Eudema Universidad, 1993), pp. 23–25.

[7]   Richard Gillespie, *The Spanish Socialist Party* (Oxford: Clarendon, 1989); Donald Share, *Dilemmas of Social Democracy: The Spanish Socialist Workers Party in the 1980s* (New York: Greenwood, 1989), esp. chap. 5.

[8]   The state subsidized political parties in relation to the vote they received. The banks provided credits to the parties in advance and in this sense gambled on the electoral outcome. Data on the credits extended by specific banks to different parties are offered in Jesús Rivasés, *Los banqueros del PSOE* (Barcelona: B-Grupo Zeta, 1988), pp. 30–40. Rivasés cites one banker who explains that "there are two types of electoral credits: those provided in the hope of being recovered, and those that are given without such expectation." See also the opinion on González of the AEB official quoted in the *New York Times*, January 4, 1983.

[9]   PSOE, *Programa 1982* (Madrid, 1982) p. 15, and *Mercado Financiero*, September 1982.

ment without a decline in real wages, the new government preemptively devalued the peseta immediately after taking office and embarked on an unprecedented austerity program designed to repress inflation. The reformers' new clout also meant that the alternative approach to financial reform that had been outlined in the party's economic program was dismissed outright. Instead, the process of financial reform under the PSOE continued to be guided by the central bank's policy agenda, just as it had been under the centrist government and before the political transition. Having already managed to limit the influence of other state actors over the financial system, the reformers now focused on finding a way to finance a budget deficit that had gone from 1 percent of GDP in 1977 to 5.6 percent in 1982 without compromising the central bank's ability to set monetary policy.[10]

The problem of orthodox deficit financing faced by the Spanish authorities derived from the absence of a market in short-term public debt in which the Treasury could finance its shortfalls. The creation of a money market that would render day-to-day control over monetary policy subject to routine central bank operations had been one of the principal objectives of the reformers from the start, but it had been effectively blocked by the bankers, who did not want the authorities to compete with them in capturing short-term savings by issuing short-term securities directly to the public.[11] With the growth of the deficit, however, the issue had acquired much greater importance. Because of the absence of a short-term debt market, the central bank was obliged to monetize the Treasury's shortfall and then to offset this monetization by issuing its own certificates of monetary regulation (CRMs) to the banks. From 1977 to 1982 more than 94 percent of the deficit was first

---

[10] The deficit's growth was due to a rise in social transfer payments (including unemployment benefits), subsidies to public enterprises, and interest on the public debt. After 1982, however, the last of these factors came to account for 62% of the growth in public expenditures. See Julio Alcaide, "El gasto público en la democracia española: Los hechos," *Papeles de Economía Española,*" no. 37 1988, p. 12. By the late 1980s, the budget deficit thus became "a self-feeding deficit driven by the financial costs of forgoing deficits": J. M. González Páramo, "El déficit del estado en 1986 y su financiación," *Economistas* (Colegio de Madrid), no. 23, 1987. See also Rafael Repullo, "Déficit, deuda pública e inflación: Aspectos teóricos y aplicación al caso español," *Boletín Económico* (Banco de España), December 1986.

[11] Under the existing arrangement, the central bank extracted liquidity through its certificates of monetary regulation (CRMs) and injected it through short-term credits to the banks but did not have a handle on the aggregate "liquid assets in the hands of the public," or ALP, which was becoming increasingly important for monetary policy objectives.

monetized, then offset in this way. But, as the deficit grew, the central bank's ability to offset the monetization was compromised because the auctions for its certificates were restricted by law to commercial and savings banks. In the early 1980s the banks' oligopsony in public debt became a serious impediment to monetary control. A sharp rise in the budget deficit in 1981 forced the Bank of Spain to raise the return on its CRMs to more than 20 percent. In the absence of an instrument of short-term public debt, the tremendous cost of this financing had to be monetized, and could be neutralized only by further increases in the already exorbitant return to the banks. Monetization was therefore unavoidable in the medium run.

This dilemma led the governor of the Bank of Spain, José Ramón Alvarez Rendueles, to push aggressively for the creation of a short-term public debt instrument in the last year of UCD government. Protracted negotiations to get the bankers to subscribe the new debt at a rate below that which they received on the CRMs failed, and the government held the first public auction of so-called pagarés del tesoro (PTs) in early 1982. A high bidding minimum, however, continued to make the auctions accessible mostly to the banks, which boycotted them until they had forced the Treasury to raise the return on the PTs to the rate they were receiving on the central bank's CRMs.[12]

The reformers' new position of strength after the Socialist victory led to a new attempt to redress this persistent conundrum. The solution, however, was obliquely enshrined in another reform of the compulsory coefficients carried out in 1983. The centerpiece of this reform was the creation of a new compulsory ratio that obliged the banks to invest up to 12 percent of their deposits in PTs. At the same time the old compulsory investment ratio (by now restricted almost exclusively to export credit) was further reduced, and the central bank's obligation to finance the Treasury's shortfalls was abolished.[13] What had once been

[12] "La reforma de un fracaso," *Mercado Financiero,* October 1982. The coexistence of two parallel public debt instruments (the central bank's CRMs and the Treasury's PTs) produced an inverted interest rates curve in which "the most prestigious issuer in the market [the Treasury] was forced to offer much higher rates of return than many private issuers of securities." Raimundo Ortega, "Tendencias recientes y problemas inmediatos de la política de deuda pública," *Papeles de Economía Española,* no. 32, 1987, pp. 130–32.

[13] Raimundo Poveda, "Las financiaciones privilegiadas de las entidades de depósito," *Papeles de Economía Española, Suplementos sobre el sistema financiero,* no. 11, 1985; Carmen Arasa Medina, "La política monetaria española: Del plan de estabilización a la década de los 80," *Situación* (Banco de Bilbao), no. 4, 1985.

an instrument of privileged financing to favored industrial sectors was thus astutely transformed into an instrument of orthodox deficit financing. This maneuver allowed the Bank of Spain to abolish its own debt instruments (the CRMs), ending the duality of public debt instruments that had hindered monetary policy.[14]

The creation of the new coefficient appeared to represent a flagrantly interventionist way to solve the deficit financing problem. This was the position publicly taken by the head of the AEB, who criticized the new measure as an "extension of the state's empire over the financial system." Even some of the public officials responsible for its implementation lamented the new coefficient as a necessary evil because of the Treasury's inability to raise funding more directly from savers.[15] Yet what was publicly described as a setback in the reform process shrouded a new accommodation between the central bankers and their clients in the financial sector.

The reform of the coefficients was drafted in the Bank of Spain and in close consultation with the banks. It was commonly referred to by public officials as a "negotiated" solution to the problem of deficit financing.[16] Thus, for example, in order to facilitate the conversion of CRMs held by the banks into PTs, the banks received a negotiated above-market return, rather than the rate set at auction, on the debt that they acquired in compliance with the new coefficient.[17] As was the case with the original compulsory investment ratio, the new coefficient must also be understood in light of its alternative, in this case a more aggressive effort on the part of the state to raise financing directly from savers without reliance on the banks to act as intermediaries. The high popularity that the PTs attained among investors early on suggests that market conditions would have allowed the authorities to act more assertively in this regard, as in fact they did in the early 1990s.

---

[14] Ortega, "Tendencias recientes," pp. 132–33.

[15] See ibid.; Rafael Alvarez Blanco, "Endeudamiento del sector público en España," *Papeles de Economía Española,* nos. 32 and 33, 1987. The technical literature on public debt policy for this period clearly reveals that the inadequate reform of the public debt market raised the return that the Treasury had to pay on its debt, thus putting upward pressure on other interest rates as well.

[16] *El País,* June 2, 1984, and personal interviews with public officials, Madrid, Spring 1991. See also Ortega, "Tendencias recientes"; José María García Alonso, "La evolución del sistema financiero español," *Papeles de Economía Española,* no. 18, 1984.

[17] The privileged tax treatment that the banks received in this transformation seems to have been the immediate cause of the resignation of the Secretary of State for Finance in 1984. See *El País,* May 19, 1984.

In addition, there is ample evidence that in the economic climate of the early 1980s the new compulsory ratio constituted a nonbinding constraint on the banks. By 1981, the aggravated economic crisis had led to a dramatic collapse in the demand for credit by Spanish firms at the credit rate levels that the banks continued to set by way of gentlemen's agreement in the context of their monthly meetings. This left the banks with liquidity excesses in 1982 and 1983 that forced them to buy increasing amounts of PTs even before the coefficient had come into effect. From 1981 to 1985, the banks' ability to maintain their oligopolistic rates and profit margins came to depend heavily on the return that they received on their public debt investments. In fact, for 1984–86 the banks held far more PTs then the new coefficient required. The PTs clearly played a compensatory role in the banking system, as reflected in the growing weight of public securities as opposed to private assets in the banks' balance sheets.[18] The counterpart to this trend was a significant decline in the supply of investment credit by the banks, which in the four months after the initial agreement on the new coefficient decreased by 300 billion pesetas.[19]

The coefficient solution to the deficit financing problem thus created an interlude in the reform process that allowed the banks to maintain their high credit rates at a critical point in the economic cycle by offering them a high-paying, risk-free alternative for their investments. Further proof of this accommodation is offered by the banks' operating costs, which had moderately declined between 1981 and 1984, but began to rise again in 1985 (see Table 7). As late as 1988, the OECD noted that despite the cost inefficiency of the Spanish banks, "their net earnings margins are in fact the highest in the EEC [with the exception of Denmark] . . . [and] despite the regulation of interest rates on part of their assets, the same is true of interest margins, suggesting that these

[18] Carlos Contreras, "Deuda pública, desintermediación, e inovación financiera en España," *Papeles de Economía Española*, no. 33, 1987. The banks held an average of 51% of the total PTs issued by the Treasury for this period, 10% above the 41% that the coefficient obliged them to. Their dependence on the PTs was also laid bare when they tried again to boycott the Treasury's auctions after the government decided not to continue granting them an above auction return on PTs once the original ones had matured in 1985. The banks' inability to place their funds in the depressed credit market forced them to return to the auctions, and even during the boycott they continued to hold PTs well above the required percentage. *El País*, November 12, 1984, and September 8, 1985; *Financial Times*, April 3, 1985.
[19] The Big Seven and their subsidiaries reduced their credit by 450 billion pesetas, while the foreign and smaller banks increased theirs by 82 and 50 billion, respectively.

controls have not had a serious effect on profitability and that their cost has largely been borne by bank clients."[20]

It is highly unlikely that the banks could have maintained their oligopolistic credit rates or their high profit margins through the period of the Socialist austerity plan otherwise than by flight into government debt. If the new coefficient constituted a nonbinding constraint, however, the question remains why it had to be made a legally compulsory requirement. Here the apparently contradictory character of the 1983 reform reveals the more subtle aspects of reciprocal consent. The new compulsory ratio can be said to have made life easier for both the authorities and the bankers in a number of ways. For the reformers, the "negotiated"—as opposed to market—path ensured a noninflationary source of deficit financing whose cost could be predicted and controlled.[21] This solution, moreover, could be arranged within the increasingly tightly knit policy community of private and central bankers and Ministry of Finance officials. The new coefficient was in this sense fundamentally different from the original investment ratio in that it did not increase the discretionary power of other actors in the state over the financial system or create vested interests outside of the financial community. It therefore did not conflict with the reformers' underlying objective of bolstering the central bank's influence over economic policy.

The transformation of the compulsory ratios can also be said to have made life easier for the reformers by making it easier for their main partners, the banks. While the authorities secured financing for the state through the new coefficient, they also eschewed a more aggressive attempt to raise state financing directly from savers. In this regard, the new coefficient was analogous to the original investment ratio, which had been the counterpart of the state's willingness not to enable the official credit institutions to compete with the private banks in capturing deposits. The imposition of a compulsory ratio thus allowed the reformers to limit the competitive impact that orthodox deficit financ-

---

[20] OECD, *Economic Surveys: Spain* (Paris, 1988).

[21] One study estimates that the state saved as much as 1% of GDP in financial costs thanks to financing provided through the PT and Reserve Requirement ratios in 1988. Rafael Repullo, "El coste presupuestario de reducir los coeficientes bancarios: Una primera aproximación," *Hacienda Pública Española*, nos. 110–111, 1988. However, because this coefficient-based financing served as an alternative to a more aggressive development of the public debt market, the real savings to the state may have been negative.

ing had on the financial sector. The appearance of heavy-handedness toward the banks that this solution entailed masked its most significant consequence: the curtailment of the disintermediation effect that is commonly associated with the growth of public debt markets, and the consequent preservation of the banks' position as intermediaries in the Spanish financial market.

The new coefficient thus gave official sanction to a situation in which the banks were able to maintain their oligopolistic credit rates by shifting a large part of their resources into public debt at a point in the economic cycle when the fall in demand for credit by firms would otherwise have forced them to reduce their margins. Because the banks' balance sheet performance in the mid-1980s became highly sensitive to the return that they received on their public debt holdings, the existence of the state-imposed coefficient also made it easier for the authorities to make this an important criterion in the Treasury's public debt policies.[22] Foreign bankers, for example, complained in 1984 that the rates at which the Treasury issued its debt were too high to be accounted for by market conditions, suggesting that they were being biased upward by the government's awareness of the impact on the domestic banks.[23] High Treasury rates, in turn, obfuscated the extent to which the overall level of interest rates, in particular the high cost of investment credit, was attributable to the banking sector's high cost and profit margins.[24] The compulsory nature of the coefficient may thus have served to mask both a direct and indirect process of subsidization of the banks by the Treasury during this period. Thus if the creation of a new compulsory ratio at a time when the central bank had been strengthened seems puzzling, it was in fact highly compatible with the evolving relationship of reciprocal consent between the reformers and the Big Seven.

In addition to the accommodation in deficit financing, the banks' ability to maintain their oligopolistic behavior in the credit market through the years of the Socialist austerity program was sustained in a

[22] Antonio Torrero, *Estudios sobre el sistema financiero* (Madrid: Espasa Calpe, 1989), pp. 89–90.
[23] *El País*, August 19 and September 13, 1984.
[24] One board member of one of the large banks expressed the opinion that this was a critical criterion in the Treasury's policies. Interview, Madrid 1991. This is also implied by Raimundo Ortega, head of the Treasury in the mid-1980s, in "La financiación del déficit público y su incidencia sobre el sistema financiero," *Papeles de Economía Española*, no. 23, 1985.

number of other ways. Like the plan to reorganize the EOCs outlined in the PSOE 1982 electoral platform, a promise to use the savings banks as a source of privileged industrial financing—a measure that would have clashed with the Bank of Spain's agenda—was indefinitely postponed once the government took office. So, for a number of years, was capital market reform. Competition was further hindered by the government's treatment of foreign banks. Increased liquidity in the interbank market in 1985 allowed the foreign banks to offer lower credit rates that year and to increase their share of the credit market to 11 percent. But the attempt was rapidly undermined by the big domestic banks, which, through their control over the domestic interbank market, cut off the foreigners' main source of funds. Far from encouraging such competitive pressures to lower the cost of corporate finance, and despite the severity of the industrial recession, the Bank of Spain placed a moratorium on foreign bank entry in 1984, arguing that the Spanish financial market had reached its point of saturation by foreign banks (a point that was arbitrarily defined as 14 percent of the credit market). One high-ranking central bank official bluntly informed the representatives of four Japanese banks that it was a question of "having foreign banks interested in Spain come to resolve problems and not just to create them."[25] By the end of the year, and after the Big Seven's maneuvers to reduce foreign bank funding, the latter's share of investment credit had receded again to 10 percent.[26]

The Role of the Banking Crisis

The course of regulatory reform under the first Socialist term thus allowed the banks to maintain their oligopolistic interest margins at a critical point in the economic cycle, while averting the negative effect that deficit financing might have had on the Big Seven's position in the financial system. The upshot was the perpetuation of extraordinary financial costs for Spanish industry in the midst of a prolonged recession and a calibration in the process of public debt market reform that had serious consequences for Spanish economic policy through the 1980s. When pressed to explain this regulatory pattern, public officials involved in the reform process almost invariably attributed it to the un-

[25] *El País,* November 27, 1985.
[26] *Financial Times,* May 23, 1991.

folding of a crisis in the banking sector in the mid-1980s. The crisis, the most significant in the Spanish banking sector since the late nineteenth century, did acquire very serious proportions just as the Socialists took office. Yet it is questionable that it made the kind of protection afforded to the large banks in their day-to-day business necessary. What is evident, however, is that the crisis advanced the relationship between private and central bankers under the new Socialist government.

The Socialists' entry into office at the end of 1982 coincided with the forced rescue of Banca Catalana, an industrial bank group created in the 1960s by Jordi Pujol (by now the leader of the Catalan regional government) and the first major bank that was taken over by the Deposit Guarantee Fund (which had been set up at the onset of the industrial bank crisis in 1978). Just three months later, the new government, in a largely unexpected move, summarily expropriated RUMASA, an industrial holding company also created during the 1960s that had come to control twenty industrial banks, in response to the central bank's discovery of a state of insolvency at the holding. RUMASA, which was to become the center of a heated political controversy during the PSOE's first term,[27] was highly unusual in two respects: it was the only newcomer ever to challenge the Big Seven (in part through its purchases of failing industrial banks and savings trusts in the late 1970s), and its banks belonged to its industrial concerns and had clearly been put at their service.[28] With 4 percent of the banking system's deposits, their potential failure also represented the first real threat to the sector's stability, a fact implicitly acknowledged by the Spanish Association of Private Bankers (AEB), which did little more than express "strong concern" at the government's choice of methods.[29]

During the next two years, virtually all of the remaining industrial

---

[27] The expropriation measure was challenged in court, but the Constitutional Court eventually ruled in the government's favor, and RUMASA's founder and head executive, José María Ruiz Mateos, was convicted of fraud.

[28] The RUMASA banks had been used to provide unbacked borrowing to the holding's nonfinancial companies to cover a mounting negative worth. An Arthur Anderson audit eventually revealed a $1.67 billion shortfall at the expropriated holding.

[29] *Financial Times*, April 13, 1984. There was a widespread perception in the media that "some [bankers] were happy with the Rumasa expropriation," as "Ruiz Mateos, with his banks and unorthodox practices had become a bothersome competitor who any moment might buy a package of stock in one of the big banks . . . and demand his admission to the 'club of Seven'": Rivasés, *Banqueros del PSOE*, p. 35. The *Financial Times*, May 27, 1983, reported that the chairman of Banco Santander "sent a note to congratulate Boyer on his performance" following the expropriation.

banks had to be rescued by the Deposit Guarantee Fund, and by the time the crisis ended it had involved 51 of the 102 banks existing in Spain in 1977. The crisis also affected the Big Seven, some of which suffered significant losses as a result of the failure of their industrial subsidiaries, and at least one of them (the Hispano-Americano) was forced to suspend its annual dividend payment in 1984.[30] However, although the dimensions of the crisis in the banking sector should not be understated, it is unclear that it required the kind of continued suppression of competition in the market for corporate finance that was maintained during the Socialists' first term. As the head of the AEB would later write, the episode never really threatened the stability of the system because it consisted of a series of discrete individual bank crises and did not extend to the sector as a whole. It is therefore questionable that the sector's stability would have been jeopardized by a measured increase in competition in the credit market from either the foreign banks or a reorganized public banking sector. The persistence of gross and net earning margins that remained well above the OECD average for the whole period suggests that the sector's profitability was quite independent of the problems faced by individual banks with failing subsidiaries (which were in any event being resolved through the massive socialization of losses). There seems to have been greater room for competition in the credit market than the automatic link so often drawn between the crisis and the government's approach to financial reform suggests.

Indeed, the new government's response to the banking crisis closely fit the pattern of accommodation in other areas of financial regulation. Despite the PSOE's electoral promise to keep rescued banks in public hands, Boyer and his team hastened to privatize both the Banca Catalana and the RUMASA banks.[31] The Big Seven's tender for Banca Catalana was quickly accepted, and the holding's banks ended up in the hands of the Vizcaya.[32] The RUMASA holdings were disposed of at a "negotiation table" attended by the Minister of Finance, the president

---

[30] The problems of the Hispano-Americano stemmed from its attempt to rescue the Banco Urquijo, an industrial bank with which it had strong ties. The government offered the Hispano assistance to absorb the Urquijo, rather than have it go the normal route of the FGD.

[31] The head of the AEB reported just days after the measure that González had assured him that the RUMASA banks would be reprivatized. *Financial Times*, March 1, 1983.

[32] La Caixa, a major Catalan savings bank, presented a tender for Banca Catalana, but it was refused in favor of one presented by the Big Seven.

of the AEB, and the presidents of the two largest banks; their new ownership was apportioned among the Big Seven in strict compliance with the cartel's internal ranking, along with a small participation by five medium-sized banks.[33] Foreign banks were excluded from the consortium of buyers, despite their expressions of interest.[34] From the beginning, the government thus forwent any leverage afforded it by the crisis to influence conditions in the credit market. The upshot was a new round of concentration that allowed the Big Seven to boost their share of the sector's resources at the time this share was being challenged by the domestic savings banks. The cost to the banks ultimately was little more than symbolic.[35]

The banking crisis, in fact, seemed to encourage the pattern of accommodation observed so early on under the Socialists, by bolstering the sense of cohesiveness in the financial policy community that now included the PSOE's economic team. It clearly made it easier for public officials to engage in policy measures that protected the banks, because the threat of instability in the sector constituted such a compelling argument that it was hardly ever questioned. It also brought the Big Seven into immediate and close negotiations with the reformers in the new government, emphasizing the element of mutual dependence be-

---

[33]   In what an editorial in *El País* (April 1, 1984) termed the "merry-go-round of the RUMASA debt," the government agreed to issue 440 billion pesetas in public debt, which the Big Seven subscribed in direct proportion to their deposits and for which they received a return of 9.5%. With the collected 440 billion, the state then extended an interest-free loan to the RUMASA banks to cover the unrecoverable debts contracted by the holding's other companies. The RUMASA banks then deposited that money with the acquiring banks at an interest of 13.5%. Through this accounting maneuver, the Big Seven acquired the RUMASA banks at a symbolic real cost that amounted to the difference between the 9.5% received from the state and the 13.5% paid on the RUMASA deposits, 121 billion over twelve years, compared to the cost to the state of 550 billion pesetas. See *El País*, March 4, May 5, July 10, and July 13, 1984. RUMASA's nonfinancial holdings, by contrast, were auctioned off to the highest bidder.

[34]   *El País*, April 1, 1984. It was only later in the decade that sales of some of the smaller failed banks to foreigners were approved. In all cases, it involved banks that were in such bad shape that the domestic banks had refused to take them over. Credit Lyonnais in 1991 purchased one smaller bank from Banco Santander for what was estimated at "an astronomical 19.5 times [the banks] historical earnings." The going price for a Spanish bank in the early 1990s was estimated to be at least twice its book value. See *Banker*, April 1992.

[35]   According to one estimate, the crisis cost the private banks 365 billion pesetas, for which price the Big Seven were able to increase their share of deposits from 70% to 82%. The cost to the public sector, by contrast, was of 1.215 trillion (an amount almost equal to the public deficit at the time). Alvaro Cuervo, *La crisis bancaria en España, 1977–1985: Causas, sistemas de tratamiento y coste* (Barcelona: Ariel, 1988), pp. 190–91.

tween the bankers and the authorities and more clearly establishing the central bank as a trusted "friend of the banking sector." This new sense of affinity now went well beyond the Bank of Spain to include the high-ranking Ministry of Finance officials who were directly involved in the resolution of the crisis, as indicated by the growing number of finance officials who went on to high-ranking jobs in the banking sector during the PSOE's tenure.[36] The most notable was Miguel Boyer, who after his resignation in 1985 became head of the semipublic Banco Exterior, and was the first president of that institution invited to participate in the Big Seven's monthly luncheons.

The upshot of the crisis was thus a reinforced sense of identification between public officials and the banking sector, or, in the words of one central bank official, a "peculiar sensitivity" on the part of officials toward the sector.[37] This identification outlasted the crisis years and set the stage for an almost single-minded preoccupation among Spanish officials with the banking sector's ability to face up to foreign competition in the late 1980s.

EC Membership and New Priorities

The course of financial reform in Spain discussed so far was driven by the agenda of a network of reformers whose principal aim was to bolster the position of the central bank in Spanish policymaking and who sought to establish a compact of reciprocal consent with the private banks as a means to that end. The ensuing pattern of accommodations maintained during the Socialists' first term, shifted the burden of adjustment from the banking sector to other sectors of the Spanish economy, aggravating and deepening a recession that sent unemployment skyrocketing to over 21 percent in 1985. The end to this dire economic scenario came only with Spain's admission to the EC in June 1985.

EC membership altered the dynamics of Spanish financial reform in two important yet somewhat contradictory ways. The first was the prospect of European financial integration, which introduced an ex-

---

[36] Among others, the first two heads of the Treasury, two director generals of financial policy, and the Secretary of State for the Economy who oversaw the reform of the stock market all went on to high-level jobs in the banking sector.

[37] Quoted in *Financial Times*, May 29, 1990.

ogenous motivation into the reform agenda and forced the government to act in areas that had long been neglected (most prominent among them capital market reform). After a decade of limiting the competitive impact of credit deregulation and disintermediation on the banking sector, the authorities were now forced to worry about preparing the national banking sector for external competition. The manner in which these issues were addressed was nonetheless strongly conditioned by the relationship between the reformers and the banks that had come into being during the previous years.

The second way in which EC membership affected the dynamic of reform was through the tremendous impact it had on the level of economic activity. In the three years after its entry into the Community, the Spanish economy went from a deep and prolonged recession to a four-year boom that was driven by massive inflows of foreign capital. This turnaround in the domestic economic context ended the nonconstraining character of the compulsory Treasury ratio introduced in 1983 and was followed first by its reduction in 1987 and eventually by its abolition. Yet foreign investment also became a palliative for the long-running problems of the Spanish industrial sector, and thus facilitated the further dissociation of financial reform from the problems of other sectors in the minds of Spanish policymakers.

The result in the late 1980s was a sharp contrast in the policy stances adopted by the Socialist government toward finance and industry. While manufacturing firms were sold off to foreigners at an unprecedented rate (the proportion of firms in foreign hands rose from 17.0 percent to 31.5 percent between 1985 and 1990), Bank of Spain and Ministry of Finance officials became almost single-mindedly concerned with safeguarding the national character of the banking sector. This concern produced a distinctive brand of financial nationalism at the end of the 1980s, manifested first in a failed attempt to restructure the sector from above and later in a policy of supporting the banks' capacity to fend off foreign takeovers, even at the expense of forgoing improvements in the efficiency of the financial sector.

The Belated Bang of the Spanish Stock Market

Perhaps the single most important manifestation of the biased course of financial reform pursued in Spain through the first half of the 1980s was the long postponement of capital market reform. As long as the reform effort was motivated solely by the central bankers' domestic policy agenda, the political logic of strengthening their principal partners, the Big Seven, had advised against any radical alteration of the status quo in the stock market.

The existing institutional structure of the Spanish stock market in the mid-1980s centered on the *agentes de cambio y bolsa,* publicly licensed agents who held a monopoly on trading that allowed them to charge a fixed commission of 0.25 percent on every transaction. Since the *agentes* acted only on behalf of their clients, there were no market makers in this system. The actors that commanded the market were the banks, which not only were its main issuers and investors but also placed the vast majority of the *agentes'* orders. Their indirect dominance contributed to a very low level of transparency. As lenders, the banks received privileged information that, with no legal restrictions on insider trading, they were able to turn to their advantage as shareholders. "Outsider" trading was seen to be "largely confined to small private investors."[38] This situation not only entailed profits for the banks but also allowed them to control the fate of their own stock. As one business journal explained, it was "an open secret that most of [the banks] place employees on the exchange floors, who go from *agente* to *agente* before the trading round . . . checking on the orders they have. Armed with this preview, the banks could then opt to intervene" by buying and selling stock to ease liquidity or by "turning their stock over from one subsidiary to another, although the latter is expressly against Bank of Spain regulations."[39]

The old institutional framework thus offered some obvious guarantees for the banks' control over the financial market. For the rest of the economy, the main consequence of this institutional control was the stock market's narrowness and manipulability, which made it an unviable source of long-term financing for industry. In 1987 only three hundred companies were listed on the four stock exchanges (of which Madrid accounted for 80 percent) and their total value of shares was just over half that in Italy. Seventy percent of the total capitalization of the exchanges, moreover, was accounted for by the banks and a small number of utilities. Industry accounted for barely 30 percent, setting

---

[38] *Economist,* August 22, 1987, p. 76.
[39] *Euromoney,* June 1988, special suppl., p. 11. The *agentes* traded each share only once a day in a ten-minute voice auction.

the Spanish stock market apart not just from those of the Anglo-Saxon countries, but also from those of France and Italy. Despite the extreme inadequacies of the existing setup, no significant reform measures had been implemented for almost a decade after the report on capital market reform that had been commissioned in 1977 and published in 1978.

EC membership became the catalyst for such reform. Foreign investors, who turned Madrid into the hottest stock market in Europe after 1986 (driven largely by the extraordinary undervaluation of Spanish industrial stocks, which had experienced a 90 percent decline in real share prices between 1974 and 1983), demanded better market services, offering significant profits to anyone who could deliver them.[40] These profit opportunities created an interest in capital market reform from some of the banks who stood to benefit and from the government which was eager to support foreign investment. At the same time, the prospect of a single European market in financial services introduced by the Single European Act of 1986 turned capital market reform into a sine qua non if Spain was to avoid falling behind other European countries in the rush to attract securities investors and if the banks were to be accustomed to operate in a more sophisticated marketplace.

These factors finally led the government to pass a major stock market reform law in 1988. Yet change continued to be shaped by the search for accommodation. Although stock market reform was portrayed as a standoff between the government and the *agentes,* the more important line of cleavage turned out to be that between the *agentes* and their old clients, the banks. Despite the benefits that the old institutional setup had afforded them, the bankers swiftly caught on to the fact that if they were to profit from the boom in foreign investment, they would have to offer a wider range of stock market services. The *agentes,* for their part, were aware that if they lost their monopoly, they would be incapable of competing with the firms set up by the banks. Thus the final draft of the reform law of 1988 was endorsed by the AEB but opposed by the heads of all four bourses, who argued that it would lead to a further "bankarization" of the markets.[41] Once the banks had become willing partners

[40] Trading by foreigners multiplied fivefold, and share prices rose by 144% in 1986. Foreign investment also continued to account for approximately 28% of the trading in the market in 1987 and 1988.

[41] The head of the Madrid Bolsa complained publicly that the *agentes* had had no input in the formulation of the reform. See *El País,* July 11, 1987.

in the government's reform effort, however, the agents could do little to influence the course of reform.

These factors were reflected in the law of July 1988. Along with major technical changes (the introduction of an electronic continuous trading system linking all four regional exchanges), the law introduced three major institutional changes: (1) an end to the *agentes*' privileges and the establishment of stock exchange firms;[42] (2) the establishment of a new regulatory commission charged with defining and imposing the rules of the market; and (3) the outlawing of insider trading. The banks were singularly positioned to attain a dominant position in this modernized market, having anticipated the changes by creating dealership firms of their own. They also drew advantage from two other legal specifications: a requirement of 750 million pesetas in capital for the establishment of market-making firms (an amount that virtually restricted the creation of this type of firm to the banks, since non-EC firms were excluded from participating until after 1992); and a decree that prevented firms that did not have the backing of a bank from gaining a banking license, thus limiting their operations to the regional level.[43] These measures allowed the Big Seven to establish a dominant position in the reformed stock market before its opening to foreign competitors. In addition, the Bank of Spain was given a major voice in the new regulatory commission of the capital market (though it would not be long before the governor of the Bank of Spain, Mariano Rubio, would fall victim to the commission's investigative powers and be found guilty of insider trading in 1994).

The belated reform did achieve a categorical transformation of the Spanish stock market once it came into effect in 1989. Yet it also entailed some significant limitations. Discriminatory tax treatment of mutual funds delayed the single most important source of new capital that could boost the market's role for almost two years. When the law was changed in 1991, it led to an almost immediate quadrupling of mutual fund savings to 7.75 percent of GDP. By then, however, the market had essentially been cornered by the banks. All eight of the largest funds, accounting for 59 percent of the total, were sponsored by the banks and only 5 percent of the money was being invested in the

---

[42]   The new law allowed for both single-capacity brokerage firms and broker/dealer (i.e., market-making) firms.
[43]   *El País,* October 10, 1988, p. N22; *Banker,* April 1988, pp. 72–74.

stock market, with the rest going mainly into public debt.[44] Though this investment pattern may to some extent have reflected the slow-down in economic activity in 1992, it also concurred with the banks' traditional ambivalence toward the markets, because "bringing firms to the Bolsa meant providing information, and probably losing power."[45] As with other areas of financial reform, capital market reform was thus calibrated to allow the banks to gain a head start, a pattern that limited the role that the stock market would play as a source of long-term finance well into the 1990s.

It is also worth returning briefly to the development of the Spanish public debt market. The late 1980s witnessed some significant changes in this area. The most important ones were the creation of a book entry system for public debt at the Bank of Spain and eventually (and with significant delay) the creation of a new long-term debt instrument (so-called *letras*) for the Treasury. The period also witnessed an increasingly explicit conflict between the monetary policy objectives of the central bank and the public debt policy objectives of the Treasury. The conflict occurred because the Treasury's principal debt financing instruments (the short-term PTs) were included in the very wide monetary aggregate that the central bank began to target in 1987 ("liquid assets in the hands of the public," or ALP). As two observers explained at the time,

> when the Treasury places downward pressure on the interest rate on Treasury bills, it increases the incentive for the banks to pass on their holdings of PTs to the public, and to take the role of commission takers rather than rentiers [of public debt]. This complicates the control of liquidity because the public debt is converted into a source of liquidity, and in addition loses effectiveness as an instrument of open market operations. But when a premium is placed on the interest rate paid by the Treasury, monetary control is recovered as the incentive for the

---

[44]　*Financial Times,* June 24, 1992.
[45]　José Manuel García Hermoso and Sebastian Ubirría Zubizarreta, "Reforma y trans-formación del mercado de valores," *Papeles de Economía Española,* no. 44, 1990, p. 138. When the central bank imposed draconian credit restrictions in an attempt to control speculative capital inflows in 1989, the banks had been far more willing to promote the commercial paper market (which they were able to control more thoroughly and in which the cost of financing was much higher) than to take companies on to the equity market, which would have allowed them to raise cheaper financing. See *Financial Times,* May 29, 1990; OECD, *Economic Surveys: Spain,* 1992, p. 28.

banks to pass on their public debt holdings to the public is reduced, and open market operations can be limited to the portfolios of financial institutions; of course, this raises the cost of deficit financing.[46]

Despite the reforms of the late 1980s, this conflict between the central bank's efforts to gain a handle on liquidity and the Treasury's efforts to reduce the high cost of financing its debt persisted through the 1980s.[47] Indeed, it seemed to be exacerbated by the Treasury's decision to promote its new long-term debt instrument (which was not included in the ALP) more aggressively on international markets, in an effort to alter the short-term structure of its debt.[48] Seeking to take advantage of massive demand by foreign investors for its international "matador" issues in 1991, the Treasury cut its rates progressively as far as the markets allowed, even though the Bank of Spain refused to bring its own interest rates in line. Yet, the discrepancy in the two interest rates led to a fall in the interbank money rate and put downward pressure on the peseta in international currency markets, a development that went against the Bank of Spain's policy objectives.[49]

Eventually the Treasury stepped back from its more aggressive stance, officially because it had been forced to raise rates by a lack of demand in the markets. This explanation, however, is contradicted by the fact that the Treasury repeatedly faced more orders than it could fill during its weekly auctions in 1991 because, as one official explained, it was offering returns above the market-clearing level to support the central bank's interest rates.[50] This lack of autonomy in the Treasury's operation manifests the persistent contradictions incurred by the reformers in eschewing a more aggressive attempt to develop the public debt market to shield the banks' position as intermediaries in the financial system. It also reflects the predominant weight of the central bank's policy objectives in Spanish economic policymaking, even when this

---

[46] Carlos Cuervo-Arango and José A. Trujillo, La política monetaria y la evolución reciente de los flujos financieros," *Papeles de Economía Española*, no. 32, 1987, pp. 7–8.
[47] *El País,* March 5 and 19, May 24, June 2, and June 16, 1991; *Financial Times,* June 19, 1991.
[48] OECD, *Economic Surveys: Spain,* 1992, pp. 37–38.
[49] *El País (Internacional),* March 4, 1991; *El País,* March 19, 1991; *Financial Times,* June 19, 1991.
[50] Interview, Madrid, Summer 1991. See also *El País,* March 15, March 19, May 24, and October 4, 1991.

pressure raised the cost of financing the public debt and thereby increased the public deficit.

From Financial Liberalization to Financial Nationalism

By the end of the PSOE's first term in office in the mid-1980s, the effort to bolster the central bank's position in Spanish economic policy-making launched in the early 1970s by a small number of academic economists had given way to a broader policy community of private bankers and public officials who identified strongly with the fate of the domestic banking sector. EC membership would rattle this community not just by forcing the pace of capital market reform but also by introducing the prospect of a single European financial market after 1992. The 1992 horizon generated an almost single-minded preoccupation among Bank of Spain and Ministry of Finance officials with preparing their domestic policy partners for the challenge ahead. Overtaken by events at the European level, the shift within the policymaking elite that had started in 1969 and driven the anti-interventionist reform agenda thus produced a distinctly nationalistic stance toward the financial sector at the end of the decade. This development was all the more striking because it contrasted sharply with the stance toward other sectors of the economy, in which foreign capital was not just offered an open door, but indeed became the centerpiece of the government's economic strategy.

The differential treatment of the banking sector was already patent in Spain's 1985 treaty of accession to the EC. Membership in the Community was an indisputable political imperative for any post-Franco government in Spain and led the Socialists to accept what many foreign observers regarded as a punishing treaty for domestic industry and agriculture.[51] By contrast, Spanish negotiators stood firm on behalf of the banking sector, negotiating a seven-year interim period in which the authorities could invoke an "economic necessity" clause to limit discretionally the entry of foreign banks while maintaining the existing lim-

---

[51] *Economist*, March 1, 1986. The treaty required an immediate and significant reduction in Spanish tariffs on industrial goods while phasing in equal treatment for Spanish agriculture only over ten years.

itations on foreign banks already in Spain until the end of 1992.[52] Foreign banks thus continued to be limited in practice to wholesale banking, the most competitive, and therefore most unprofitable, sector of the market, for the remainder of the 1980s.[53] No other sector in Spain could claim such advantageous treatment in the late 1980s, with the exception of energy (a sector in which the banks and the state continued to be the largest stakeholders).[54]

The contrast in the accession treaty, however, was only the first element in an increasingly paternalistic stance by the government toward the financial sector in the late 1980s. It was followed by the central bank's effort to limit the incursion of foreign capital into the shareholding of the Big Seven through a gentlemen's agreement whereby the banks agreed not to sell troubled subsidiaries to foreigners at a time when foreign banks were willing to pay substantial premiums to gain a retail network.[55] Only in the early 1990s, when the Big Seven began to seek out share swaps with other EC banks as a way to establish international alliances and fend off hostile takeovers, did the Bank of Spain give its assent to significant bank stock purchases by foreigners.[56]

Most notable, however, was the Bank of Spain's attempt in the late 1980s to direct a series of mergers among the Big Seven, with a view to restructuring the sector for the European market. Despite their oligopolistic hold on the domestic financial system (and in fact because of it), the Big Seven were small by international standards, the largest among them, Banesto, ranking only seventy-third by assets in the world in 1986.[57] The central bank's effort is commonly associated with the

---

[52] Banks of other EC countries were limited to three branches for the first four years after accession, and thereafter were allowed to open only two additional branches per year until 1993. The limit on the amount of deposits that foreign banks could raise in Spain was maintained at 40% for two years and thereafter increased by 10% per year to reach 100% in 1993. See Rafael Termes, "Consequencias de la adhesión sobre nuestro sistema financiero," *Papeles de Economía Española,* no. 25, 1985, and Luis A. Lerena, "La banca española en el proceso de integración en la CEE: Dirigismo frente al mercado," *Situación* (Banco de Bilbao), no. 4, 1985.

[53] *Euromoney,* July 1986, p. 102.

[54] For an analysis of the politics of Spanish energy policy in the transition, see Thomas D. Lancaster, *Policy Stability and Democratic Change: Energy in Spain's Transition* (University Park: Penn State Press, 1989).

[55] *Economist,* August 22, 1987.

[56] The exception to the rule was the 1983 share swap agreement that had given Commerzbank of Germany a 10% stake in Banco Hispano-Americano.

[57] *American Banker,* July 31, 1987; "Spanish Banks: Best of the Bunch," *Economist,* April 6, 1991.

1987 "Revell report," which had been commissioned by the government and drew two basic conclusions: that the number of banks that made up the core of the Spanish financial system was too great for the size of the Spanish economy, and that there had come to be a growing divergence among the Big Seven between those banks that had acquired more dynamic and aggressive managements and those whose management practices had changed little.[58] The four smaller banks in the cartel (Bilbao, Vizcaya, Santander, and Popular), the report suggested, were more efficiently managed than the three largest banks (Central, Banesto, and Hispano-Americano). The ideal strategy for the sector thus would be to pair the more dynamic banks with the more traditional ones.

Yet such a strategy was not likely to be initiated by the banks themselves. Indeed, the mergers being recommended were "of a sort rarely, if ever, seen before," as they paired "small relatively efficient banks with large and relatively inefficient banks." Most mergers, the report noted, involve "a dominant partner, which is almost invariably the larger of the two banks. When the dominant partner happens to be less efficient than the bank it is absorbing and to be less well managed, the result is rather more likely to perpetuate the existing inefficiencies than to create a wind of change in the new bank." Hence "the situation in Spain [did] not favour the merger solution to achieve greater efficiency in the banking system unless the authorities [were] prepared to take the bull by the horns and to impose the more efficient management on the less efficient in any mergers irrespective of the size of the banks concerned."[59]

The Revell report was released just before the Banco de Bilbao made a hostile bid (the first ever among the Big Seven) to take over Banesto in late 1987. The Bank of Spain not only gave its backing to the bid but is widely believed to have instigated it. The outcome, however, highlighted the limits of the central bank's ability to interfere directly in the internal business of the banks. The Banco de Bilbao's bid was thwarted by a ruling of the Madrid stock exchange (at the time still the corporate representative of the *agentes*), which, in a last-ditch effort to gain support in its efforts to influence capital market reform, ruled that the

---

[58] Jack Revell, *Mergers and the Role of Large Banks*, Research Monograph in Banking and Finance, no. 2. Institute of European Finance (University College of North Wales, Bangor), 1987, chap. 8. See also William Chislett, "From Minnows to Big Fish?" *Banker,* April 1988, p. 67, and *Euromoney,* July 1986.
[59] Revell, *Mergers,* p. 280.

Banco de Bilbao's shareholders had to approve the share issue that the bank was offering to Banesto's stockholders, thus giving Banesto's board time to defeat the bid.[60] After the fiasco, the central bank is believed to have backed off from promoting a similar bid by Banco de Vizcaya toward Banco Central. Although the incident was followed by two mergers among the Big Seven, they were far from the ones that the central bank had envisioned, pairing the two more dynamic banks, Bilbao and Vizcaya, and two of the so-called mammoths, Hispano-Americano and Central.[61] Both mergers, in the opinion of most observers, were intended to guard against future hostile bids and to take advantage of the government's tax forgiveness on the huge capital gains revaluations that the mergers made possible.[62]

The hostile bid by the Bilbao severely shook the modus operandi among the Big Seven and had strong reverberations on the financial policy community in Madrid. Press accounts began to speak of a cleavage between the BBV (Bilbao-Vizcaya), identified by some observers as the government's "bank of choice," and Banesto, the renegade of the 1987 failed takeover bid. Thereafter Banesto received less than amicable treatment from the Bank of Spain on several occasions before it was taken over by the central bank when an audit showed massive overvaluation of assets in late 1993. It was sold to the Banco Santander five months later.[63] The monthly luncheons attended by the heads of the large banks, however, continued after the events of 1987. They came to an end only in 1990, after the Banco de Santander began to offer interest on current accounts in response to a similar move by foreign banks, setting off an unprecedented deposit war among the

---

[60] *Economist*, December 19, 1987.

[61] A merger between Central and Banesto, the third of the so-called mammoths, fell apart in 1989.

[62] Alvaro Cuervo, "La evolución del sistema financiero español," *Papeles de Economía Española*, no. 43, 1990, p. 187, and *Euromoney*, July 1989, p. 54.

[63] "¿Es el BBV el 'grosse Bank' del PSOE?" *España Económica*, January 1990. The "black hole" discovered in Banesto's assets exceeded $4 billion. The Santander beat its two contenders, BBV and Argentaria, with a bid of $2.5 billion, establishing itself as the largest bank in Spain. Banesto's problems were attributed to the aggressive industrial dealings and unorthodox accounting operations of its management, headed by Mario Conde, a self-made entrepreneur and outsider who had come to the rescue of the bank's board during the Bilbao's 1987 hostile bid and who was eventually convicted for fraud. See "Who Busted Banesto?" *Institutional Investor*, February 27, 1994. In spite of the much-publicized animosity of the central bank toward Conde, Banesto was granted a tax break of $180 million on the asset revaluation that Conde devised by consolidating its industrial shares into a large holding company. See *Financial Times*, April 24, 1990.

banks that seemed to bring an end to the days when foreign competition could be largely ignored.[64] Nevertheless, by late 1990 the banks had managed to curtail the deposit war. Moreover, the competition over deposits did not spill over into the credit market, as seen in the very modest decline in the banks' financial margins in the early 1990s (see table 7 in chapter 1).

Despite the internecine conflict set off by the central bank's attempt to restructure the sector, the basic character of the financial policy community in Madrid survived the EC challenge well into the 1990s. One manifestation of the degree of intimacy in this community was the role taken by the central bank in 1990 in a succession crisis at the BBV, whose newly merged board could not agree on a new president until the governor of the Bank of Spain stepped in to make the choice. As the *Financial Times* noted, "the bottom line [was] not that the BBV did exactly as the governor ordered. It is that the bank did so because it had asked [the governor] to arbitrate in the first place, and had undertaken to abide by his ruling."[65] Another illustration was the central bank's handling of the Banesto fiasco in 1994. According to several accounts, the new central bank governor, Angel Rojo, called in the heads of two of the private banks (BBV and Santander) on the eve of the takeover to arrange a rescue that would leave Banesto's assets and branch network in the hands of what by this time were the remaining Big Four private domestic banks. Although other EC banks were eventually allowed to bid for Banesto after the illegality of restricting the auction only to Spanish banks was brought to the government's attention, the difficulty posed by the size and intricacies of Banesto's problems, as well as the speed with which the selloff was scheduled, made it far too risky for anyone without the inside access granted to the BBV and the Santander to participate.

Indeed, the one source of tension between the central bank and its clients at the end of the 1980s was the bank's zeal to prevent a foreign takeover of one of the large banks. This determination also lay behind its promotion of mergers because, as the Revell report noted, "the real advantage of size" was not efficiency but its ability to "protect a bank from being taken over."[66] In the early 1990s, the authorities thus reacted with considerable alarm to the decision by some of the large

---

64 *Financial Times*, February 26 and May 29, 1990.
65 *Financial Times*, May 29, 1990, p. v.
66 Revell, *Mergers*, p. 275.

banks to reap extraordinary profits by selling off troublesome subsidiaries to foreigners and to accept incursions by foreign capital into their boards.[67] This discrepancy between the viewpoints of the private banks and the central bank and the latter's almost single-minded concern to preserve the national character of the banking sector may best be understood as an attempt to maintain the cohesiveness of the policy community that the reformers had worked so hard to establish.

The nationalistic stance toward the financial sector, ironically, also led the Socialist government to do in 1991 what it had previously avoided: to transform the EOCs into a commercial banking entity. After the central bank's frustrated attempt to orchestrate mergers in the sector, the government in early 1991 merged the EOCs with the Postal Savings Bank and the Banco Exterior (the only commercial bank in which the government held a controlling share) into the Corporación Bancaria de España (CBE), which, in terms of total resources, became the largest financial institution in Spain. However, contrary to the PSOE's 1982 electoral program, which had cast such a reorganization as a way to exert competitive pressure in the credit market and to improve credit conditions for industry, the principal motivation behind the CBE's creation was the authorities' desire to compel further mergers among the private banks that would shield them from foreign takeovers.[68] The gamble proved at least partially successful; it was followed just a few weeks later by the surprise announcement of the creation of the Banco Central Hispano (BCH), whose combined resources surpassed that of the new public holding. The government enthusiastically furnished the BCH with a tax break similar to the one extended to the BBV, despite the fact that the wisdom of the merger of the two mammoths was strongly questioned by banking experts.[69]

---

[67] Sales of bank stock and share swaps had placed 15.79% of the big banks' stock in the hands of foreign investors by early 1991, although, with the exception of Commerzbank's 10% participation in Banco Hispano-Americano, no foreign investor had a controlling share.

[68] This objective was made explicit by both the minister of finance, Carlos Solchaga, and the head of Banco Exterior, Francisco Luzón, who designed the merger and went on to become its first president. *ABC*, May 5, 1991; *El País*, March 3, 1991; *Financial Times*, May 23, 1991. The Revell report also suggested the creation of a large public bank as a way to force the private banks into mergers, and the creation of the CBE was apparently carried out based on the blueprint of a second report commissioned from the British academic. *El País*, May 5, 1991.

[69] The BCH experienced very significant difficulties, which led its profits to fall far below the sector average for several years after its inception.

On the other hand, and despite official assertions that the new public holding company also would be used to offer better credit terms to industry, the CBE displayed limited zeal in this area. The public holding's capacity to do so was curtailed by the fact that the original institutions were not truly merged, but simply placed under a common institutional structure until 1993, when the government moved to privatize the holding, turning it into a commercial bank, called Argentaria, which was responsible to its shareholders and hence obliged to maximize profits within the existing market structure, rather than seek to change it.[70] In theory, the activities of the conglomerate might have been coordinated through the Ministry of Finance before its privatization. In practice, the same desire that led to the CBE's creation—to strengthen the domestic banks—also led the government to forgo a more aggressive use of the CBE in the credit market.[71] Before the Socialists' electoral defeat in 1996, Argentaria had thus become the fifth member of a now-reconstituted Big Five group of Spanish commercial banks.[72]

Rather than seek to augment competition in the market for corporate finance, the strategy the Spanish authorities adopted on the eve of 1992 was thus to support the banks' ability to exploit the existing degree of oligopoly in the credit market so that they could enter the single market with the greatest possible amount of capitalization (an attribute critical to preventing takeovers), while prodding them to merge and modernize their management.[73] This approach was encouraged by the realization in the early 1990s that the banks' staying power and their ability to marginalize foreign competitors in the domestic market rested precisely on what also made them less cost-efficient: their inordinate branch

[70] The government sold 48% of Argentaria's shares in 1993 and another 25% right before the 1996 election.

[71] Argentaria was the third bank to bid on Banesto in 1994, although it was not deemed to be favored by the central bank. See *Financial Times*, April 23, 1994.

[72] Illustrating the continuity in the banking sector's modus operandi, Argentaria was involved in what the *Financial Times* (May 23, 1995) described as a "neat share-out of the telecommunications sector," along with BBV and La Caixa, the Barcelona-based savings bank that also had become a member of the club of big banks in the early 1990s. By 1995, Argentaria, BBV, and La Caixa were set to replace the state's shareholdings in the public telecom operator, Telefónica, and Santander-Banesto and Banco Central Hispano were granted the sole license to set up a second mobile telephone network.

[73] After 1992, Spain would be one of the slowest of the twelve signatories to the Second Banking Directive of 1988 (along with Germany) to implement the single banking market directive. See Gary C. Zimmerman, "Implementing the Single Banking Directive in Europe," *Federal Reserve Bank of San Francisco Economic Review*, no. 3, 1995.

networks, which created a formidable cost barrier to entry into the highly profitable retail market.[74] As late as the early 1990s, foreign banks that had entered the Spanish market at the beginning of the 1980s were still far less profitable than Spanish banks, even after some of them had managed to acquire small retail networks.[75] With the exception of Manufacturers Hanover, moreover, less cost-efficient European banks fared better than the American banks, whose competitive advantage rested precisely in their cost efficiency, and several of which (including Chemical and Chase) eventually withdrew from Spain.[76]

The government's stance of benign neglect was reflected at the end of the decade in the behavior of the large banks, whose efforts focused far more heavily on shifting their lending to the least cost-sensitive borrowers (households and construction) than on cutting costs so that they could offer better credit terms to business. Although the prospect of the single market clearly placed pressure on the system, that pressure came far more heavily from the threat of hostile takeovers by foreign interests seeking a piece of the sector's high profit margins than from market competition (though competition for deposits outweighed competition in lending). In addition, the banks in the late 1980s began again to expand their industrial holdings after two decades of steady divestment. This strategy was exemplified by Banesto, whose new management, after foiling the Bilbao's hostile bid in 1987, consolidated its industrial stocks into a holding company to revalue the bank's book worth and then went on to sell shares in its "Corporación Industrial" to raise profits. Most of the other banks followed Banesto's lead. Thus in 1990 and 1991, "extraordinary items" accounted for more than a third of the pretax earnings of the large banks, and surpassed 50 percent of profits at Banesto and 60 percent at Santander.[77]

The banks' return to and subsequent sell-off of industry in the early

---

[74] "Defending el Dorado," *Euromoney,* July 1989.

[75] Even a bank such as Barclay's, which with over two hundred branches had the largest network of any foreign bank in Spain, was hard-pressed to compete with a bank such as Banco Popular, the smallest of the large Spanish banks, which had over 1,600 branches. The Spanish banks, moreover, proved very adept at imitating and overtaking the market innovations brought by the foreign banks, as in the syndicated loan market. See *Euromoney,* July 1986; *European Banker,* June 1995, October 1996.

[76] *El País,* March 11, 1991; *Financial Times,* May 23, 1991. Other American banks that retreated from Spain included First National of Chicago, First Interstate, and Continental Bank Corp. By 1993, all fifteen of the largest foreign banks operating in Spain were European banks. See *Banker,* April 1992; *Euromoney,* April 19, 1993.

[77] *Cinco Días,* May 8, 1991; March 20, 1992.

1990s was consistent with their highly procyclical investment behavior of the past. A number of observers have argued that it also constituted a strategy to increase their capitalization in order to fend off possible hostile bids on the eve of the single market.[78] Whatever the dominant motivation, the strategy allowed the banks to maintain their high profits despite their still very high costs. In 1990, Banco Popular ranked as the world's most profitable bank (a place it maintained for over three years), and even Hispano's 0.9 percent profit margin, the "lowest post-tax return on assets [ever] reported" by one of the large Spanish banks, was "roughly three times the average of Britain's clearers."[79] And Spanish banks as a group continued to lead European banks in profitability in 1991, 1992, and 1993, remaining remarkably unaffected by a new recession that was sharply cutting bank profits elsewhere and producing another wave of record bankruptcies among nonfinancial firms at home.[80]

[78] See Jordi Blanch, Antoni Garrido, and Esteve Sanromá, "Las relaciones banca-industria y su incidencia sobre la eficiencia bancaria," *Economía Industrial,* no. 272, 1990, p. 93; Carlos Chuliá, "Las participaciones del sistema bancario en las empresas no financieras," *Papeles de Economía Española,* no. 44, 1990, p. 79.

[79] *Economist,* April 6, 1991, p. 79.

[80] See *Banker,* September 1992; *Financial Times,* Nov. 4, 1992; *European Banker,* January 1994.

7

From Meso To Macro:
The Rise and Fall of the Peseta

The persistent protection afforded to the domestic banking sector in Spain from the beginning of this century through various regulatory overhauls was not a simple function of the sector's economic clout. It was made necessary by the objectives of contending state elites who sought to advance particular political agendas and institutional outcomes through a strategic partnership with the banks. In the 1980s, with the Spanish Socialist Workers' Party (PSOE) in office, domestic financial flows were therefore liberalized in a manner that minimized competition in the supply of corporate finance and preserved the position of the banks as intermediaries in the economy. These outcomes in the regulatory arena were reflected in the character of economic policy under the PSOE, in particular in the differing stances that the government took toward finance and industry as it sought to integrate Spain into the single European market, and as developments at the European level began to overtake the domestically crafted process of regulatory reform.

The upshot of the accommodation between the domestic banking sector and the central bank reformers was that the oligopolistic structure of the Spanish financial system was extended through the 1980s and in some respects (as in the calibration of stock and public debt market reform) into the 1990s. Economic policy, meanwhile, came to center increasingly on the maintenance of a high interest-rate differential vis-à-vis the rest of Europe and an appreciating currency, through which the government could maintain the necessary foreign capital inflows to compensate for the failures of domestic reform. Like financial reform itself, this strategy reflected the preferences of the central bank. Yet in a hampered domestic financial market, the strong-currency course had highly contradictory consequences. The additive effect on interest rates of the central bank–led financial reform process and policy strategy, compounded in a seemingly counterintuitive way by developments in the European Monetary System (EMS), produced a strong bias in favor of speculative capital inflows and against investment in productive capacity or technological innovation. By the early 1990s, the Spanish economy thus began to exhibit "Dutch disease" characteristics and was riding on a bubble that would inevitably burst with the crisis of the European Exchange Rate Mechanism (ERM) in 1992–93.

Economic Performance and New Policy Dilemmas

The year 1990 was a watershed for the Spanish economy. After four years of euphoria, and with the onset of a new world recession, business profits declined by 30 percent, the sharpest fall since the PSOE had taken office. The decline continued in the next two years and was accompanied by virtual stagnation in the rate of productivity growth and a rapid worsening of the current account deficit that Spain had begun to carry since joining the EC. Equally important, though it received less attention, was a shift in the way this deficit was financed. The share of long-term direct foreign capital declined sharply and was replaced by short-term capital inflows and foreign debt.[1] Various reports on the Spanish economy noted the worrisomely low pace of technological innovation in industry, the sharp loss of competitiveness suffered over the preceding years, and the almost complete halt in the modernization process that Spanish firms had begun in the

---

[1] Net long-term capital fell by well over $2 billion during the first four months of 1990. See Analistas Financieros, "La financiación del déficit corriente español: Qué ha cambiado en los flujos de capital a lo largo de 1990?" *Cuadernos de Información* (FIES), June 1990; *Informe Mensual* (La Caixa), January 1992, pp. 69–73.

mid-1970s.[2] Inflation, on the other hand, remained stubbornly above the EC average despite draconian monetary measures and a new turn toward austerity in 1989. Unemployment, which had remained above 16 percent during the boom years, began to rise again dramatically, surpassing 24 percent in early 1993. By then the Spanish economy was once again, as in the early 1980s, immoderately hard hit by a downturn in the world economy.

In addition to these signs of underlying economic weakness, the Spanish economy was characterized in the late 1980s by growing tension between internal and external macroeconomic balance. This tension was captured in a paradox. Although Spain's current account worsened almost continuously after it joined the EC in 1986, going from a surplus of $3.9 billion in that year to a deficit of $10.9 billion in 1989 and of over $16 billion in 1990 and 1991, the peseta appreciated sharply both in nominal and in real terms over the same period.[3] This appreciation, which ended only with the onset of the 1992–93 crisis in the ERM, was driven by massive inflows of capital (over $30 billion in 1991) which served to finance the current account deficit but had a strong inflationary impact on the Spanish economy. It therefore presented Spanish authorities with a new policy dilemma as their objective of fighting inflation suddenly appeared to conflict with their commitment to capital liberalization.

The peseta's enduring appreciation in the face of a sharply deteriorating current account was made possible by the rapidly changing context of the EMS at the end of the 1980s and by the effect of Spain's high real interest rates in that context. After the partial lifting of external capital controls that came with EC membership in 1986, Spain experienced very large inflows of long-term direct investment that sought to take advantage of the undervaluation of Spanish industrial stocks and the relatively skilled and cheap labor force. Yet there also was a substantial amount of portfolio investment, about half of which is estimated to have responded principally to Spain's high differential in short-term interest rates and therefore to have been highly speculative and vol-

---

[2] *El País*, November 12, 1990; Juan Antonio Maroto, "La situación empresarial en España (1982–1989)," *Cuadernos de Información Económica* (FIES), nos. 44–45, 1990.
[3] In real (unit labor cost) terms, the peseta is estimated to have appreciated between 25 and 30% from 1987 through 1991. See Philippe Bacchetta, "Por qué es necesaria una devaluación de la peseta," *Cuadernos de Información* (FIES), July 1991; OECD, *Economic Surveys: Spain* (Paris, 1991), p. 9.

atile.[4] Because this speculative element in capital inflows also came to be driven increasingly by the rising value of the Spanish currency, it acquired a self-reinforcing character. It forced the central bank to engage in a progressive tightening of domestic credit and hiking of interest rates to compensate for the inflow of external liquidity. Yet these measures encouraged further short-term capital inflows and placed further upward pressure on the peseta. By late 1988, this circle had become vicious enough to prompt the government to impose a draconian credit squeeze and, in 1989, unprecedented restrictions on capital inflows, which included a 30 percent deposit on borrowing raised by Spanish firms abroad and a 25 percent withholding tax on foreign purchases of Spanish public debt.[5]

The dynamic created by high interest rates, however, was complicated by the government's decision to join the ERM in June 1989. ERM membership, advanced by the Bank of Spain as a way to discipline wages and add credibility to the government's anti-inflation stance, was also expected to force a greater balance between interest rate hikes and fiscal policy, to ease the strong upward pressure on the peseta.[6] The very success of the EMS in increasing the peseta's credibility in international markets, however, intensified the speculative element in capital inflows. The decision to enter at a relatively high rate of 65 pesetas to the deutsche mark and with a 6 percent fluctuation band (as opposed to the standard 2.25 percent) produced an immediate and massive influx of short-term capital that pushed the peseta up against its upper band limit. From virtually the moment it entered the ERM and for almost three years thereafter, the peseta thus became the "strongest" currency in the system, pushing steadily up against its upper ceiling, despite an inflation rate that was 2 points above the ERM

---

[4] OECD, *Economic Surveys: Spain,* 1991, p. 24; Jaime de Piniés, "Vulnerabilidad externa y la autopista," in *La política española en el contexto internacional hoy previsible para los años 90* (Madrid: Círculo de Empresarios, 1990), pp. 355–56; *El País,* March 24 and October 6, 1991.

[5] Guillermo de la Dehesa, "Las incógnitas macroeconómicas de 1991," *Anuario de El País,* 1991. The increase in foreign borrowing by Spanish firms was spearheaded and intermediated by the domestic banks in response to the government's credit squeeze. See also *El País,* May 29, 1992.

[6] *Financial Times,* June 7, 1989; OECD, *Economic Surveys: Spain,* 1991. For an explanation of the decision to join the ERM in 1989, see José Luis Malo de Molina and José Pérez, "La política monetaria española en la transición hacia la unión monetaria europea," *Papeles de Economía Española,* no. 43, 1990.

average and the continuing sharp deterioration of the Spanish current account.[7]

The peseta's nominal appreciation became a source of sharp tension between the Spanish central bank and its ERM partners, fueling speculative pressures that ultimately contributed to the system's crisis and eventual crash in 1992–93. The ERM's bilateral parity grid—designed to protect the independence of the Bundesbank within the system—in practice forced weak-currency countries (those whose currency approached the lower limit of their bilateral band against any other currency) to adjust before strong-currency countries (those whose currency approached the upper limit of their bilateral band) had to do so.[8] Spanish interest rates therefore soon began to act as a direct constraint on policy in countries such as France, the Netherlands, and later Britain (which joined the ERM in 1990), putting them in the position of having to raise interest rates (or not being able to cut them) to keep their currencies in line with the peseta.[9]

This effect of the ERM's rules of adjustment was aggravated by developments at the time of the peseta's entry. The lifting of capital controls in the late 1980s by countries such as France and Italy, coupled with the 1987 Basel-Nyborg Agreement, which committed governments to maintain their currencies' parities within the system without recourse to devaluation, produced a dramatic rise in short-term capital flows into currencies that offered positive interest rate differentials with little regard for economic fundamentals (such as inflation rates or public deficit levels). Economists referred to this phenomenon as a "new EMS," characterized by high capital mobility, the apparent disappearance of a risk premium on currencies with worrisome fundamentals, and the phenomenon of "undeserved credibility," which was reflected in the remarkable performance of the peseta and in the somewhat shorter-lived appreciation of the Italian lira at the end of the

[7] It became the second strongest currency after the April 1992 entry into the system of the Portuguese escudo, whose value in the system was a close function of that of the peseta. See "Tres años de la peseta en el SME," *Informe Mensual* (La Caixa), June 1992.
[8] The ERM's asymmetric adjustment rules centering on the bilateral parity grid are discussed in John B. Goodman, *Monetary Sovereignty: The Politics of Central Banking in Western Europe* (Ithaca: Cornell University Press, 1992), pp. 191–201.
[9] See *Financial Times*, October 24, 1989, and May 7, 1991; *El Sol*, February 17, 1991; *El País*, March 24, April 30, and May 17, 1991; *Investment Daily*, March 18, 1991; *Independent*, June 17, 1991; *Times*, December 20, 1991.

1980s.[10] In this context, attempts by the Bank of Spain to stem the appreciation of the peseta through intervention in currency markets in support of the deutsche mark and dollar proved powerless when stacked against a 6.7 percent positive interest rate differential between the peseta and the deutsche mark.[11] Just three months after the peseta's entry, the Bundesbank thus began to call openly and adamantly for a devaluation of the peseta; a development met with dismay by Bank of Spain officials who argued that it was impossible to devalue "against the markets."[12]

Spanish interest rates contributed to the growing instability in the ERM, but membership in the system also perpetuated the vicious circle in Spanish policy. The surge in short-term capital inflows after the peseta's entry came just as the central bank was attempting to stave off credit growth. To counter this trend, Spanish authorities raised interest rates further and imposed a 10 percent ceiling on credit growth, reversing the reformers' decade-long drive to shift monetary policy away from credit controls and into the money market. Such measures were symptomatic of a growing intractability in the government's fight against inflation. As the *Financial Times* put it at the time, "Spain's monetary policy options [had] probably been exhausted by EMS membership, the existing high rates, and credit restrictions. Every time the Bank of Spain [had] to intervene to soften the currency by placing pesetas in the [currency] market, it damage[d] progress made on controlling the supply of money and delay[ed] any fall in interest rates."[13]

Having joined the ERM at a high parity rate with the intention of placing a damper on inflation, Spanish authorities thus came to face an unexpected policy dilemma. The peseta's strength appeared to conflict with the government's commitment to keep it within the 6 percent

[10]   Francesco Giavazzi and Luigi Spaventa, "The New EMS," in Paul De Grauwe and Lucas Papademos, eds., *The European Monetary System in the 1990s* (London: Longman, 1990); and Patrick Artus and Henri Bourguinat, "The Stability of the EMS," in Afred Steinherr, ed., *Thirty Years of European Monetary Integration: From the Werner Plan to EMU* (New York: Longman, 1994).

[11]   The day after the peseta's entry into the system, the Bank of Spain began to intervene heavily in favor of the deutsche mark and dollar in an attempt to brake the peseta's advance. See *New York Times*, June 20, 1989; *Financial Times*, June 20 and October 31, 1989.

[12]   *Financial Times*, October 24, 1989.

[13]   *Financial Times*, June 20, 1990. Contrary to the experience of other member countries, EMS membership thus did not have an observable effect on inflation in Spain. See Ana Revenga, *Credibility and Inflation Persistence in the EMS*, Bank of Spain Working Paper no. 9321 (Madrid, 1993).

ERM band. Yet it was believed that to redress this situation by allowing a cut in interest rates would be to compromise the central bank's anti-inflation stance at home. For a relatively high-inflation country such as Spain, ERM membership thus suddenly appeared to conflict with domestic price stability.

The Spanish authorities' dilemma reflected the ERM's growing susceptibility to what economists refer to as the Mundell-Flemming condition, according to which monetary policy autonomy is not possible in the context of both fixed exchange rates and free capital flows.[14] Yet this condition is generally expected to imply that in a fixed exchange rate zone with high capital mobility, a country with higher than average inflation will need to raise its interest rates to maintain its exchange rate. The perversity of the Spanish case lay in the fact that it had an appreciating currency despite somewhat higher-than-average domestic inflation and despite a rapidly deteriorating current account balance. The unexpected consequence of the peseta's participation in the ERM from 1989 to 1992 thus reflected the biases that high interest rates had created in the Spanish economy even before it had entered the system. As one foreign observer put it, despite the fact that the real interest rate differential between Spain and Germany narrowed to just 3 points after 1990 (thanks principally to the rise in German rates), Spain's "structural problems [made] high Spanish interest rates a far more dependable bet" for foreign investors than those of other European countries."[15]

High Interest Rates and Spanish Economic Policy

The paradoxical experience of the Spanish peseta in the EMS was linked directly to the high real interest rate differential that Spanish financial assets offered vis-à-vis those of other ERM member states. Economists generally interpret this differential as the unintended consequence of two other problems: a lack of fiscal restraint and inflation. Spain's macroeconomic policy mix in the late 1980s and early 1990s was characterized by the combination of a tight monetary policy stance

[14] See Jeffry A. Frieden, "Invested Interests: The Politics of National Economic Policies in a World of Global Finance," *International Organization*, no. 45, 1991.
[15] *Financial Times*, March 15, 1991. The lifting of some of the controls led purchases of Spanish public debt by foreigners to quadruple in just one month when the 25% withholding tax was lifted in early 1991.

and a laxer fiscal policy stance. The prevalent interpretation of this policy mix is that monetary policy was forced to compensate for a lack of fiscal restraint in the government's fight against inflation.[16] The persistence of inflation (which rose from a low of 4.8 percent in 1988 to 6.8 percent in 1989 and leveled off at 5.9 percent in 1991) despite very high interest rates is commonly attributed to wage growth, which, given the phenomenal level of unemployment in Spain, is in turn attributed to certain features of Spanish labor laws and industrial relations practices. Most often cited are the prevalence of centralized bargaining at the sectoral level, the practice of backward-looking wage indexation, and the comparatively high level of dismissal costs for workers with non-time-limited contracts.[17] Spain's high real interest rate differential is thus understood as a risk premium imposed by currency markets on the peseta, because of the perceived inflation-proneness of the Spanish economy.

To be sure, all of these factors played a role in determining the level of Spanish interest rates in the late 1980s and early 1990s. If fiscal policy had been tighter, the Treasury's financial costs and the crowding-out effect on credit rates would both have been lower. If wages had grown less, inflation might not have increased again after 1988, and the loss of competitiveness experienced by Spanish firms as a result of the overvaluation of the peseta would have been mitigated. If the cost of firing workers with open-ended contracts had been lower, unemployment might have placed greater downward pressure on wages, and businesses might have deemed the creation of new long-term jobs more profitable at the margin.

The prevalent interpretation of high interest rates in Spain, however, entails some serious inconsistencies. The level of the Spanish public deficit before the 1992 currency crisis (averaging 3.6 percent from 1987 to 1991) and the level of the public debt (at 47 percent in 1991, well below the European average) do not seem to explain the high cost of financing the public debt. The notion that Spain's real short-term interest rate differential vis-à-vis Germany simply reflected a risk pre-

---

[16] See, for example, José Luis Raymond and José Palet, "Factores determinantes de los tipos reales de interés en España," *Papeles de Economía Española*, no. 43, 1990.

[17] OECD, *Economic Surveys: Spain*, 1991, pp. 66–68; Juan Dolado and S. Bentolila, "Labour Flexibility and Wages: Lessons from Spain," *Economic Policy*, no. 18, 1994; Olivier Blanchard et al., *Spanish Unemployment: Is There a Solution?* (London: CEPR, 1995), Annex 4.

Table 17. Cost components of inflation, 1981–1990

	1981–1983	1984–1986	1987–1988	1989	1990
GDP deflator	12.5%	10.0%	5.7%	7.0%	7.3%
Unit labor costs[a]	6.0	2.9	1.9	2.1	3.2
Unit profits[b]	5.4	5.7	3.6	4.0	4.0
Indirect tax rate	1.1	1.6	0.2	0.9	0.3

[a]Percentage change at annual rate.
[b]Percentage point contribution to GDP deflator at annual rate.
Source: Adapted from OECD, *Economic Surveys: Spain*, 1990–91, p. 59.

mium on the peseta related to public debt and inflation also seems to be contradicted by the fact that up until 1991, this differential was higher than the one sustained by the Italian lira, despite Italy's far higher public deficits and debt, far lower level of foreign reserves, and very similar inflation performance. The exclusive focus on labor market variables in explanations of Spain's inflation-proneness also is problematic. Despite the apparent rigidity of wages in the face of Spain's extremely high unemployment rate, unit labor costs until 1989 grew far below the rate of growth in unit profits. They thus had a moderating effect on the rate of inflation (see the cost components of inflation in Table 17). Even between 1989 and 1991, when wage growth accelerated after the breakdown of social concertation between the government and the unions, the real wage per person in Spain still grew well below the European average (1.8 percent as opposed to 5.2 percent), and the rise in unit labor costs during this period was due largely to the sharp drop in productivity rather than to the growth of wages.[18] As late as 1991, the OECD noted that "international comparisons of gross wage levels" and the record of wage moderation were among Spain's principal points of attraction for foreign investors.[19]

Labor market–centered explanations also fail to recognize the extent of change that took place in this area during the 1980s. Although Spanish labor law offered workers with permanent contracts a very high level of protection against dismissal, measures taken by the Socialist government early on significantly altered the terms of employment and labor-cost determination. With the legalization of temporary em-

[18] Agustín García Laso, "La dinámica salarial de los años ochenta: De la política de rentas al 'pacto de competitividad,'" *Información Comercial Española*, no. 705, 1992, p. 194–97; OECD, *Economic Surveys, Spain*, 1992, p. 59.
[19] OECD, *Economic Surveys: Spain*, 1991, pp. 62–65.

ployment contracts in 1984, businesses could hire new workers and shed them in response to market conditions with virtually no dismissal costs. By the early 1990s, more than 30 percent of workers in Spain were employed under temporary contracts (the EC average was 9 percent), and Spain had one of the highest labor turnover rates in the OECD.[20] Some economists argue that this flexibility in employment did not translate into real wage flexibility, because the unions' wage demands were determined by permanent workers, who did not face the threat of dismissal in a downturn. Yet empirical tests of this hypothesis suggest that the purported "insider effect" on wages was very small. It therefore hardly offers a sufficient explanation of the stickiness of inflation in Spain.

The most important fact that tends to be overlooked in accounts of Spain's economic problems, however, is that the inflation-proneness of the Spanish economy at the end of the 1980s had a very strong sectoral component. As one report pointed out, "unlike developments in the rest of the OECD, the rate of inflation in services (excluding rents) exceeded that of manufactures by 7 percentage points" in the second half of the 1980s, and it was this "abnormally large cumulative rise in the price of nontradeables relative to tradeables" that was the principal cause of inflation in Spain.[21] Thus, while the inflation rate of Spanish tradeables (food and manufactures) edged toward the EMS average, the inflation differential in services increased. The divergent trend in sectoral inflation rates reflects the exceptionally rapid growth of the services sector in relation to the tradeables sector (where unit labor costs grew very modestly even after 1988). Yet this structural transformation of the Spanish economy was exacerbated rather than mitigated by high interest rates and a strong currency, because both of these factors encouraged resources to flow into precisely those sectors that were better able to pass on their costs to consumers (i.e., nontradeables) and away from those sectors that were forced to compete with cheap imports (i.e., tradeables). As the 1992 OECD report acknowledged, the government's policies thus were producing a "shift of resources from the sectors exposed to foreign competition to the sheltered sectors," and the renewed acceleration of inflation after 1988 was overwhelmingly due to this shift.[22]

---

[20] See the section on labor market reform in OECD, *Economic Surveys: Spain*, 1994.
[21] OECD, *Economic Surveys: Spain*, 1992, pp. 62, 65.
[22] Ibid., pp. 21, 28.

Indeed, if in the late 1970s the Spanish economy had displayed the features of an overdraft economy as a result of decades of cheap credit, by the early 1990s it had acquired many of the features of a Dutch disease economy: poor export performance, rapid growth of the less competitive sectors of the economy, and the combination of an over-valued currency, high interest rates, and inflation.[23] The persistence of inflation was perhaps the most striking of these factors, given the government's commitment to fight it. Yet, as the OECD analysis suggests, inflation was rooted in a shift of investment from competitive to less competitive sectors, which was being spurred by high interest rates and the overvaluation of the peseta. High interest rates and an overvalued currency thus undermined not only the competitiveness and productivity growth of Spanish firms but also the one objective that Spanish policymakers were focusing on: disinflation.

These observations raise the question of just how Spanish policy-makers ended up facing this conundrum. Standard economic accounts tend to overlook two factors behind this outcome. The first is the strategic role that interest rates acquired in Spanish economic policy at the end of the 1980s. The second is the way in which the government's policy strategy was both encouraged and hampered by the nature of the domestic financial market.

Although the high level of Spanish interest rates is commonly interpreted as an unintended outcome of other policy failures, the interest rate differential between Spain and other EC countries served an important strategic purpose in Spanish policy during the late 1980s. The appreciable effect of partisan politics on public spending (as reflected in the renewed expansion of social transfers after the Socialists' narrow victory in 1989) and the ability of the unions to raise their members'

---

[23] The source of overvaluation in a Dutch disease economy is a sector that is experiencing explosive growth, thereby producing large inflows of foreign capital. The overvaluation of the currency and the inflation caused by capital inflows create a bias against investment in other tradable sectors and are thus associated with deindustrialization. Typically, the term has been used for economies in which a natural energy source has played this role (as with the discovery of natural gas in Holland or the windfall profits for oil-producing countries after the OPEC price shocks). In the Spanish case, however, what played this role was the sale of national assets to foreigners, both industrial and real estate, and the inflow of speculative capital to take advantage of high Spanish interest rates. See Cándido Muñoz Cidad, "Un ajuste febril," *El País*, March 27, 1991. For a general discussion of the Dutch disease concept, see W. M. Corden, "Booming Sector and Dutch Disease Economics: Survey and Consolidation," *Oxford Economic Papers* 36 (1984).

wages in the face of massive unemployment after 1988 cemented the perception among the PSOE's economic policy elite that high interest rates were the only way to wage battle against inflation. This conclusion was strongly influenced by the particular economic outlook, or "optic," that had become so dominant under the first Socialist administration. One critic summarized this outlook as follows:

> The European challenge has to be met. Nationalistic economic positions make no sense in the face of relentless European integration. Spain must prepare for that integration by aligning itself with the central or hard core (more and more, that is to say, with Germany), and since the essential characteristic of that core is a low level of inflation, this must be the overriding priority. . . .
>
> Given these basic ideas, and taking into account the existing current account deficit, it is necessary to count on high interest rates to encourage capital inflows that can compensate [for that deficit], and to bolster the peseta's value in order to cheapen imports. . . . The scheme thus requires higher interest rates than [those of other EC] countries.[24]

This argument, equating adjustment with eliminating the inflation differential between Spain and the ERM's low-inflation (and low-growth) core countries, justified the strong currency course pursued in the late 1980s. It was premised on the notion that the nominal exchange rate could be used to enforce desired changes in economic fundamentals. High interest rates were the sine qua non of such a strategy, not just because they underpinned the strong currency but also because they were needed to attract sufficient foreign capital inflows to finance the resultant trade and current account deficits. In this sense, the level of interest rates that the government's tight monetary policy stance created in the Spanish economy in the late 1980s must be seen not just as an unintended outcome but also as entailing a policy choice. The government rejected the option of easing monetary policy in a manner commensurate with the very significant reduction in the public deficit achieved between 1986 and 1988. Had it pursued this option, it might have had to accept a more gradual disinflation between 1986 and 1988 (when inflation was cut from 8.8 to 4.8 percent). Yet it might also have averted the speculative appreciation of the peseta, and the intense

---

24   Antonio Torrero, "El poder de las ideas," *El País,* December 19, 1990.

shift of resources toward sheltered activities that reactivated inflation in 1989. Such a choice, however, would have implied forgoing the advantages vis-à-vis domestic actors (in particular the unions) that the government associated with the strong peseta. Spanish policymakers' unshakable belief in these advantages is revealed in the notion that a strong currency, even if overvalued, would boost competitiveness by countering the ability of domestic producers to rely on a weak currency, and by facilitating "the productive re-equipment of the Spanish economy" through cheap imports. It is also reflected in the Bank of Spain's insistence that it was "not uncomfortable" with the peseta's appreciation in the face of a deteriorating current account, even as this appreciation was clearly undermining Spanish monetary policy.[25]

The strategic policy choice behind the high interest rate/strong-currency outcome also is reflected in two other aspects of Spanish economic policy in the late 1980s and early 1990s: (1) the government's decision to forgo the collaboration of the unions in its fight against inflation; and (2) its increasingly untenable position on the issue of Spanish participation in European Monetary Union (EMU) after the ERM crisis of 1992–93.

The government's strong-peseta policy course had dour implications for Spanish unions. The appreciation of the peseta after 1986 rapidly eroded the international competitiveness of Spanish firms. The reliance on high interest rates to attract sufficient capital inflows to finance a growing account deficit thus required wages to compensate not just for the higher financial costs carried by Spanish firms but also for the lowered profitability that this loss of competitiveness entailed. As critics argued, the government's strategy turned wage moderation into the "central" and apparently only "variable in the performance of the [economic] system."[26] With unemployment failing to decline below the 16 percent mark despite an average growth rate of almost 5 percent between 1986 and 1990, one of the consequences of this stance was the

---

[25] See the views on Spain's ERM entry by the deputy finance minister, Pedro Pérez, in *Financial Times,* June 20, 1990; Daniel Manzano, at FEDEA/Fundes-Club Conference, Madrid, June 13, *Cuadernos de Información* (FIES), July 1991; *Financial Times,* June 13, 1990.

[26] Jesús Albarracín and Pedro Montes, "La única política posible?" *España Económica,* January 1991, p. 25. The point was continuously emphasized by government officials, who tended to cast competitiveness as a simple function of wage moderation. See, for example, *El País (Internacional),* June 4 and December 31, 1990, and May 16, 1991; and *El Independiente,* October 24, 1991.

collapse of the Spanish experiment with incomes policy that had been initiated with the 1977 Pactos de la Moncloa.[27]

The failure of negotiations between the unions and the government after the expiration of the first (and only) global wage agreement signed between the Socialist government and the Socialist union (UGT) in 1984 was influenced by the divided character of the Spanish labor movement. But it also reflected the one-sided outcome of previous negotiations, the government's tendency not to keep promises made to the unions, and its willingness to proceed without their support. In the two years covered by the 1984 agreement, the UGT experienced a continuing fall in real wages without any appreciable effect on unemployment (see the wage agreement and inflation outcome figures in Table 18). It also suffered stunning losses in works council elections to the Communist Comisiones Obreras (CC.OO.), which had agreed to a slight real wage cut in a 1982 pact with the employers to give the new Socialist government some room for maneuver, but had refused to sign the 1984 agreement after the severity of the government's austerity measures and the extent of its industrial restructuring program had become clear. The UGT's position within the labor movement was further complicated by the government's failure to expand unemployment benefit coverage to 48 percent of jobless workers (as promised in 1984), and by the employers' failure to meet their commitment to raise wages above the agreed targets in line with productivity increases at the firm level. In the 1986 round, the union's leadership therefore insisted on an upper wage range limit that was two points above the government's inflation assumption. The government, however, preferred to walk away without an agreement to cover private sector wages for 1987–88, a decision that appears to have been influenced by the experience of 1984, when wage growth remained below inflation despite the absence of a concertation agreement for that year.[28] It took a similarly hard line in 1988, after insisting on a very low inflation assumption (3 percent) for public sector wages. The UGT leadership, who had

[27] The Pactos were followed in the 1980s by a series of agreements that varied in form. Some included both the Socialist and Communist unions (UGT and CC.OO.), the government, and employers, some only one union (the UGT), and some did not include the government as a signatory. The formula for negotiation remained the same, however, with the government seeking wage moderation in return for policy concessions in the form of transfer payments and other public spending.
[28] Alvaro Espina, "Política de rentas en España, 1977–1986," *Papeles de Economía Española*," no. 22, 1990, p. 274.

Table 18. Nationwide wage agreements and inflation targets, 1980–1990 (percent change at annual rates)

	1980	1981	1982	1983	1984	1985	1986	1987	1988	1989	1990
National pact target											
From	13.0%	11.0%	9.0%	9.5%	6.5%	5.5%	7.2%	n.p.	n.p.	n.p.	n.p.
To	16.0	15.0	11.0	12.5	n.p.	7.5	8.6	n.p.	n.p.	n.p.	n.p.
Wage agreements	15.3	13.1	12.0	11.4	7.8	7.4	8.1	6.5	5.4	6.7	8.1
Inflation											
Target	14.5	14.0	12.5	12.0	8.0	7.0	8.0	5.0	3.0	3.0	5.7
Outcome	15.3	14.4	13.9	12.3	9.0	8.2	8.3	4.6	5.8	6.9	6.5

n.p. = no pact covering wages.
Source: Adapted from OECD, *Economic Surveys: Spain, 1992*, p. 58.

agreed to just such a limit in the 1988 public sector wage round, only to see actual inflation rise to almost double the assumption, rejected the proposal.[29] That same year, the government also refused to allocate any part of a windfall surplus from taxation and social security contributions to social spending, despite the fact that the proportion of unemployed receiving benefits continued to fall far below its 1984 commitment. It chose instead to allocate the surplus to lowering the public deficit to 2.7 percent in 1989 (a level well below the EC average). The result was a complete rupture between the PSOE and the UGT and the latter's alliance with the CC.OO., which culminated in the general strike of December 1988.[30]

The government decided in essence to "ignore the unions and take the risk" despite the fact that until 1989 (and hence until the break) wages had continued to have a clear moderating influence on inflation.[31] Contrary to the authorities' expectations, however, the unions would manage to extract greater wage concessions from employers after the collapse of the concertation process in 1988. This seems to have been an important element in the government's decision to enter the EMS a year ahead of schedule in 1989—and to do so at an exchange rate that signaled its willingness to live with an overvalued currency.

The pressure exerted on Spain by its ERM partners and its growing inability to impose wage restraint through interest rate hikes eventually spurred the government to attempt to revive concertation in the early 1990s. In early 1990 the IMF began to call on Spanish authorities to seek an incomes policy agreement with the unions that would tie real wage growth to productivity growth. The government moved on the recommendation a year later, when the Bundesbank again raised the possibility of a two-speed EMU and officials began to worry that if Spanish interest rates were not cut and the peseta not moved to the standard 2.25 percent ERM band, Germany and France might try to keep Spain out of the first phase of such a union. In 1991, shortly after the Bank of Spain had cut interest rates 20 points in response to a request from the Bank of England (which was seeking to cut its base rate), the government proposed a "competitiveness pact" along the

[29] OECD, *Economic Surveys: Spain*, 1991, p. 67.
[30] Richard Gillespie, "The Break-up of the 'Socialist Family': Party-Union Relations in Spain, 1982–1989," *West European Politics*, January 1990, p. 53.
[31] OECD, *Economic Surveys: Spain*, 1992, pp. 58–59.

lines set out by the IMF.[32] By then, however, trust had been seriously eroded, and the unions refused to resolve the external and internal contradictions of the government's strong-peseta strategy by agreeing to limit their wage demands.

The government's reliance on the overvalued currency to enforce adjustment was also highlighted in its response to the 1992–93 crisis in the ERM. Intent on having Spain included in a fast-track Europe, the government drew up a "convergence" plan of fiscal and monetary measures in early 1992 meant to allow Spain to meet all of the requirements set out in the Maastricht Treaty. Included were across-the-board cuts in unemployment benefits and a doubling of the work time required to qualify for benefits, which were imposed by decree and virtually without consultation with the unions.[33] Although the plan strongly overestimated the rate of capital formation in Spain and was thrown off track by the subsequent crisis in the ERM, Spanish officials continued to "treat convergence towards economic and monetary union as an article of faith" in 1993. A *Financial Times* article on the Spanish response to the currency crisis noted that, "as usually occurs among those embracing a dogma," the government was "quite unaware of the disbelief among others." Having "fixed its sights on converging with the rich Community economies," it had "worked out how to reach its target in closed doors meetings of motivated policy makers and relentlessly set out on its course although it [might] scorch the earth it treads on."[34]

If the government's response seemed entirely out of touch with reality to foreign observers, it represented a desperate attempt to rescue a policy course it had pursued since the mid-1980s. To pay off economically and politically, that policy course (including the standoff with the unions) required continued capital inflows. These, however, had come to depend increasingly on the credibility of an overvalued peseta, which in turn was now closely tied to the prospect of European currency union and to Spanish participation in it. The point was poignantly illustrated when foreign purchases of Spanish public debt dropped

---

[32] *Financial Times*, March 15 and June 19, 1991; *El Independiente*, October 24, 1991. Such fears also led the government to depart momentarily from its staunch pro-EMU stance in late 1990, when it proposed a one-year delay in the movement toward monetary union, only to be rebuffed by its EC partners. See *El País* (*Internacional*), September 10 and 24, 1990.

[33] *Financial Times*, April 13, 1992.

[34] Tom Burns, "Markets Distrust Dogma," *Financial Times*, April 2, 1993.

sharply in response to the Danish "no to Maastricht" vote in June 1992. It was fully driven home by the ERM currency crisis two months later, when, despite its long-held position as the highest valued currency in the system, the peseta became the subject of a massive speculative attack that forced the government to devalue and to impose sharp interest rate hikes and spending cuts just as domestic demand was contracting. Remaining in the system, and not following the British and Italian governments out, was viewed as critical to maintaining the foreign capital lifeline. The government therefore threw its weight behind an ever more doubtful project of early monetary union, continuing to portray Spanish participation as a simple function of mustering the necessary "tenacity."[35] Such commitment might have seduced foreign investors as long as the European project was not challenged, but it now began to be perceived as sheer "dogmatism" by the markets, forcing two further peseta devaluations on the government before the ERM's effective suspension in August 1993.[36]

The excesses of the Spanish policy course were captured in the dramatic consequences of the ERM crisis for the Spanish economy. The government did manage to keep the peseta in the EMS, but only through severe adjustment measures that cut public consumption to 1.6 percent of GDP in 1993 (the lowest level since 1969) and pushed the unemployment rate up from 18 percent at the end of the second quarter of 1992 to over 24 percent by the first quarter of 1994. The string of forced devaluations and subsequent depreciation of the peseta (by as much as 30 percent in nominal terms by 1995), on the other hand, did allow a radical transformation of the Spanish balance of payments, reducing the current account deficit from over 3 percent of GDP in 1992 to less than 1 percent in 1993, one of the fastest external adjustments ever experienced by an OECD country. Inflation, so persistent in the days of the strong peseta, also declined substantially to 4.6 percent in 1993. Despite the government's refusal to take advantage of the opportunity to restore competitiveness afforded to the British and Italian economies by their exit from the ERM, the system's crisis thus offered some relief to an economy that had been made to endure a policy strategy that sought "the achievement of the final results [of the

---

[35] Felipe González, quoted in *Wall Street Journal*, August 5, 1992.

[36] *Financial Times*, April 2, 1993. Once the future of the EMU was questioned, foreign speculators no longer believed that the government could in the long run avoid devaluation.

core EMS] countries, i.e., low inflation and strong currency, through the use of the financial lever, placing the whole burden of adjustment on the productive apparatus."[37] More than three years of severe over-valuation nonetheless left a lasting mark, and by the time of the PSOE's electoral defeat in 1996, unemployment still hovered around 23 percent.

Back to the Financial System

The costs that the government's strategy imposed on the economy and its self-defeating effect on the fight against inflation bring us back to the question why it was so insistently followed. One answer may lie in the choices imposed on Spanish authorities by the EU's move toward monetary union. Given the oft-noted deflationary bias of the ERM, which Spain would have to join to participate in EMU,[38] the idea of promoting the reequipment of industry by cheapening imports through a strong currency rather than seeking to minimize the loss of competitiveness of Spanish exporters might be seen as a rational response. Because the ERM was more effective at constraining monetary policy than fiscal policy, countries willing to endure a significant overvaluation of their currencies resulting from an unbalanced macroeconomic policy mix could maintain higher growth in the late 1980s than countries seeking to fit both their fiscal and monetary policy to German interest rates.[39] The notion that a high nominal exchange rate could be used to enforce convergence toward the economic fundamentals of core EMS countries also was not unique to Spain. Italian authorities relied heavily on such a premise at the end of the 1980s, when they sharply tightened monetary policy to address Italy's extremely large budget deficits.

The ERM may indeed have warped the incentives for policymakers in the late 1980s. At the very least, it failed to discourage the lack of balance in the Spanish policy course. However, the costs of allowing the

---

[37]   Torrero, "Poder de las ideas."
[38]   On the ERM's deflationary bias, see Stefano Vona, "Real Exchange Rates and Trade Imbalances in the EMS," in Piero Ferri, ed., *Prospects for the European Monetary System* (New York: St. Martin's Press, 1990).
[39]   Such a conclusion can be read from Vona's analysis of growth and balance of payments developments in the ERM (ibid.), particularly from the contrasts he draws between the experience of Italy and that of France, where fiscal consolidation was taken much farther in the late 1980s.

Spanish economy in essence to "live off other people's money while paying the highest interest rates in Europe for the privilege"[40] were staggering, and seem to belie the notion that the government's reliance on high interest rates simply reflected a coolheaded dose of supply-side socialism.[41] With the exception of Italy in the late 1980s, no other government in the ERM relied so stubbornly and unilaterally on the exchange rate lever in its fight against inflation. France's policy of "competitive disinflation," which also is sometimes referred to as the *franc fort* policy, involved a far more balanced policy mix. It was guided by the criterion of keeping interest rates high enough to maintain the franc within the lower end of its ERM band until the actual disinflation process allowed it to move gradually to the center of its band in the late 1980s.[42] And in the case of Italy, where public deficits surpassed 10 percent of GDP in the late 1980s and appeared virtually intractable, the decision to lean on the nominal exchange rate as a last-ditch effort seems more understandable than in the Spanish case, where the overall public deficit had been cut from 7 percent in 1985 to 3.1 percent in 1987 and where the public debt was still one of the lowest in Europe.

Another explanation lies in the character of the Spanish policymaking community and in the extraordinary sway that the central bank's views had gained in policymaking circles by the mid-1980s. These factors account for the obsessive tendency to view inflation as a simple function of wage growth even when the empirical record clearly showed that the sources of inflation were of a different nature. They also help explain the extent to which any course that might have lowered the value of the peseta came to be seen as a capitulation to the unions. The strong currency strategy also conformed with the central bank reformers' long-held objective of altering the institutional bases of

[40]   *Financial Times*, March 15, 1991.
[41]   *New York Times*, February 13, 1989. This interpretation of the Socialists' policies also is challenged by the paltry character of other supply-side policies. Thus, although the Socialists increased R&D expenditures in the public sectors, these expenditures continued to average only 0.7% of GNP from 1985 to 1990, compared to a 2% average in the EC. Expenditures on vocational training in relation to GDP remained less than half the OECD average, despite the relevance of such policies in the context of Spain's extraordinary unemployment levels. See *El País* (Internacional), November 12, 1990; OECD, *Economic Surveys: Spain*, 1992, p. 70.
[42]   Vona's analysis suggests that whereas Italy and Denmark tolerated a significant real appreciation of their currencies, disinflation in France was based on internal cost cutting rather than on the use of the exchange rate. See "Real Exchange Rates," pp. 70–75.

Spanish policymaking. Thus, even if reliance on the exchange rate lever was ultimately counterproductive in the fight against inflation, it had the virtue of preserving the influence of the central bank over national economic policy.

The central bank's ability to define the thinking behind Spanish policy played an important role in the late 1980s. Yet the course of Spanish policy also responded to the particular constraints and incentives that derived from the structure of the domestic financial market. The manner in which financial liberalization had been pursued had persistently limited competition in the supply of corporate finance and therefore placed extraordinary financial costs on Spanish firms. Even before the rapid appreciation of the peseta at the end of the 1980s, the Spanish economy thus was subject to a bias against investment in productive capacity in competitive sectors and in favor of a reallocation of resources toward sectors and activities that could better absorb such costs. This bias is reflected in the high return that firms were able to attain from their financial investments (see Table 3 in chapter 1), and in the nature of foreign investment. After Spain's entry into the EC in 1986, foreign capital had first flown predominantly into manufactures, as foreign investors sought to take advantage of lower wages and the extreme undervaluation of Spanish industrial stocks. Yet a large share of foreign money was quickly rerouted toward the financial services sector, which became the main beneficiary of foreign capital inflows after 1987.

The strong currency strategy pursued by the Socialist government sought to turn this preexisting high interest rate bias in the economy into an instrument that would allow it to curb wages and fight inflation while simultaneously attracting the necessary foreign capital inflows to finance the resulting current account deficit. Yet in such an economy interest rate measures could have only a limited impact on inflation (as they encouraged the resource allocation that made the economy inflation-prone). This limitation was ultimately reflected in the government's resort to credit ceilings and controls on capital inflows starting in 1988. Because the central bank reformers in charge of economic policy were unwilling to impose a more radical transformation of the domestic financial market, Spanish policy in the late 1980s thus became caught up in an attempt to suppress the inflationary consequences of this underlying bias through a policy strategy that could do nothing but exacerbate the inflation-proneness of the Spanish economy.

The hampered structure of the Spanish financial market also contributed to the high interest rate policy course in other ways. One was the persistent malleability of the Spanish public debt market, whose development had been retarded in the mid-1980s by the search for "negotiated solutions" that preserved the banks' position as intermediaries in the economy. The banks' control over the public debt market raised the cost of financing the public deficit. It was also responsible for the conflict between central bank and Treasury interest rates that marred Spanish policy in the early 1990s. The Treasury's attempt to lower its costs through foreign issues of long-term public debt, which was obstructed by the central bank in 1991, received a further setback when the ERM currency crisis sharply eroded the interest of foreign investors in Spanish securities. Just the first devaluation of the peseta in September 1992, moreover, instantly added over 300 billion pesetas to the cost of the public debt.[43] The compromises made between public officials and the banks on developing the public debt market in the 1980s thus continued to contribute to the cost of deficit financing in the early 1990s.

However, the most evident way in which the financial sector contributed to the excesses of the Spanish policy course in the late 1980s was through its direct role in promoting the sectoral shift of resources that made the Spanish economy so inflation-prone. Not having been forced to cut their costs during the recession years, the banks at the end of the 1980s maintained their oligopolistic interest margins by massively shifting credit to those sectors and activities that were least sensitive to high interest rates and most likely to pass on their costs to consumers. The galloping pace at which the banks were extending credit to sheltered sectors, speculative ventures, and consumers in 1988 and early 1989 allowed demand for services during this period to grow twice as fast as overall consumer demand.[44] This development was what lay behind the re-acceleration of inflation that prompted the government to risk the collapse of the social concertation process and the complete alienation of the unions.

One can of course still argue that if the deficit had been cut further in the 1980s, or if wage growth had not picked up after 1988, Spain

---

[43]   Analistas Financieros, "La financiación del déficit corriente," *El País*, September 22, 1992.

[44]   OECD, *Economic Survey: Spain*, 1992, p. 63; *Financial Times*, February 24, 1989.

would have had lower interest rates and lower inflation in the early 1990s. All these explanations, however, neglect how the failure to reform the domestic financial market drove the intractable inflationary process in Spain and overdetermined the views and choices of Spanish policymakers through the end of the 1980s.

Conclusion: The Politics of Financial Liberalization

The trend toward market-oriented reform in formerly interventionist states is commonly interpreted as the result of systemic market forces that force societies to alter their regulatory institutions in a manner that allows them to allocate resources more efficiently. Such a market-driven view relegates political and historical factors to a second order, and leads us to expect that, other things being equal, reform is likely to support the competitiveness of national economies. The Spanish experience challenges these assumptions by suggesting that the political dynamic behind liberalization may be quite independent of the dictates of competitive market forces, and that this dynamic can produce a reform process that fails to support an economy's competitiveness.

The protracted and biased course of financial liberalization in Spain is the direct consequence of the domestic historical dynamic that brought such reform about. The way liberalization was carried out and its consequences for the Spanish economy were the result of strategic choices on the part of anti-interventionist reformers whose first priority was to alter the institutional structure of Spanish economic policymaking to give greater influence and leverage to the central bank. These outcomes reflect a pattern of accommodation between state elites and the private banking sector that can be traced back to the beginning of the twentieth century, and that was just as pervasive in the neoliberal reform drive of the 1970s and 1980s as it was in the creation of an interventionist regulatory framework under the Franco regime. The prolonged privileging of the banking sector in Spain, however, was not just a secondary domestic effect in an independently driven process of change. It was the consequence of the same developments in the Spanish state that brought about the early turn to market-oriented reform.

Much of my analysis relies on the contrast between the Spanish experience and that of France, the country on which the interventionist framework of financial regulation introduced in Spain in the early 1960s was modeled. The adoption of the French regulatory model in Spain, I have suggested, was not just a matter of institutional mimicry. It reflected important underlying similarities in the politics of postwar economic policy between the two countries. The similarities, however, stop precisely at the point at which the market-driven view leads us to expect greater convergence: when governments move to abandon interventionism in favor of a market-based system of capital allocation. What insights can we draw from this contrast between the Spanish and French experiences about the politics of domestic financial liberalization?

The French–Spanish Contrast and the Politics of Regulatory Reform

The story of Spanish financial reform highlights the primary role of state elites rather than economic actors in bringing about the regulatory shift away from interventionism. With the exception of foreign banks, no domestic sectoral actors exerted any significant pressure in favor of liberalization when it was initiated, and the interests of foreign banks were all but relegated to insignificance for well over a decade after the reform process was initiated. The Spanish case also highlights the primacy of monetary policy considerations over other economic objectives in bringing about the shift away from interventionism, as do analyses of the French experience by other authors.[1] Yet in France the

---

[1]   Michael Loriaux, *France after Hegemony: International Change and Financial Reform* (Ithaca: Cornell University Press, 1991); Jacques Melitz, "Financial Deregulation in France," *European Economic Review* 34 (1990); Stephen S. Cohen, James Galbraith, and John Zysman, "Rehabbing the Labyrinth: The Financial System and Industrial Policy in France," in Cohen and Peter A. Gourevitch, eds., *France in the Troubled World Economy* (London: Butterworth, 1982).

course of reform conformed broadly to the objective of supporting the adjustment of French producers to new international conditions by accompanying credit deregulation with substantial financial market reform. Although French governments resisted abandoning the principle of discretionary credit regulation that allowed them to provide financing at low interest rates to favored users until the mid-1980s, once they decided to do so, credit deregulation was accompanied by an assertive and simultaneous effort to boost the role of the capital market as a source of long-term investment finance. Indeed, preliminary steps that would bolster the capacity of the capital market to play such a role were undertaken in France well before the regulatory turnabout of the 1980s. The Spanish reform effort, by contrast, failed to support the ability of Spanish producers to adjust to international competition in very important ways, replacing one set of economic problems (an overdraft economy in which producers relied heavily on institutional credit) by another (a Dutch-disease economy in which resources were redirected away from productive investment in tradeables and toward investment and consumption in sheltered sectors).

These differences in the actual course of reform were accompanied by some more subtle but nonetheless telling differences in how the regulatory shift away from interventionism was ideologically packaged and conceptualized in the two countries. Though the arguments for credit deregulation were based largely on the efficiency of capital allocation in both countries, the French reform effort was intended to emulate the German (or, as popularized by Michel Albert, the Rhennish) model of organized capitalism, which centered on the institution of universal banking.[2] In practice, reform in France produced a far greater shift toward reliance on the capital markets, and in this sense seems to have approached the Anglo-Saxon model more than the German.[3] But the choice of Germany as an ideological referent is nonetheless significant because it illustrates the consideration given to the problem of industrial finance in a process that was driven primarily by monetary policy considerations. As Philip Cerny puts it, reform in France was ultimately based on "the convergence of two logics," a financial policy and an industrial policy logic.[4] It was clearly influenced

---

[2] Loriaux, *France after Hegemony,* pp. 206, 227, 237.
[3] Melitz, "Financial Deregulation in France."
[4] Philip Cerny, "The 'Little Big Bang' in Paris: Financial Market Deregulation in France," *European of Political Research* 17 (1989): 182.

also by a strong awareness that being able to keep up in Europe (specifically with Germany) required that attention be given on a structural
(financial market) level to the investment requirements of French producers, even as French governments chose to subject macroeconomic
policy to German direction.

The reform effort in Spain, by contrast, was conceptualized far more
strictly as a domestic political battle against the enemy within, as com-
bating the historical scourge of government interventionism in Spain.
Once the French model (so closely associated with authoritarianism in
Spain) had been discarded, no other European referent took its place.
Spanish reformers appeared convinced instead that they could achieve
convergence with Europe only by approaching the solutions spelled out
in monetarist and neoclassical economic theory and generally identified
with the United States. As in the French case, however, the external
referent, while connoting something important about the politics of
reform, served more as an ideological tool than as a guide to action.
The issue of industrial finance was virtually exorcised from the problem of financial reform in Spain. The advantage of a market-based
financial system was taken as a matter of faith, even though the structure of that market went unreformed for well over a decade after credit
deregulation was initiated. Only in the late 1980s, when developments
at the European level overtook the Spanish reform process and created
a new set of concerns for state elites, was reform of the capital market
(so central to the Anglo-Saxon model of corporate finance) finally
addressed. By then, however, Spanish policymakers had become so
focused on the challenge that lay ahead for the domestic private banks
that even this reform effort was calibrated and directed largely at boosting the profits and staying power of the banks, rather than nonfinancial
firms, in a single European market.

What these contrasts and paradoxes illustrate is the extent to which
reforms that are commonly seen as driven and determined by competitive market pressures respond to historical developments within the
state. The critical difference in the two reform processes lies in the
character of the state actors who controlled it, and in the way financial
reform fitted into their broader set of objectives. In Spain, financial
reform was promoted and controlled by a network of reformers anchored in the central bank, and it became a vehicle for furthering that
institution's influence over policy. In France, central bank economists
also did much of the intellectual groundwork and participated in the

drafting of proposals for regulatory reform. But the process was controlled and coordinated by the Treasury, a part of the state bureaucracy
that had been "the economic apex in a centralized state" for four
decades and that combined responsibility for both monetary and industrial policy.[5] The Bank of France remained in a subordinate position at
the time of the reforms, and the Treasury continued to set the overall
direction of monetary policy when France focused on disinflation in the
mid-1980s.[6] The French central bank, moreover, did not become the
object of a contending network of policymakers who defined themselves in opposition to other parts of the state. It was embedded in an
overarching network of high-ranking civil servants that centered on the
Treasury and served to integrate the industrial and financial policy
communities. The career path of high-ranking Bank of France officials
thus typically went from the Treasury to the central bank. Other parts
of the financial policy community, notably the large commercial banks,
were also run by civil servants designated by the Treasury or belonging
to its bureaucratic corps.[7] This pattern contrasts strongly with that of
Spain, where the opposite path, from the central bank into top positions in the executive, became so emblematic during the 1980s, and
where the men in charge of designing the reform effort had come to see
their mission as that of elevating monetary policy and financial regulation to a plane apart from other policy concerns.

To be sure, these differences in the identities and objectives of state
reformers worked themselves out in interaction with other structural
aspects of the domestic political economy. The imbalance within the

[5]   John Zysman, *Governments, Markets, and Growth: Financial Systems and the Politics
of Industrial Change* (Ithaca: Cornell University Press, 1983), p. 114. See also Andrew
Shonfield, *Modern Capitalism: The Changing Balance of Public and Private* (Oxford:
Oxford University Press, 1965), pp. 129–30; Stephen S. Cohen, *Modern Capitalist
Planning: The French Model* (Berkeley: University of California Press, 1977), chap. 4; and
James K. Galbraith, "Monetary Policy in France," *Journal of Post-Keynesian Economics*
(Spring 1992): 399–400. There are varying positions on just how dominant the Treasury's
position is. Some observers argue that French policymaking is more pluralistic than I have
suggested. In general, however, they question the extent of the Treasury's dominance
rather than its position as first among equals. See Jack Hayward, *The State and the
Market Economy* (Brighton: Wheatsheaf, 1986), pp. 22–25; Cerny, " 'Little Big Bang' in
Paris."
[6]   John B. Goodman, *Monetary Sovereignty: The Politics of Central Banking in Western
Europe* (Ithaca: Cornell University Press, 1992), pp. 131–41. The Bank of France attained formal statutory autonomy in 1994 in preparation for European Monetary Unification (EMU).
[7]   Ibid., p. 109; *Banker,* May 1995.

Spanish policymaking elite and the extent to which financial reform came to center on compromises between the central bank and the private banks were exacerbated by the weak position of Spanish industry vis-à-vis the financial sector.

By the mid-1970s, the great majority of large private industrial firms were under the control of either the banks or foreign capital. Because foreign-controlled firms had greater access to external financing, the position of industry as an independent political pressure group was weak when it came to an issue, such as financial regulation, were its interests conflicted with that of the banks.[8] The influence of public industry, on the other hand, was curtailed by the fact that the sector was saddled with so many firms in decline as a result of the socialization of losses that took place in the 1970s. In France, by contrast, the public sector included a significant number of industrial champions that were still regarded as indispensable to the country's economic success. It also encompassed the large commercial banks, which had been effectively nationalized since 1945.

These structural factors may have contributed to the divergence of the Spanish and French reform processes, but they are not sufficient to explain that divergence. French industry included more international heavyweights in the 1980s than did Spanish industry. Yet these firms were the ones least in need of domestic financial restructuring, because they had access to international markets. If the reform process addressed the needs of industrial firms to a far greater extent in France than in Spain, it was not because of organized sectoral pressure on the state. It was rather because reform in France was advanced by a network of state elites that integrated, rather than separated, the financial and industrial policymaking communities. To be sure, public ownership of the financial sector facilitated reform in France, because French policymakers, unlike their Spanish counterparts, did not have to contend with a private cartel. Yet I have shown that post-Franco governments in Spain had several tools at their disposal to exert leverage over the private banks (including the legal regime governing the operations of foreign banks and the official credit institutions), but that they chose consistently not to pursue these options. The Socialist government also chose to forgo the opportunity afforded to it by the banking crisis of the

---

[8] This situation is reflected in the fact that the Spanish Banking Association (AEB) was granted disproportionate voting power in the Spanish employers' organization (CEOE).

early 1980s, which left a substantial portion of the banking sector's deposits and the infrastructure of those industrial banks rescued with public funds in its hands.

These observations bespeak the importance of the identities and motivations of state elites in explaining the course of reform in the two countries. Yet it might be argued that the differences I am describing simply represent residual variation in a process of market-induced convergence of regulatory institutions. There is little doubt that the international economic context changed significantly for the French and Spanish economies sometime in the late 1960s as a result of the adoption of an overtly expansionist monetary policy stance in the United States, new competition in product markets, the growth of offshore financial markets, and eventually the supply shocks of the 1970s. Such changes created specific policy challenges for governments that had been able to pursue relatively expansionary policies since the 1950s. There was now less balance-of-payments leeway for monetary expansion, so that governments had to pay greater attention to restricting the overall level of liquidity as opposed to directing liquidity flows, or in effect rationing credit selectively rather than selectively expanding it.

These changes in the international context, however, are often emphasized in a way that obscures the endogenous political limits of the strategy of defusing social conflict and maintaining the profitability of firms through cheap credit policies in the late 1960s in both France and Spain. More important, although the changing economic context limited the room for expansionary monetary policies, raising the political costs of a regulatory framework that now forced governments to allocate openly the costs of adjustment to external shocks, it did not determine any particular course of reform. The shift away from interventionism is best understood as involving two separate kinds of objectives and motivations. The basic one, which is responsible for the cross-national trend away from interventionism, constitutes an essentially negative choice on the part of political or elected authorities to extricate the state's authority from allocating the costs of adjustment by getting rid of selective credit regulation. Whether or not such credit deregulation is accompanied by adequate "market reform," however, is a function of the motivations of reformers within the state bureaucracy and of the character of the domestic policymaking community.

Unpacking the cross-national trend away from interventionism in this way also explains the different timing of the decisions by political authorities to abandon selective regulation in France and Spain. In both cases, the move occurred when elected authorities became convinced that austerity was unavoidable but perceived that it entailed substantial political risks, so that proposals for market-oriented reform suddenly offered an important political advantage. In Spain this moment came at the height of the political transition, when the Suárez government had to face up to the simultaneous tasks of thwarting a mounting balance-of-payments crisis while inaugurating a democratic political process. In France, it came only after 1983, when François Mitterrand was convinced that there was no alternative to austerity and to keeping the franc in the ERM. By differentiating the decision to abandon interventionism from other facets of reform, we also can better account for the difference in the extent to which liberalization was accompanied by market reform in the two countries. In Spain, a network of reformers anchored in the central bank, for whom reform represented a vehicle for increasing the bank's influence over policy, rejected any assertive attempt to use the resources at the state's disposal to increase competition in the credit market. Reform was guided instead by a series of compromises between these reformers and the private banks that were intended to secure the central bank's principal reform objectives and to preempt any attempt by other political actors to usurp its leadership in the reform process. In France, by contrast, where the reform process was coordinated by the Treasury and coincided with a different, less divisive, configuration in the domestic policymaking community, the monetary policy decision to abandon selective credit regulation was accompanied by much more aggressive market reform.

The historical displacement of an industry-oriented policy outlook in the Spanish policymaking community and the more balanced perspective on adjustment that persisted in France are critical to an understanding of the course of reform in the two countries. It also is important to note, however, that developments within the state were not determined solely by ideology. The relative success of market-oriented reform in France was facilitated in important ways by the fact that the state ultimately had control over the banking sector. Public ownership made it easier for public officials to abolish regulatory practices that limited competition in the credit market. It also allowed the state to use the banks as a compensatory mechanism to aid industry after the 1987 stock market crash and the 1992 ERM crisis. Indeed, this relationship persisted in the early 1990s, even after the privatization of two of the three large commercial banks (Société Général and BNP), and may have contributed to the state of bankruptcy discovered in 1994 at Crédit Lyonnais.[9] Hence what may have been more important is the way state control of the banking sector informed French policymakers' perceptions of the problem of adjustment.

The nationalizations of 1945 contributed to the emergence of relationships between the French policymaking elite, the banks, and industrial firms which ensured that the abandonment of interventionism would not be seen as a solution in and of itself. In Spain, where a few large commercial banks emerged from the interwar period far better capitalized than their French counterparts and still in private hands, financial regulation became the object of a different set of cleavages and identities within the state policymaking elite, contributing in the 1980s to a reform process that took place largely at the expense of Spanish producers. The comparison of the two cases therefore suggests that the comprehensiveness of financial reform in France may have been due largely to the way the state's control of the banking sector had shaped the character of the French policymaking elite.

Finance and the Socialist Experiment in Spain

The analysis in this book has centered on exposing the historical background and consequences of financial reform in Spain, and on secular shifts within the state's policymaking elite. It also, however, has important implications for our understanding of the economic strategies pursued by post-Franco governments, particularly by the Socialist government that came to office in 1982 and held an almost unchallenged parliamentary majority until 1993. As I have noted, the individuals in charge of economic policy under the PSOE, particularly the two finance ministers, Miguel Boyer and Carlos Solchaga, were intimately linked to the network of academic reformers at the central bank. But their policy preferences and views also became part of what the PSOE

---

[9] The Socialist government persuaded the commercial banks to swap shares with large industrial firms in the early 1990s, in an effort to encourage their involvement in industry and create core shareholdings to fend off hostile takeovers. After the ERM crisis, the government persuaded the large commercial banks not to pass on the full cost of the interest rate hikes instituted by the Bank of France to their core industrial clients, at significant cost to the banks' profits. See *Institutional Investor,* July 1994; *Financial Times,* October 9 and November 3, 1992, and March 2, 1993.

leadership came to regard as a social democratic policy strategy suited to the specific situation of the Spanish economy in the 1980s. This orientation, which some observers have designated as "supply-side socialism," involved an almost categorical rejection of countercyclical demand management as a solution to Spain's unemployment problem. It favored instead a long-term strategy of boosting competitiveness through macroeconomic rigor, wage moderation, and fiscal consolidation to raise the level of public savings and to shift resources in the state budget away from social transfers into capital investments in infrastructure.[10] In the view of the government's economic team, this combination of policies aimed at boosting profitability constituted the best strategy for integrating Spain into the European economy and for solving the problem of structural unemployment in the long run.

If this strategy was not to result in an increase in unemployment, it required continued moderation and even a reduction in real wages. During the years covered by social concertation agreements, the pace of wage growth met this condition. Nominal wage agreements remained below actual inflation and unit labor costs fell continuously from 1978 until the late 1980s.[11] Starting in 1989, however, wages accelerated, as the unions sought to recoup some of the concessions made during the previous years. The government's decision in the late 1980s to allow concertation to end was motivated by the perception of insufficient union cooperation in the fight against inflation and by the belief that an adequate reduction in real wages might be better achieved if the unions were forced to negotiate without the benefit of a social pact. The failure of this expectation is commonly attributed to the institutional features of the Spanish labor market, which are believed to exacerbate the insider-outsider conflict among workers by encouraging a predatory pursuit of benefits for union members at the expense of higher unemployment.[12]

This prevailing focus on labor market institutions is consistent with the comparative literature on social democracy, which stresses the "strategic capacity" of unions to engage in a solidaristic wage stance as

[10]   See Carles Boix, "Political Parties, Growth, and Equality," unpublished manuscript, 1995, pt. 2.
[11]   Juan Dolado and S. Bentolila, "Labour Flexibility and Wages: Lessons from Spain," *Economic Policy*, no. 18, 1994; Blanchard et al., *Spanish Unemployment*, Annex 4; OECD, *Economic Surveys: Spain*, 1992, pp. 66–70.
[12]   Olivier Blanchard et al., *Spanish Unemployment: Is There a Solution?* (London: Centre for Economic Policy Research, 1995), pp. 56–57.

200 BANKING ON PRIVILEGE

the key to successful disinflation based on social concertation.[13] Some organizational characteristics of the Spanish unions (such as ideological division and low membership) were indeed not conducive to this kind of "strategic capability." Other aspects, however, such as the primacy of bargaining at the sectoral level and the fact that Spanish labor law amplified the unions' influence in the wage-setting process (so that they could in fact predict the effect their demands would have on the economy), also can foster solidaristic wage restraint. Moreover, while aspects of Spanish labor law inherited from the Franco regime, such as the high level of dismissal costs, militated against a solidaristic wage stance, the UGT was willing to go along with substantial alterations of this legal framework during the Socialists' first term and moderate its wage demands to support the government's policies. The divorce between the government and the UGT at the end of 1988 was thus not so much over the distribution of costs as over the distribution of profits, as the union leadership felt it was time to reap the rewards of its earlier collaboration.[14]

The analysis offered in the preceding chapters suggests that the government's conflict with the unions and the failure of incomes policy in Spain were determined significantly not by labor market features but by the state's compromised approach to reforming the structure of the financial market. The very significant contribution of wage moderation to the fight against inflation up until 1989 was undermined by the shift of resources into consumption and sheltered sectors that took place during the 1980s. This dynamic of the credit market, exacerbated by large inflows of short-term capital responding to Spain's high interest rates and to its appreciating currency, also lay behind the government's failure to reach the inflation targets to which the unions had agreed to peg wages in the public sector in 1988. The fact that inflation was overshot again, by more than 3 points, in 1989, despite the draconian credit squeeze and capital controls imposed in that year, further eroded the government's credibility with the unions, undermining its attempts to revive concertation in the early 1990s.

[13] Fritz Scharpf, *Crisis and Choice in European Social Democracy* (Ithaca: Cornell University Press, 1991), pp. 176–78, 187–92.
[14] José María Maravall, "Politics and Policy: Economic Reforms in Southern Europe," in Luiz Carlos Bresser Pereira, Maravall, and Adam Przeworski, *Economic Reforms in New Democracies: A Social-Democratic Approach* (New York: Cambridge University Press, 1994), pp. 119–20.

The dynamic of the Spanish financial market thus persistently and repeatedly undermined the government's ability to deliver on its part of the deal in its attempt at social democracy. Voluntary wage restraint requires a belief in a " 'social memory' for all necessary contributions and sacrifices, so that participants [are] relieved of the need to seek immediate compensation."[15] The persistence of inflation and unemployment in spite of the UGT's cooperation eliminated any chance that labor could hold on to such a belief. In this context, the government's shows of socialist tough love became indistinguishable from a hostile and conservative monetarism, and its determination to use an overvalued currency to keep pressure on the unions was bound to backfire.

[15] Scharpf, *Crisis and Choice*, p. 178.

Index